Graham Coster was born in 1960 in Croydon. He read English at
Cambridge, and then from 1983 to 1987 was assistant editor of Granta.
He is the author of a novel, *Train, Train*, and of another travel book, *A
Thousand Miles from Nowhere*, and the editor of *The Wild Blue Yonder*,
an anthology of writing about flying. His travel journalism has appeared
in the *Daily Telegraph*, *GQ*, the *Independent on Sunday* and *Condé Nast
Traveller*. He now works as an editor for the publishing house Aurum
Press. He lives in London.

Corsairville

The Lost Domain of the Flying Boat

GRAHAM COSTER

PENGUIN BOOKS

PENGUIN BOOKS

Published by the Penguin Group
Penguin Books Ltd, 27 Wrights Lane, London w8 5TZ, England
Penguin Putnam Inc., 375 Hudson Street, New York, New York 10014, USA
Penguin Books Australia Ltd, Ringwood, Victoria, Australia
Penguin Books Canada Ltd, 10 Alcorn Avenue, Toronto, Ontario, Canada M4V 3B2
Penguin Books India (P) Ltd, 11 Community Centre, Panchsheel Park,
New Delhi – 110 017, India
Penguin Books (NZ) Ltd, Cnr Rosedale and Airborne Roads,
Albany, Auckland, New Zealand
Penguin Books (South Africa) (Pty) Ltd, 5 Watkins Street, Denver Ext 4,
Johannesburg 2094, South Africa

Penguin Books Ltd, Registered Offices: Harmondsworth, Middlesex, England

First published by Viking 2000
Published in Penguin Books 2001

3

Lines from Stephen Spender's 'The Landscape near an Aerodrome' in *Collected Poems
1935–1965*, are quoted by permission of Faber & Faber Ltd.
Lines from W. B. Yeats's 'The Wild Swans at Coole', in *Collected Poems*, are
included by permission of A. P. Watt Ltd and Michael Yeats.

Set in Adobe Caslon
Printed in England by Clays Ltd, St Ives plc

For my Dad,
who took me on plane journeys
even before I went flying

'He left a Corsair's name to other times'
                    – Byron, 'The Corsair'

A

CERTIFICATE OF

CONTEMPORARY TRAVEL

This is to certify that

Mrs V.R. HOLME

has flown over the equator in the *Empire* flying-

boat the ___ *CIRCE*

thus becoming one of the progressive band of

travellers who cross the line by air. Over the waters

of Lake Victoria, the Lingga Archipelago, the *Empire*

flying-boats pass in a moment from hemisphere to

hemisphere, beyond the zone whose dwellers recognize

no alteration in the length of night and day

'Born with the sun they travelled a short way towards the sun,
And left the vivid air signed with their honour'

Stephen Spender

Longitude 34° 15' E

Latitude zero

22 4 1939

Commander

CONTENTS

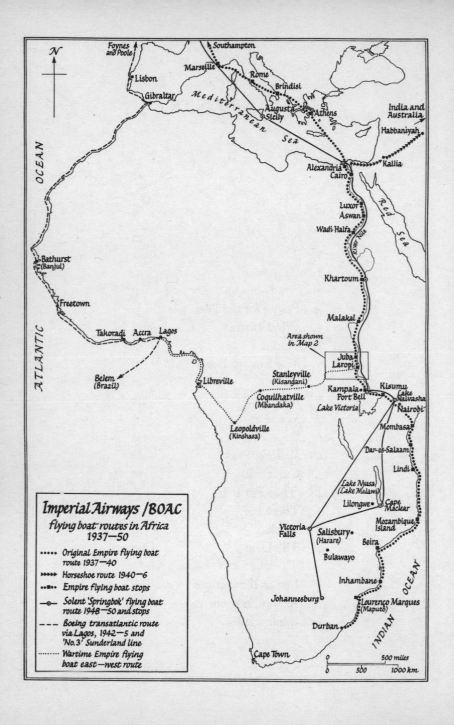

N

Foynes
and Poole
Southampton
Marseille
Lisbon
Rome
Gibraltar
Brindisi
Mediterranean
Augusta
Sicily
Athens
India and
Australia
Habbaniyah
Alexandria
Kallia
Cairo
OCEAN
Luxor
Aswan
Wadi Halfa
River Nile
Red Sea
Bathurst
(Banjul)
Khartoum
Freetown
ATLANTIC
Malakal
Takoradi Accra Lagos
Area shown
in Map 2
Juba
Laropi
Belem
(Brazil)
Libreville
Stanleyville
(Kisangani)
Kampala
Port Bell
Kisumu
Lake
Naivasha
Coquilhatville
(Mbandaka)
Lake Victoria
Nairobi
Mombasa
Leopoldville
(Kinshasa)
Dar-es-Salaam
Lindi
Lake Nyasa
(Lake Malawi)
Lilongwe
Cape
Maclear
Mozambique
Island
Victoria
Falls
Salisbury
(Harare)
Beira
Bulawayo
Inhambane
INDIAN
Johannesburg
Lourenço Marques
(Maputo)
Durban
OCEAN
Cape Town

Imperial Airways / BOAC
flying boat routes in Africa 1937–50

- • • • • Original Empire flying boat route 1937–40
- ►►►► Horseshoe route 1940–6
- • ■ • Empire flying boat stops
- —○— Solent 'Springbok' flying boat route 1948–50 and stops
- — — Boeing transatlantic route via Lagos, 1942–5 and 'No.3' Sunderland line
- • • • • Wartime Empire flying boat east–west route

500 miles
500
1000 km

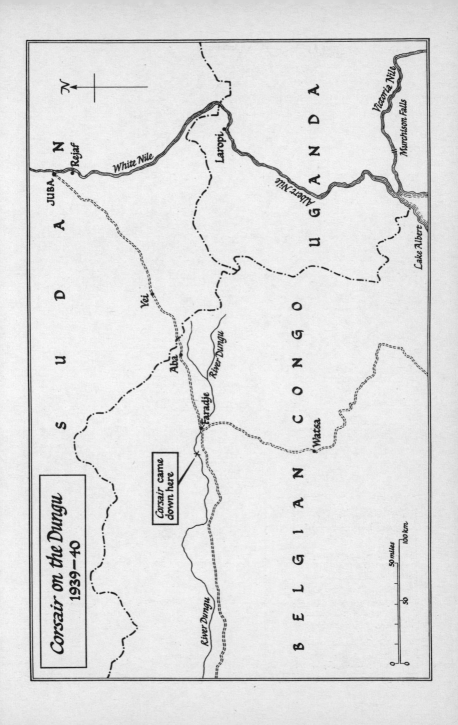

Corsair on the Dungu
1939–40

N

SUDAN

JUBA.
Rejaf

White Nile

Laropi

UGANDA

Victoria Nile

Murchison Falls

Albert Nile

Lake Albert

Yei

Aba

River Dungu

Faradje

CONGO

Watsa

BELGIAN

Corsair came
down here

River Dungu

50 miles   100 km

50

I

The Legend

'CRASH, AFRICA,' wrote one of the passengers on his telegram form. That was all. The young man had been adamant: he must wire home as soon as possible – and in his agitation this was all he could think of to write. It was greatly to the amusement of the local American missionaries who had come to his assistance. Crash, Africa, they joked: where was that?

The missionaries had seen the flying boat approaching low overhead, above their mission station – couldn't imagine what it was doing in this area. It went away, and then came back again, heading west towards the river, and this time it seemed, for some extraordinary reason, to be coming in to land.

For the thirteen passengers it had been the usual early start. The rap on their hotel-room door would have come hours before dawn – around 2.30 in the morning. They'd spent the night in Kenya, in Kisumu, its third city, a sultry freshwater port on vast Lake Victoria. But once the mosquito net had been brushed aside it would not have been far to go to report for the next leg of their long journey: the Kisumu Hotel, an old colonial pile with a corrugated roof, was right down by the waterfront – the previous evening the silver craft now waiting at its moorings for departure at 4.15 a.m. had touched down in the Kavirondo Gulf and they'd been able to walk ashore straight on to the jetty.

The flying boat was one of Imperial Airways' luxurious 'Empire' boats, delivered just two years earlier by Short Brothers of Rochester to commence the company's new Empire Air Mail services across the globe from Britain to Africa, India and Australia. Officially classified the 'C-Class', each member of the fleet was christened with a name, and every name began with C. The flying boat starting its engines at Kisumu was *Corsair*, after the privateers who had menaced the Barbary coast of Spain – and perhaps also after the extravagant hero of Byron's eponymous epic poem, a quotation from which adorned the individually badged notepaper provided for the passengers.

She was flying the northbound Africa service from South Africa to England – in those days a five-day voyage dropping down several times a day for morning coffee, lunch and tea (and most importantly aviation fuel). *Corsair* had set out from Durban, the start of the service, two days earlier, and followed the east coast of Africa up as far as Mozambique Island in Portuguese East Africa. There she had stopped for the night, and after reaching Mombasa the next morning, Kenya's ancient and dreamy fortress-port, turned inland away from the Indian Ocean to fly west to Kisumu. Today they would begin to follow the Nile northwards, bound as far as Khartoum, capital of the Sudan. There'd be a further three days' flying before *Corsair* was due to touch down on Southampton Water and taxi in to the terminal to meet the motor coach for London.

It was the fourteenth of March, 1939.

During the previous day's flight *Corsair*'s direction-finding equipment, which the wireless operator used to obtain radio bearings for navigation, had stopped working. On arrival at Kisumu he'd reported the fault, and in the morning found a note from the Imperial Airways ground engineers to say they'd installed a new apparatus. Problem solved. *Corsair* rose off the water, touched down further along Lake Victoria an hour and a quarter later at Port Bell, for Entebbe, the Ugandan capital at that time, and then took off again for Juba, in southern Sudan, 350 miles away. According to the timetable, they'd be alighting on the White Nile there two hours later. The captain, E. J. 'John' Alcock – brother of the Alcock who, with Arthur Whitten-Brown, had made the first ever flight across the Atlantic in 1919 – put *Corsair* on automatic pilot and, leaving the first officer in charge, retired to the spar compartment for a snooze.

Around the time when Juba ought to have been coming into sight, Alcock reappeared on the flight-deck to check their progress. Second-hand accounts paint a relaxed scene of the first officer reclining with his feet up on the instrument panel, a wireless operator with headset half on, half off. *Where are we?* Between Uganda and Juba the Nile flows through the Sudd, a vast swamp of clogging papyrus, endless and undifferentiated. No sign of the great river. The weather had turned bad: soon a mist was thick around them. 'Ace – king – queen – jack: we're in the shit!' is said to have been one of the comments that passed between captain and first officer. The wireless operator was instructed to get a bearing from Juba. 'We're past it' came his puzzled reply once he'd read off the signal from the direction-finding loop.

If they were already north of Juba, that meant an about-turn. And though there was nothing that looked like the Nile beneath them, the country was confusingly busy with a tangle of meandering rivers. For two hours the crew flew around seeking some recognizable landmark by which to orient themselves: none. *Corsair* was thoroughly lost. Eventually, after more than four hours in the air, the flying boat had only fifteen minutes' fuel left.

Descending through the mist, the crew spotted a straightish stretch of water. Was this the Nile after all? Nothing for it: here was where they'd have to try and land. Some of the passengers were asleep: it was decided to leave them that way, and to say nothing to the others. Alcock guided *Corsair* among the trees, and brought her down on to the water without harm – an exceedingly skilful achievement on a waterway that turned out to be scarcely wider than her wing-span. But at the end of his landing-run the flying boat hit a submerged rock. Her hull holed, *Corsair* was in danger of sinking fast. Alcock opened up all the engines to taxi as fast as possible towards the bank, and managed to beach the craft in time. Soon the plane's crew had hacked a hole in the top of the fuselage, and the uninjured but bemused passengers were being invited by the first clerk and steward to clamber to safety ashore.

Where were they? The country around the river was flat, swampy bush. No human settlement was visible. But after five minutes a white man appeared on the scene. He was a Belgian, M. Appermans, the local provincial commissioner, who'd beheld from his residence the unlikely spectacle of a huge flying boat looming low overhead, jumped in his car and hurried to the water's edge. You have just alighted, M. Appermans informed the crew, on the River Dungu. Juba was 200 miles away, in another country. They had inadvertently been flying south-west. *Corsair* had come down in the Belgian Congo.

The provincial commissioner took the passengers to his house, furnished those who'd got their feet wet wading ashore with slippers, and all of them with sun helmets and umbrellas to ward off the overhead noonday sun, of whose fierce effects they were apparently unaware. ('I happen to know,' reported Imperial Airways' Central African Area Manager Mr Vernon Crudge, sadly, in a memo to London a fortnight later, 'that hardly any of these items have found their way back to him and his wife.') M. and Mme Appermans 'then regaled the passengers with food and drink . . . at no small expense', and drove them to a small hotel some 50 miles away in the border town of Aba. From there the party, their luggage and the mail, also retrieved from the stricken flying boat, were conveyed to Juba. A couple of days later *Centurion*, the Empire boat flying the next northbound Africa service, arrived, and the passengers, at least, were able to fly away.

Which left *Corsair*. A huge, four-engined passenger flying-boat, less than two years old, she now languished sunk up to her water-line in thick mud, her hull stove in and flooded with stale water, on the foreshore of a claustrophobically narrow river in remote Central Africa. It had been that troublesome direction-finding gear, investigation later revealed, that had led her so badly astray. The ground staff hadn't checked the polarity of the replacement set they'd installed at Kisumu, and neither had the wireless operator: because the voltage had been reversed, the radio bearing he'd read off for Juba had been out by 180°. Quite simply, *Corsair* had turned left instead of right. Now what was to be done with her?

Take a trip to the Imperial War Museum's vintage aircraft collection at Duxford in Cambridgeshire, where one of only three large flying boats left in Britain has been preserved, and, putting all nostalgic sentiment aside, imagine yourself as a pre-war loss adjuster to the civil-aviation industry. You would not need long for your assessment. Walk around the gleaming white Short Sunderland – military sister of Imperial Airways' Empire boats – and let its sheer size, its great *bulk*, register. Climb the steps beside its tall flanks and clamber through the fuselage. From wing-tip to wing-tip: nearly 40 yards. Almost 90 feet long. Mounted on its beaching wheels, its flight-deck stands higher off the ground than the top deck of a bus. To get this particular Sunderland back from France, where it had been converted into a nightclub, to Britain for restoration, it had to be cut in half – sliced horizontally from nose to tail like filleting a fish – to fit on to the largest trailers that could be hauled by road. *Corsair* was just as big.

A flying boat like this, then: stuck fast in several feet of mud with a great gash in its hull. Gracefully weightless in the air, buoyant on water, a flying boat is at home in two elements. Stranded on land, like a swan it is helplessly heavy and immobile. Or think of a whale washed ashore – killed by having to bear its own weight. Fallen to earth, a plane is deserted by aerodynamics. It becomes dumb, inert metal. And we haven't even begun to address the question of trying to fly it off a minor and improbably narrow African river. No chance. No argument. Abandon it to nature in its oozy grave and collect on the insurance – why not?

But that was not what happened with *Corsair*. Imperial Airways decided otherwise. At that time its fleet of Empire boats was the most modern in the world. Imagine one of British Airways' 747–400 series Jumbos coming down somewhere inaccessible: writing off a plane of that size would saddle the underwriters with a replacement bill of £40 million. In 1939 a cost of £50,000 to order a new C-Class boat was of equivalent import. But it was not only the insurance company that wanted to see if *Corsair* could be salvaged.

Imperial Airways had been unlucky with its prestigious new fleet. Delivered in 1937, by the end of the year three of the flying boats had already been lost – the first, *Capricornus*, crashing in a snowstorm in France only eight days after arriving from the manufacturers, and with just ten hours' flying on its log. The company had ordered replacements, but the following year the losses continued. *Calpurnia* crashed at night during a sandstorm at Lake Habbaniyah in Iraq. In 1939, two months before *Corsair* came to grief, *Cavalier* had had to put down in the North Atlantic when her engines iced up, and sunk when the high waves tore a hole in the hull. On 12 March 1939, indeed, just two days earlier, *Capella* had been wrecked in Batavia Harbour in Indonesia.

The new Empire Air Mail service had in any case been such a success that the previous Christmas, to cope with the amount of post now being sent to Britain's colonies and dominions, Imperial Airways had had to call into service every aircraft it could get its hands on, both from its own fleet and by chartering others, to get it all through. Even flying boats' floats were packed with mail to maximize the load. Now the continuing losses of the flying boats it relied on just to run its regular services across the Empire ruled out any question of simply throwing away *Corsair* and sitting back to wait for Shorts to make a new one.

And the question was, in any event, being swallowed up by larger history. On 15 March 1939, the day after *Corsair* made it down on to the River Dungu, Hitler sent his troops into Czechoslovakia. Britain was already preparing for war. Back in 1934, at the same time that it had commissioned the Empire boats from Short Brothers, Imperial Airways had ordered for its European services a fleet of landplanes from the Armstrong–Whitworth company. It took four years – as the airline's chairman complained ruefully to his share-holders in 1938 – for the first to arrive. Armstrong–Whitworth was already busy building Whitley bombers for the RAF. Shorts were now making Sunderlands for Coastal Command's U-boat patrols. Imperial Airways might order another C-Class, but it wouldn't get one.

The leader of Short Brothers' salvage team, Hugh Gordon, had recently been sent to Naples to repair another Empire boat, one that had taxied into a submarine in the harbour, and found himself caught amongst huge crowds welcoming Hitler as a guest of Mussolini. With a brief to see if *Corsair* could be brought back into service, Gordon caught an Empire flying boat to Juba.

'It is not clear,' booms the author of *Merchant Airmen*, the HMSO's wartime history of civil aviation, pondering the Central African backwater where *Corsair* had come down, 'why so desolate a spot should ever have been dignified with a name.' Crash, Africa, indeed, was probably about right for the middle of nowhere, which was where Gordon was headed. But in fact the name of the place was to become everything. Captain Alcock's log-book, now in the archive of the Southampton Hall of Aviation, recording the bald details of the flight in his confident hand, reveals its official designation:

Time of departure: 0618, Port Bell
Time in air: 4 hours 28 minutes
Time of arrival: 1026, Faradje

Faradje, then: this was officially where *Corsair* now lay, and from where Hugh Gordon and his team would have to try and salvage her.

It was not, however, the place from which she finally flew away. By the end of 1939 she was still on the River Dungu. And when, early in 1940, a full ten months after her thirteen startled passengers had found themselves clambering out through a hole in her roof on to a muddy riverbank, *Corsair* finally gathered speed down the river, rose on the water and flew away into the Central African sky, Crash, Africa, or Faradje – the place too desolate to be worthy of a name – had acquired yet another. 'Many aircraft have taken their names from places,' writes John Pudney in *The Seven Skies*, his affectionate history of Imperial Airways and BOAC. 'It was the unique distinction of one of the Empire flying boats to give her name to a place.' The Empire boat dwindling to a silver speck in the sky had left behind a place called Corsairville.

How *Corsair* finally escaped from the Dungu, so far as it has hitherto been written down, is an epic saga. It tested two separate salvage teams, battling heat, flies and illness, who mended the flying boat and refloated her, and then found they had to mend her all over again. It drew in the local gold-mine, and hundreds of native convicts. It led to the building of new roads, the trucking-in of rocks and tree-trunks from a 100-mile radius, the damming of the River Dungu and the creation of a lake, and even the construction of a new African village. Amidst all this, the world also went to war. Where there had been just a cross on a map, *Corsair*'s salvagers created a settlement. In order that the flying boat might leave this corner of the African landscape, they had to remake the landscape.

Or so runs the legend. It is hardly a well-known tale – you have to hunt for it in specialized and sometimes frankly esoteric works of aviation history. It first appears in *Merchant Airmen*, published by the HMSO in 1945, where a photograph of *Corsair* serenely at anchor at Gwalior in India, several years after her sojourn in the Congo, is captioned THE PLANE THAT BUILT A VILLAGE. Perhaps writing biographies of Galsworthy and Chesterton had schooled its author, Dudley Barker, in fable and saga. 'In Central Africa,' he pronounces, 'there is a memento of those nine months of toil. At Faradje, on the Dangu [*sic*] river, there stands the new mud village built for native labourers. It is named Corsairville.' John Pudney's *The Seven Skies* reprised the story in 1959. I came across it in C. H. Barnes's compendious, 560-page history of *Shorts Aircraft since 1900*, unfanciful as it is authoritative, published eight years later.

Not only has the legend been handed down over fifty years, however: half a century also seems only to have embroidered the fable of Corsairville, and deepened conviction as to its veracity. As recently as 1995 A. S. Jackson, in *Imperial Airways and the First British Airlines 1919–40*, was adamant about the survival of *Corsair*'s picturesque legacy:

As a result of the ten-month period which the flying boat spent on the River Dangu [*sic*] a new village community grew there. It was (and is) called Corsairville. The artificial lake is still there, and the village depends for supplies on the road which the rescue team and their helpers hacked through the bush to reach the aircraft.

A remote African backwater picked out by chance; an engineer setting out to assess the feasibility of patching a hole in a metal hull – and then, with the passage of almost a year, the random has become planned, emergency expedient has spawned a civic legacy, the temporary has become permanent. Retrospectively, there had been a destination for the lost flying boat after all, somewhere to inscribe in the gazetteer.

Corsairville. It isn't on the map – but then, with President Mobutu's Africanization of his country's placenames once the Belgian Congo became independent Zaire, it wouldn't be. But how had it come about? Who had been the members of the cast in this extraordinary play? And who would have visited since? Would anyone from there remember the story of the great metal whale that fell from the heavens and wallowed in the Dungu for the best part of the year? Would *Corsair* have inspired an African cargo-cult? Were the dam and the lake actually still there?

Then again, maybe Corsairville's literal survival was only wishful thinking on the part of these historians of the last fifty years. Certainly the author of *Shorts Aircraft since 1919* came to have second thoughts. 'It is unlikely,' C. H. Barnes was writing in 1973, 'that any trace remains today of "Corsairville".'

But let us keep those inverted commas, for in that sense, at least, Barnes was wrong. As we have just seen from A. S. Jackson's 1995 book, the trace of 'Corsairville' is as pronounced as ever – in fact in its most picturesque manifestation yet – as a place on a psycho-historical map. 'Corsairville': an imaginative region; an invisible city; a potential place.

It is the story of this story that is just as fascinating to me – for the assumptions and longings that seem to have led to its inception and embellishment. It is as though all these – British – writers who have retold it and passed it on *wanted* the story to be true. Behind it there is a myth of beneficence and civilization: the sleek, futuristic aircraft descending from the sky and, during her stay, conferring a lasting legacy of community, communications and shelter on a primitive, isolated corner of Africa. John Pudney was no plane-spotter, nor a sentimentalist – rather, a distinguished and sensitive poet. His most famous poem, 'For Johnny', made the plangent epigraph for Terence Rattigan's film about the wartime bomber crews, *The Way to the Stars*. But here he is unafraid to jump to a very large conclusion and point a grandiloquent moral. 'No type of machine,' he eulogizes, 'more justly earned the honour of giving its name to a place.'

What does he mean? What kind of a place is 'Corsairville'? To find an answer to how someone could write a sentence like Pudney's, one would have to tell a whole era, and travel thousands of miles, of history. Above all, one had better get to grips with the question of flying boats.

Camilla

2

Croydon

'The first time I went out on a flying boat – how wonderful!' said
Victor Pitcher. 'The sea breeze, going out in a launch . . .' A cheerful,
youthful man, now living in retirement in Bournemouth, Victor
had written several standard textbooks on navigation, and in the
1960s had been the only British chairman of the International Airline
Navigators Council. But during the war he'd been a young navigator
on the giant Boeing flying boats BOAC had bought from the
Americans to run its air service across the Atlantic. 'It was something
to do with the British tradition,' he went on, 'the sea tradition. It
was a great feeling when you walked on a flying boat – just the water
lapping against the keel . . . We were taught to calculate the tides
from the phases of the moon – knowledge that was hardly ever used,
but part of the mystique in a way. *We knew all this*. The landplane
chaps didn't! And the engineers would go down and *check the bilges*,
things like that – it was just like a boat! And we used nautical terms
such as "hatches" – we didn't use "windows". And we used to do
watches – on the Boeing flying boats legs of twenty-two hours
without landing. It was the third element: land, air . . . and water.'
Victor's verdict on those three years on the Boeings was emphatic,
but not, I was to find, unusual: 'Those flying-boat days were the
highlight of my life.'

A flying boat. Still, when one considers the term, one naturally
thinks – or I do: an aeroplane that can land on water. But is the
flying carpet in *The Arabian Nights* a plane that can cover your

lounge floor? No: it's a carpet that can fly. Equally, a flying boat is just as much a boat that can fly. It is an improbable, even a perverse notion – something doing what it isn't supposed to, like a fish riding a bicycle. When the Empire boat *Clyde* touched down at Lagos during the last war, carrying members of de Gaulle's Free French Army to win over French Equatorial Africa for the Allies, the Nigerian natives who assisted with its refuelling dubbed it 'the canoe that goes for up'. But if it is a cranky idea, it is also rather fabulous: an aeroplane walking on water; a boat defying gravity – as magical as a flying pig.

Not all seaplanes, of course, are flying boats. There is also the floatplane, a – small – usually single-engined craft with the wheels on the end of its undercarriage replaced by floats. Floatplanes hop from lake to lake in northern Canada; Supermarine's famous floatplane of the thirties – forerunner of the Spitfire – set a world air-speed record of over 400 m.p.h. But floatplanes are pond-skaters, mere water-skiers, not pelagic voyagers. A flying boat's fuselage is also its hull. The two functions, boat and plane, are truly integral.

And not so long ago, the rationale for a flying boat was as obvious as the use of cavalry in warfare. Three-quarters of the earth is covered by water. An aircraft capable of touching down on it could land just about anywhere. Landplanes required an airfield, which means expensive earth-moving, civil engineering and drainage for flat run-ways and taxi-aprons – all of which, grass or dirt, could be turned to quagmire overnight in the tropics by a monsoon. Seaplanes just needed the driftwood and the odd crocodile cleared away. A runway was only so many hundred yards long, and just a few yards wide – hazardous constraints in the days when flying machines' reliability could not be presumed upon. On Lake Victoria in Central Africa you had the length of Ireland for your take-off run, and could touch down on a runway the sides of which were invisible in the far distance.

Before the last war the world – and particularly Britain – thought first about water. Long-distance travel meant a sea passage: the White Star Line or Cunard's *Queen Mary* for an Atlantic crossing; the Union Castle steamer for a leisurely voyage out to the Dominions. Trade meant cargo ships sailing down the river from the city docks and out on to the open sea. International mail caught the boat. At the end of the twentieth century, small, island nation, we are among the last to retain a maritime heritage. Only in 1997 was our Royal Yacht finally decommissioned, and even later still the decision taken – merely on strict financial grounds – not to order a replacement. In the *QE2* Britain still has a national flagship ocean liner. R. M. Ballantyne, Joseph Conrad, C. S. Forester, William Golding – our writers have long written about the sea. Think, even today, of the popularity of Patrick O'Brian.

But Britain was also early into aviation, and Alcock and Brown's pioneering 1919 crossing of the Atlantic in their Vickers Vimy established a primacy which, at least with wonders of the air like the vertical-take-off Harrier, or even *Concorde*, it retains. Aeroplanes are not part of, say, France's national mythology, as the Spitfire or the Lancaster are part of ours. When Britain's national security was most perilously threatened by Hitler in 1940 in the Battle of Britain, it was aeroplanes that saved us.

Perhaps to the British sensibility, then, there is even now an immediate serendipity about flying boats. Aviation, in its rapid and relentless technological march, only looks forward. But flying boats connect us with our past, and a long history we don't want to lose. They lead us to our landscape: a seaside no one in Britain is ever far from; the great riparian cities; the harbour, the haven. In old age, as the American writer Paul Theroux noticed on his journey around Britain's coastline, we are a nation looking out to sea. Theroux thought that what held these elderly retirees' gaze was the numinous infinite – a confronting of their own imminent death. You could also say it was a recognition, a choice, of home.

Home for me, however, was a long way from the sea. Croydon, where I grew up, was by then no longer a Surrey town: it had become a dormitory suburb of London. Alternatively, place it as half-way between London and Gatwick Airport. 'Shop like you mean it' ran the slogan I once saw blazoned outside a shopping mall in Wichita: Croydon was good for shopping. What German bombs had not obliterated, sixties planners had finished off: Croydon's town centre was a gusty canyon of high-rise office blocks, its architectural foci the Underpass and the Flyover. From D. H. Lawrence, fuming with boredom during the brief sentence of teaching at its Davidson Road School, to slighting references in John Betjeman, Martin Amis and David Lodge, Croydon had become a literary archetype of all that was anodyne, anaemic, atrophied. To a schoolboy it seemed somewhere devoid of history.

When I was twelve, however, my parents decided to move, and one Sunday afternoon we went to view a house in South Croydon. It was set back from the road behind a row of dark fir trees. You entered under a gloomy porch; the interior was lightless, stuffy and old-fashioned – or so it seemed to me at the time. In the unmodernized kitchen was a square porcelain sink and a scrubbed-wood draining board. There was even an elderly and ailing woman bedridden in one upstairs room. I know now, of course, that it is precisely someone's absence, disappearance, that ages the shabby furnishings, sucks the air out of a house to leave it older and tireder than they ever were. Besides, it was a dank autumnal day.

'When Wilkie was here . . .', the woman housekeeper who showed us round reflected sadly – 'Captain Wilcockson. He was an airline pilot.' She spoke of him as a grand, much-loved man. It was his death that had forced the sale. But I didn't care. I couldn't get out of that still, dark, suffocating house fast enough. We could never live there.

It was nearly twenty years later before I discovered who Captain Arthur Wilcockson was. He had been one of Imperial Airways' most famous pilots. In the early thirties he'd flown its giant Handley–Page biplanes on the luxurious 'Silver Wing' service from Croydon to Paris, booming along with thirty-six passengers aboard – a huge number for the time – served at damask-covered tables on blue and white bone china by wing-collared stewards. These Handley–Page HP-42s, named *Hannibal* or *Hengist* or *Hanno*, nicknamed 'the Flying Banana' for the protuberant fuselage slung underneath the biplane wing like a transverse toboggan, jounced across Croydon Aerodrome's grass airstrip so enthusiastically that seatbelts needed to be fastened to enable passengers to retain contact with their seats. Wilkie had also sometimes drawn the short straw and found himself at the controls of *Scylla* or *Syrinx*, Imperial Airways' two unloved Short biplanes that, come bumpy weather, in his own words, 'wallowed all over the sky'. One day, taxiing across the airfield at Brussels with Captain Wilcockson at the controls, the unwieldy *Syrinx* was up-ended by a gale and wrecked. He returned to Croydon to be presented by his grateful fellow pilots with a large wooden medal.

A photograph from the time shows a round-faced, comfortably double-chinned, imperturbable man. The wide white-crowned peaked cap makes him look more like the captain of an ocean liner – which, in a way, is what these pre-war flying elect were, for nearly seventy years ago flying was an élite social event equivalent to a passage on the *Queen Mary*. Croydon led the way, the very first London airport, in connecting British travellers to the rest of the world: you could check in under the glass dome of its art deco departure hall, board a kangarooing HP-42 – and end up in Cape Town, or Calcutta, or even Darwin, Australia.

But then Captain Wilcockson had gone on to flying boats, and here was the genuine distinction. In 1937 he'd flown the Empire flying boat *Caledonia* non-stop across the Atlantic – a pioneering trial flight for what would be the first ever regular air service between Britain and the United States. *Caledonia* had taken off on 5 July from Foynes on the west coast of Ireland in heavy rain – 'not at all the sort of night,' its pilot airily remarked afterwards, 'that one would choose for a jaunt of this description.' The flying boat's fuselage was filled with extra fuel tanks carrying the over 2,000 extra gallons necessary to cross the ocean; the captain flew at just a thousand feet above the water to avoid ice in the clouds if he went higher. Only twice in the whole flight did they sight ships on the sea, and were able to make contact with neither to check their position. Not until they'd been flying for nine and a half hours did Wilkie and his first officer gain a glimpse of any stars in the sky – but at last they were able to position the planet Jupiter and the star Arcturus in the sextant to fix their latitude and longitude. Fifteen hours and ten minutes after leaving Ireland they finally alighted at Botwood in Newfoundland.

On to Montreal, and thence to New York, where Imperial Airways' Sales Adviser was concerned to choreograph the historic arrival for maximum publicity. When you're over the George Washington Bridge, he told Wilkie over the phone before the departure from Canada, hold back as much as possible to let the aerial photographers get some good pictures.

'How do I know where the George Washington Bridge is?' was the captain's admirably lofty response.

Get a map, came the terse advice.

The following year saw Captain Wilcockson instrumental in another flying-boat first. Imperial Airways had not yet solved the problem of flying its planned airmail service across the Atlantic: either the extra amount of fuel required would, as with *Caledonia*, preclude any payload, or the addition of freight would prevent the craft getting airborne. Another solution, similar to NASA launching the early Space Shuttles from a 747, was a piggy-back. On 20 July 1938 a small floatplane, christened *Mercury*, with half a ton of newspapers, newsreels and mail aboard, lifted off over Foynes from the Empire-type flying boat *Maia* that had given it a leg-up into the air, and twenty hours later delivered the first ever transatlantic air cargo to Montreal. Each pilot had to take care when the two aircraft jumped 15 feet apart that, unable to see his sister plane, he didn't fly into it. 'The sensation,' wrote *Mercury*'s pilot, the formidable Australian Don Bennett, who once wrote a complete textbook for flying-boat pilots, *The Air Mariner*, during a five-day layover in Brindisi and went on to found Bomber Command's Pathfinder force, 'is exactly the same as dropping a heavy bomb.' Down below Bennett, at the controls of the heavy bomb, had been 'dear old Wilkie'.

History, moreover, now made sense of something I *had* liked and taken for granted about Croydon. It had always been great for aeroplanes. When I was only five or six, my father had taken me for the first time to the International Air Fair at RAF Biggin Hill, the famous Battle of Britain fighter station fifteen minutes' drive east. Kenley, ten minutes south, where my father played cricket, had been another Battle of Britain base. Biggin Hill was where I learnt to watch planes – not the number-ticking of the spotter but the wondrous ballet of powered flight; physics become grace. We still go every year, my father and I, and where the small boy was frightened by a thunderous Lightning back in the sixties, and sheltered from the rain with his father under the delta wing of a mighty Vulcan, now it's the once-in-a-blue-moon honeyed mesh of a Constellation, or a screaming Harrier bowing to the crowd.

One year I saw the last airworthy Short Sunderland in the world making serene, burring passes over the runway, sailing the air in slow galleon turns on a blazing day at Biggin Hill – the one and only time it ever came – and that is as close as I've ever come to the flight of a great flying boat. The wonder of that sight, which has never left me, is that, of all the planes I'd seen at the Air Fair over all the years, this was the only one – I'd even watched Concorde touch its wheels down and then pulverize the air again in ascent – that couldn't land. The Sunderland had come from the sea, and to the sea it must return. Water seemed an impossibly long way away: even now the image of that Sunderland seems as strange as seeing a pelican over Croydon – or, indeed, as finding that one of the most illustrious flying-boat pilots had lived all his life in leafy Croham Manor Road.

To the question, Why are you fascinated by flying boats?, I'm tempted to answer, How could anyone not be? But Croydon, perversely, has something to do with it. Flying boats were always other, in every way. Writing now, in east London, looking out over the Regent's Canal, I know how even a narrow stretch of water opens the sky, makes you look up (an HS 146 airliner is just climbing north out of London City Airport). My hard, slabby, landlocked home couldn't accommodate them – they came from elsewhere, from the edge of the world.

I am, of course, too late. I missed Captain Wilcockson, and I missed the flying boats, too. The last ever flying-boat service in Britain taxied out on to Southampton Water two years before I was born. I never flew in any of the great flying boats. I shan't get the chance now. You always wonder about the life you weren't given, the stations closed by the time your train passed through. And just as one is struck by the certainty of John Pudney's conviction about 'Corsairville', so I admit my equal certainty that, in Victor Pitcher's place on the transatlantic Boeings, I would have said the same as he, and I wish I could have, and wonder why. The nearest I could get now would be to stand on the quayside waving goodbye and strain my eyes for a glimpse of a dwindling speck on the horizon, but at least I could do that. Though Captain Wilcockson had never left Croydon, within a few years the international air departures had: in 1937 the flying boats took over. The only place to start, then – in Britain certainly the nearest glimpse – was Southampton.

Centurion

3

Southampton

Ocean Village was not a village, and commanded no view of the ocean. It was a shopping mall of recent vintage, echoingly empty – one of those waterfront regeneration schemes where what had replaced the derelict docks retained, despite the Caribbean-sounding soubriquet, something of their melancholy desertion. But it was a nearby source of a cup of coffee before I visited the cafeteria-free Hall of Aviation, and it turned out to be hiding a splendid and instructive view.

Occasionally, that morning in Southampton, a Fokker airliner of KLM or Air UK had buzzed overhead, gaining height after taking off from the airport out at Eastleigh; but here was no aviation landscape – no treeless greensward, or crouching huddle of buildings, or flat tarmac and concrete. This was the Eastern Dock. Half a mile west, the *QE2* had just docked for a refit, her first in Britain for years. The container port was a forest of cranes, derricks and gantries. And up here in the Ocean Village 'food court' one looked out over one's coffee on to the River Itchen, and at a marina of bobbing yachts, rigging tinkling in the breeze, floating boardwalks, the sporadic sunlight crinkling on the lapping water like foil. To the south was the harbour mouth, further still the invisible Solent, beneath a tall sky. Even on an unsettled October day, flurried with torrential showers, the dominant facet was the light. Light is never still on water. It breaks and fissures and glints and flashes and fades, and its ceaseless play continually throws a scene into different emphases. *Here*, it beckoned, and *here*, and *here*, and *here* – and each was elsewhere. I was glad I'd come here before I went to see the flying boat. It had made me look at – indeed, *watch* – water, but also it had shown me a nautical prospect: not a plane in sight, not a plane's world.

'You've got to remember,' Norman Powell was explaining, 'when this thing was in the sea the water'd be up to that main rivet line. When it was on its take-off run the water'd be up over the windows. You needed this great tall hull to keep the propellers out of the water. And look at the shape of that hull – it's not built to be aerodynamic! It's built to be a boat!' A small, slight, neat man, as he pointed up at that main rivet line encircling this huge metal hippo – it was level with his head – he was his own gauge of its gigantism. Mr Powell had flown Short Sandringhams like this for Aquila Airways, who until 1958 had run Britain's last scheduled flying-boat services. He'd taxied them out from Berth 50, just a few minutes away in the Eastern Dock – there were photographs in the museum of them being backed in between the floating pontoons – and taken off from Southampton Water to fly down to Nice, Madeira and Lisbon. This aircraft, built in 1943 and later christened *Beachcomber*, had done its flying out in the Antipodes, finishing its service life plying between Sydney's Rose Bay and Lord Howe Island, before ending up in the Virgin Islands to be rescued for preservation. Now, gleaming white and red in the livery of Ansett Flying Boat Services, mounted up on its beaching chassis and denied even a glimpse of the sea, it was landlocked here in Southampton, where Mr Powell and the other retired volunteers who ran the Hall of Aviation museum showed people over it, the last passenger flying boat in the country.

Inside, we climbed a steep narrow ladder up through a trapdoor on to the flight-deck. Cockpit is definitely a better word for the flight crew's cramped compartment on a modern jetliner: as little headroom, as snug a fit, as in a small saloon car. But here was just what it said it was: a deck, the deep glass of the screen canopy all round a spacious, light observatory above the waves. 'You need good visibility,' said Mr Powell – I was now sat in the first officer's seat – 'there's twenty feet of wing *beyond* that far propeller.' And, like a ship's captain up on the bridge, you wanted to be high above the waves – there might be small boats drifting too near, flotsam lying in your path. 'As soon as one of these touched down on water,' he continued, 'by maritime law it was a boat.' It had to display the flag of its country of origin as an ensign, and another bearing BOAC's speedbird motif, or Aquila's eagle. He pointed aft: the flight engineer would stand on the navigator's map table there, open the top hatch and fix the flags to the top of the fuselage. 'And remember': it was Mr Powell's characteristic admonition – there was a lot you definitely couldn't afford to forget if you were at the helm of a flying boat – 'something like this has no brakes. You can only go forward.' Just like a boat: the best you could do was cut the engines, but if you'd misjudged the distance to the quayside you could only sit tight and wait for the impact.

But push those throttle levers forward, open up the engines, and as soon as you were off the water you'd turned into a plane – though a flying boat like this would take four or five minutes just to haul itself up to a thousand feet. Everything about its thick-set, pendulous profile said *heavy* – but weight was not *Beachcomber*'s problem. She weighed less than 17 tons: construct her like a German ironclad and she'd never have got off the water. Indeed, a flying boat was a remarkably delicate thing, made of very thin metal – 18-gauge, only slightly more than a millimetre thick. 'I've seen a .303 bullet pass through this,' said Mr Powell, tapping at the fuselage with his elbow. Any collision with even a small boat would tear the hull open like a tin can and sink the flying boat. Until the jet engine was invented all large aeroplanes, labouring under propeller-generated horsepower, were in retrospect underpowered, but a flying boat was also handi-capped by its shape. Not a sleek aerodynamic pencil, but that lantern-jaw hull to keep the propellers dry. 'The amount of power required to get one of these into the air, and then keep it flying,' said Mr Powell, 'that's a lot of parasite-induced drag . . .'

I followed Mr Powell back down that precipitous ladder. The passenger cabin was rather dark – no sunlight bouncing in off the water here – and more like a train compartment than the inside of an aircraft, the seats arranged in groups of four facing one another: planned not on the assumption of a swift translation from A to B, but a leisurely, congenial, communal journey. 'And remember' – one last thing, as we stood beside *Beachcomber* again – 'this hull is made of aluminium.' It was a strong, light material – wood, which flying boats had previously been made of, tended to soak up water and increase the weight for take-off. 'What's the greatest enemy of aluminium? Salt. It was a constant battle. After every flight they'd have it up on the slipway, and clean off all the salt incrustation. The engineer would go round inside before every flight, around the main rivet line, coating it with beeswax, and tightening every rivet. Because they'd always leak. Water'd always come in. And you have to have water in the bilges, anyway. And once the hull had fallen prey to corrosion that was that . . .'

Watch a cormorant, the scruff-headed black seabird, squatted on a rock, its long wings outstretched like sheets on a line: if it didn't let the water dry off, its whole life of diving for food would wash the oils out of its plumage and drown it by waterlogging. It's a contest the bird can never conclusively win. Being light enough to fly made a flying boat a fragile boat, and being boat-shaped enough to float made it a laborious flyer. And the very element in which it spent half its life – the salt water of the sea – was fatal to its existence.

We've grown used to the impersonal efficiency of modern aviation.

Today's airliners are not supposed to remind us of flying: better, for customer equanimity, that we are able to give our attention to the film, the headset-music schedule in the in-flight mag, to 'Red or white, sir?' during the meal. 'Mechanical failure', 'pilot error' – we don't want, and almost never need, to be reminded that the metal conveyance whizzing us through the sky at 40,000 feet has been built and operated by mere mortals. To look out of an Airbus window and see a greasy handprint on the silver wing is a shock: *mechanics* in *overalls*, like the men who MOT my car, service this thing!

Every one of those rivets shaping the white-painted panels into *Beachcomber*'s flanks, on the other hand, had – not just evidently but deducibly – been punched in by hand. An Airbus might have computer-generated design tolerances and fly-by-wire avionics: the flying boat could only be the product of human agency. You didn't need to anthropomorphize this old seaplane to see a pathos in what it was. What it managed to do had been earned at a price. In its ungainliness, its crudity, its vulnerability – for even a single loose rivet the craft be lost – it bowed to a natural world that technology had not yet been able to shut out or conclusively overcome. Like Victor Pitcher (and all flying-boat people, I was to find), Mr Powell pronounced the term in a particular way. Not, as you'd have thought, 'flying *boat*', with an emphasis on the wonder of it, but familiarly, as though one word: '*fly*ingboat' – both things at once, inextricable. 'Very cumbersome,' admitted Mr Powell when I asked him what these Sandringhams were like to fly. 'It's horses for courses – and the flying boat was always a compromise.' You paid a price for – but you also earned – your passage across the water and into the air. You couldn't love perfection: cherishing began with the recognition of imperfection.

Look at many extinct beasts and, in the austere light of today, their clumsy anachronism mocks itself. That model of a dodo in the Natural History Museum: stupid ugly thing – who could ever love a dodo? Many of the earliest biplanes: a collection of packing crates tied together by wire. Helplessness, the lame duck, is not attractive. But this flying boat couldn't be dismissed as merely a neither-one-thing-nor-the-other or a bit-of-both. Rather it seemed to hark back to a rarefied world that ought to have existed – where a flying machine might skid down on to the water as gracefully as a swan, and spend a life bobbing on the waves as oblivious as an eider. It brought news of the kind of kingdom that would accommodate – *need* – unicorns, or centaurs. It was our compromised, brackish world that hadn't measured up.

'Finger trouble.' That was Captain Vic Hodgkinson's unsentimental verdict on the mess flying boat *Corsair* had got into at Faradje: digit lodged somewhere it shouldn't have been instead of being more gainfully employed. The Hall of Aviation's archive was less a room than a cubicle, so I'd settled myself down beside the flying boat to rummage through the box of Africa memorabilia, and had just come across Captain Alcock's log-book with its fluently inscribed Remarks about Direction Loops. Oh, yes, Vic revealed: he'd once seen a 16 mm black-and-white ciné film about the *Corsair* salvage. It had been shown to his group of recruits while they were cooling their heels after the war at nearby Calshott, waiting to begin their civil flying-boat training with BOAC. That must have been the So You Still Want To Be A Flying-Boat Pilot? lesson. 'They tied its tail to a tree,' he told me – to prevent the flying boat drifting on the narrow river, or going too fast before it was stabilized for take-off. 'It acted like a brake': they'd get the engines' torque up, the pilot would stabilize the trim, and then – Vic swung an imaginary axe *chop!* on the rope – *Corsair* would be off. He'd since tried to track down the film through the RAF Museum at Hendon and various avenues, but without success. 'It must have deteriorated by now.'

Captain Vic Hodgkinson had led the team that had restored *Beachcomber* to its present condition here in Southampton after its arrival from the Virgin Islands, and written a small book about its history. A warm and friendly Australian, full of wheezing, honking laughter, Vic had flown flying boats throughout the war for the Australian Air Force. He'd trained on the old Supermarine Walrus, an amphibious plane designed for catapulting off the decks of ships – 'I could talk all day about those.' (Nowadays we have Tornados and Fighting Falcons, aircraft named to inspire international arms buyers with intimations of pitiless kills and whirlwinds of damage. Back in those quixotic days you could actually, if you wanted – no image consultant or market analyst would stop you – you could actually call a plane a Walrus.) Vic had first come over from Australia to Britain early in 1940, on the Empire boats *Carpentaria* and *Corio* – it took two weeks from Sydney to Poole – to join the new 10 Squadron for Coastal Command.

'The Australian Air Force had bought nine Sunderlands,' Vic recalled. 'They were £80,000 each in those days – and they paid for them through the whole war. It was one of the biggest contributions to the war effort. Our squadron was run purely by Australians: it was the only Commonwealth squadron to serve in the UK during the war.' They'd flown twelve-hour operations from Oban in Scotland protecting the Atlantic convoys, laid flare paths in the sea at night, hunted submarines in the Bay of Biscay, patrolled the Straits of Gibraltar, and ferried tyres and ammunition for Bristol Beaufighters to Alexandria during the 1941 desert campaign. Posted back to Australia in 1942 he'd flown Catalinas – American-made flying boats – from Cairns in the north to bomb the Japanese airfields in the Solomon Islands, and on one operation, in the air continuously for 25 hours 50 minutes, he'd seen the sun come up twice – but the record was 42 hours, Vic added, and that didn't include all the time before you took off or touched down. The fatigue of crews during such epic endurance missions was intense: one wartime pilot is said to have radioed that he had just sighted a man riding a bicycle across the sea.

Then, with the end of the war approaching, a total of 217 wartime operations flown, and the prospect of the air force asking him to drive a desk, Vic had seen an advertisement for fifty flying-boat pilots, and come back to Britain to fly BOAC's flying-boat services from Southampton until their withdrawal in 1950, before finally retiring on 707s.

I'd asked him if he'd show me Southampton's old flying-boat haunts down at the waterside – but first, while I browsed among old timetables and crackly rolled-up posters, he had some fluorescent lighting tubes to replace inside *Beachcomber*'s cabin. Besides continuing to devote his spare time to looking after the flying boat, Vic also carpentered superb items of furniture. Such craftsmanship and hands-on practicality was, I came to find, typical of flying-boat people. Even those now well into their eighties – perhaps approaching ninety – weren't letting up in their industry: time and again I'd phone to be told, 'Oh, just a minute – he's out in his workshop . . .' Flying boats were hands-on contraptions. They either attracted doers, or they made men learn to use their hands, to pitch in. For those who'd spent their working lives maintaining or repairing them, it was a constant task, and those whose job was to fly them had had to do just that.

Vic Hodgkinson had done his basic training on a landplane called a Wapiti (more wonderful nomenclature: christened after a North American species of red deer – one tries to imagine an aircraft with shy brown eyes), and contrasted the experience of then finding yourself at the controls of a flying boat out on the water. 'Instead of something nice and smooth, here was something that was pitching round all over the place. You had a boat to take you out, and in bad weather you'd get soaked before you even got on board – and it was quite difficult to get on board, because it'd be swinging on its mooring. No brakes, no steering – not like modern land aircraft which you can turn anywhere you like – and it wanted to weathercock in the wind all the time. They call it the romance of flying,' Vic mused. 'People look back, think it was marvellous . . .' But he wasn't really debunking the myth: he was celebrating the actuality. At the age of eighty, flying boats were still his passion. There was no fun in doing something easy. 'It was more of a challenge,' he said. 'It was seat-of-the-pants stuff.'

As I drove us down to the waterfront Vic pointed out the serrated awnings of the old Harbour railway station. In the days of the flying boats passengers would check in at Airways House in Buckingham Palace Road in central London, walk straight out on to a dedicated adjoining platform at Victoria Station, and the train would bring them to within yards of the berth. And if news had reached London that the flying boat had been delayed by the weather or an engine problem, a tea-dance would be laid on for them down in Airways House's art deco ballroom. Today cars were parked under the canopies where the tracks would have been. On the corner of the street, in front of the old railway terminus, was a grand wedding-cake of a building: the former South-Western Hotel, said Vic, where the passengers would stay overnight before the customary crack-of-dawn start. The BBC had taken it over after the station and hotel had closed, but now it was an empty hulk. The Empire boats had left from Berth 108, further west along the River Test near the ocean-liner terminal, but the entrance turned out to be a noisy container depot now, behind high fences. Vic got out and chatted to the gateman while articulated trucks roared in and out and huge spread-eagled tractors squatted over containers like weightlifters, to prise them deliberately up off the ground. No good, was the news on his return: no access, but nothing to see, either – no trace left of the old berth.

We parked out on the Town Quay, where the Hythe ferry docked, to see if there was a view across to Berth 50, from where Vic had flown the later Solent flying boats in the last years of the Africa service. In the Hall of Aviation's archive I'd found the brochure for the opening of the new BOAC flying-boat terminal after the war, extolling the 'deep mushroom shade' of its seat upholstery and the glass-fronted restaurant overlooking the water – but from the road all trace of a 'New Marine Airport' was gone, and more high hoardings and security gateposts enclosed a large demolition site. The Town Quay itself had become another leisure development – a precinct of shops and an Old Orleans restaurant. From here we could see that across the water the terminal building had indeed gone altogether: huge heaps of aggregate stood in its place, awaiting some big new construction project. But there were the old flying-boat walkways still, dilapidated grey asbestos, poking down into the water to where the pontoons would once have been.

Vic and I walked to the far end of the Quay. There an old man was playing a few shuffling notes on a harmonica, casting furtive glances back at us. In the late morning the sky was grey, there was a nagging wind. It was trying to rain. Vic pointed south, showing me where the flying boats used to taxi out towards their maintenance base at Hythe, to the confluence of the Test and the Itchen, and then round the bend to port towards Calshott for take-off. The wind had whipped up a slapping, choppy sea. He looked across to the old walkways of Berth 50. It was a narrow channel that separated them from this quay. Those rocking yachts, the playful light on the marina, had led me to envision stout flying boats pleasantly riding the calm water. This, I could see now, would not have been so pleasant – trying to step off a rocking pontoon into a heaving cabin, and then bouncing about inside. You could imagine the passengers casting a glance upwards at those buzzing airliners from Eastleigh and thinking, *land*plane . . .

'In weather like this I wonder how we ever used to land a flying boat here,' Vic said. That great corpulent Sandringham higher than a bus in the museum. 'I never used to enjoy it here – taxiing up with no brakes, the tail going like this' – he swung his upright hand about like a mad weathervane – 'and trying to come into the berth. A litt-le bit hairy . . .' Forty, fifty years ago: indeed, you wondered.

Courtier

4

Planes for the Few

The night they launched the Princess, however, the harbour was like a millpond. A gale had blown up during the day: they'd waited until midnight for high tide and no wind. The black water shone around the giant hull as it was rolled in, floodlights illuminating the underside. What was above was out of frame, but the scale of all that must have been excluded suggested nothing less than a ship.

This was the twenty-first of August, 1952, across the Solent from Southampton at Cowes on the Isle of Wight. Forty-six years later its flight engineer and I were watching his video of the 16 mm news film shot by its manufacturers of the launch and first test-flights. A dense fog had descended that afternoon by the time I drove in the gates of RAF Bicester, the largely disused airfield in Oxfordshire where I was to meet Dick Stratton in the local gliding club. I nosed the car among towering locked gunmetal-grey hangars: just then the place seemed terminally deserted. It was a couple of days before Christmas, and the few people in the clubhouse – no flying today with this visibility – were saying their goodbyes and drifting away for the holiday, until it was just the two of us left, and the Princess. Listen to a man tell you, in a tone of matter-of-fact familiarity, about the years when he helped to fly a ten-engined, 220-foot-wide double-deck flying boat from Cowes Harbour in the Isle of Wight – and then drive away again an hour or so later into the fog. I could not have had a sharper sense of dislocation – of the story of the Princess coming at you out of a reverie.

'A huge aeroplane,' conceded Dick Stratton – 'by anybody's standards.' It seems a fantasy out of *Thunderbirds* that, back in the fifties, the anachronism of the seaplane – or the irrevocable pull of a maritime tradition, depending on how you look at it – was proved by Britain's launch of one of the most colossal aeroplanes ever built, and a flying boat at that. The flying boat had always been a compromise, Norman Powell had told me at Southampton's Hall of Aviation – but what could have been more gloriously extreme than, a full two years after BOAC had withdrawn its last Solents from its last flying-boat service, to unveil a leviathan fully twice as big again? Nowadays planes are designed for a market – indeed, even in those days, so were successful airliners like the Constellation. But the Saunders–Roe Princess was designed for a dream. If you wanted magnificent folly, the world of the flying boat had it in spades. It was almost a prerequisite.

Britain's giant seaplane was intended for the transatlantic run, carrying over a hundred passengers in luxury worthy of the competing ocean liners – its twin-deck cabin fitted out with cocktail bars, powder rooms and even bunks for overnight slumber. 'How the hell they ever got the money to build the Princess,' declared Mr Stratton, 'I would not know.' By the end the Ministry of Supply had invested the exceedingly luxurious sum of £10 million in the project. Problems with the development of its chosen gas-turbine engines meant it was years late, and always underpowered. Only three craft were built; only one ever flew; none was ever sold or carried a paying passenger. The bars and berths were never put in: the interior remained a hollow shell. The last flight was in 1954; cocooned in bitumen and plastic for years on the banks of the Medina river at Cowes, while ideas came and went of using the seaplanes to transport Saturn V rocket parts for NASA or as test beds for atomic reactors, the last of the three went to the breakers in 1967.

It was such a British story. The small, maverick firm of Saunders–

Roe on the Isle of Wight was a technological hothouse – could turn its hand to anything from boats to stressed roofs for Becton Gasworks, and was soon to develop the hovercraft, helicopters, a rocket-powered interceptor fighter and space probes. 'Oh, it didn't run on tramlines,' said Mr Stratton. The chief test-pilot, Geoffrey Tyson, came, felicitously, from Croydon. With the Princess the small company gave birth to a monster aircraft unbelievably advanced for its time: a pressurized cabin, the first and only time it had been achieved on a flying boat; air-conditioning. Even as it was being fitted with state-of-the-art power-operated flying-control systems, Saunders–Roe's boffins, to Dick Stratton's amazement on joining from the RAF in 1949, already had fly-by-wire technology (which wouldn't be used commercially until Concorde) up and running in its test house. But the Princess was also stunningly out of date.

In retrospect the location of Saunders–Roe, beavering away on a small island, seems all too microcosmically emblematic. Here was a plane commissioned by an insular maritime nation, hitherto insulated from a world that had changed around it. The Princess was first mooted during the war when the government, with commendable foresight, established the Brabazon Committee to prime the aircraft industry for peacetime with new products for civil orders. It got things right, eventually, with the projects that became the Britannia and the Viscount – but it also ordered a seaplane for a post-war world that would take advantage of all those long concrete runways the war was currently laying down. It presumed, too, on a pre-war moneyed and leisured élite for its customers, when the People's War was liberating a middle-class meritocracy as the major new travel market. It was a mandarin's dream of idyll.

Mr Stratton was an engineer, a direct, open man in a baggy sweater, and this was his homily: 'Everything that we do, in engineering,' he said, 'is better than better. But nobody understood market research in the British aircraft industry. Boeing have never made an aircraft that didn't sell. We had delusions of grandeur in getting passengers off the *Queen Mary* – but the idea of cocktail bars and two-berth cabins was absolute rubbish. The hard knocks of commercial aviation showed up eventually when we were overtaken by the 707 coming the other way, and people were really jammed in like sardines – it was only then you could get enough revenue out of aeroplanes to pay the bills. We were backing the wrong horse, in a big way.' The Princess was too clever by half, and not savvy enough.

And yet Dick Stratton was still travelling round the country giving lectures to packed houses about the Princess. For the Princess was an astounding, fabulous aircraft. 'There she goes,' he said: now we were watching its first ever take-off – a tricky logistical exercise, he recalled, because that week had been Cowes Week, and the harbour filled with yachts. What rose on its skirts of white spray and floated off the water – in the absence of any soundtrack the accompanying silence only heightened the grace of it – was like a vast basking shark become weightless and gliding into the air. Aboard, said Mr Stratton, it had been so smooth, so quiet, you really weren't aware of its huge bulk. 'Although it wasn't so heavy, you see. We were 320,000 lb take-off weight. A 747'll go out of London Airport nowadays at 800,000 lb – and they'll do it on four engines and we did it on ten!' An aerial camera from a shadowing Sunderland was following the Princess's dreamy passage, on a bright, clear day, above Calshott, round the south coast past Christchurch and Bourne-mouth, and then there below were the white slivers of the Needles. When you watched it now you knew it could have no use whatsoever – look at it! Something out of Jules Verne! So you could just wonder at it as a work of art, pure spectacle – that it had been built at all. I was looking at nothing other than a flying ship. 'Oh, it's all epic stuff, isn't it?' said the flight engineer briskly. 'History now.'

*

'They're going to be good planes all right, make no mistake about that,' says Fat Patrick's father in Tim Binding's 1993 novel *In the Kingdom of Air*, 'but in my opinion, and I only do the bloody sums around here, these planes are a luxury only the British would want to afford. Herr Hitler is building cars for everyone. He calls them *Volks Wagens*. We build planes for the few.' *In the Kingdom of Air* is one of a small scattering of English novels in which the flying boat makes an appearance. It opens in Rochester, the plane-making Kent town home to Shorts' seaplane works, and Fat Patrick's father is talking about the Empire boats, whose interiors he is designing. It is Dickensian in much more than its Medway setting.

One day someone will essay the thesis that needs to be written on *The Flying Boat in British Fiction*, and test my proposition that its rare literary touchdowns serve as instructive markers. Where you find a flying boat you will also find the extravagant, the quixotic, the whimsical. It inherits the Sternian tradition, not the Richardsonian. None, to my knowledge, in the fiction of Margaret Drabble. But look in the first volume of Evelyn Waugh's Sword of Honour trilogy: it is a flying boat that 'climbed in a great circle over the green land . . . and set its course across the ocean', carrying away Guy Crouchback with the corpse of Apthorpe, whose death is in some way connected with the previous booby-trapping of his treasured portable thunder-box, and the mad Colonel Ritchie-Hook, who probably booby-trapped it. Think of that most delightfully English of English authors, J. L. Carr, who published, out of his middle-England home in Kettering, such miniature classics as *Carr's Dictionary of Extraordinary Cricketers*. Of course, he did his war service on a flying-boat station in West Africa, and, in *A Season in Sinji*, wrote a novel that managed to combine flying boats and a cricket match. The Empire boats, says the narrator of *In the Kingdom of Air*, were craft that 'flew in the age of the white saxophone'. Tristram Shandy would have called it – what these rare landings of the flying boat are seeking out – the 'hobby-horsical'. It was that, as much as anything, that attracted me to flying boats. When there was a flying boat involved you knew you'd be meeting someone who followed their own agenda. We built planes for the few.

In 1991 Edward Hulton strode down Piccadilly to meet me outside the Ritz, a tall, slightly distracted figure in his forties, sporting a tweed three-piece, and with a shock of uncombed hair – the kind of person you might expect to meet in the unsaddling enclosure at Ascot. In the last thirty years he is the only Englishman to have owned a flying boat. I don't include anything with fewer than four engines, or amphibians that have wheels as well. I mean a real behemoth like a Sandringham or a Sunderland. It had been quite difficult to fix an appointment to meet: whenever Hulton's wife answered the phone any mention of flying boats provoked a frosty disinclination to pass on a message. He had business to attend to in St James's, he told me when we finally managed a date, but, once installed in a coffee shop near Fortnum's, it seemed he had time to talk all day about flying boats.

There was a magnificent vagueness to Edward's account of how, and why, he'd acquired a Second World War vintage Short Sunderland flying boat. In Monte Carlo one day he'd met a man who told him that in the British Virgin Islands they were still using flying boats on scheduled services. 'It fired my imagination,' pondered Hulton in his slow, deliberate baritone, 'and I knew I had to have one.' So he went out there and bought one. He had, it must be said, the advantage over most impulsive dreamers of an inheritance from his father, Sir Edward Hulton, the founder and proprietor of *Picture Post*. As one of the earliest exponents of hang-gliding he also had previous experience of flying by the seat of your pants – indeed, taking a leap off a mountain. But, prior to his purchase, had Hulton ever flown in – or even seen – a Short Sunderland flying boat? 'Obviously not,' came the stern reproof.

Islander, the flying boat he now found himself the owner of, was actually the sister craft of Southampton's *Beachcomber*: by the time Hulton got out to the Caribbean it was lying derelict and corroded in a hangar. Six months' work in Puerto Rico was necessary to clean it up for its flight across the Atlantic. Then it was laid up for four years under repair at Chatham, in order to convince the Civil Aviation Authority to grant a Certificate of Airworthiness (aviation's equivalent of an M O T, permitting a plane to take to the air). And then, finally rolled out on to the slipway, on the eve of its relaunch it was hit by the 1987 hurricane, and a wrecked wing took another two years to fix. 'I *very* nearly gave up then,' Hulton admitted.

But rueful longing was quite absent from his observation that 'Modern aviation is entirely concerned with efficiency. Lower the undercarriage, taxi your airliner to the gate and pay your parking fee.' He looked back, instead, to the days of wartime Coastal Command when pilots like Vic Hodgkinson had flown their marathon operations. 'Sunderland crews prided themselves on being a privileged club,' Edward continued, 'and it still is. Back then these aircraft were completely self-contained, could fly on patrol for days on end. There's a feeling of freedom in a flying boat – theoretically you can land on any calm stretch of water you see . . .'

Except that Edward had done very little of this. Other vintage-aircraft preservationists set up supporters' clubs, who collected subscriptions and did sponsored walks and gave up weekends to re-skin tailplanes. They set up stalls at airshows, sold souvenirs, and worked their elderly planes hard with a summer schedule of perhaps three flypast appearances a day to pay their way and keep them in the air. The Sunderland's brief visit I'd seen at Biggin Hill had been one of less than a handful of such airshow appearances. Hulton had taken it to the west of Ireland for the opening of the Foynes Aeronautical Museum, on the site of the old flying-boat base from where Captain Wilcockson had taken off across the Atlantic in *Caledonia*. It sounds like the start of what would have been an ideal future for *Islander*: the Irish airline Ryanair had undertaken to base it on the Shannon and maintain it in peak condition for Edward. But on the very evening of the opening day its owner suddenly upset a great many people by insisting his flying boat be brought back to England in the morning. Approaches from other parties to use Hulton's Sunderland for promotional work and pleasure trips had never quite come to anything. It seemed, from talking to those who'd tried, that you could never quite nail Edward down. 'Edward was *useless*,' sighed one person in despair. I imagine they'd all met that same distant, reserved gaze with which he regarded me, as though I was slightly to the side of his vision, and something was lingering just out of focus on the horizon.

But then, it was his flying boat. He'd gone out and bought one. When I met him, some twelve years after he'd acquired his Sunderland, it was up for sale. The novelty was wearing off. He was wryly noncommittal about how much it had all cost him. Elsewhere I heard informed suggestions well in excess of £2 million. It took him several years to find someone to take his flying boat off him – though the price he was asking was little more than the going rate for a Spitfire. Just about any aircraft would have been cheaper to look after. Eventually a wealthy American collector bought it, and in 1994 the fifty-year-old *Islander* hauled herself off Southampton Water again, made a couple of low-level passes above the coast to bid goodbye to a large crowd and, like the Wandering Jew, boomed off on another long crossing of the Atlantic to a new home on a lake in Florida. 'It would be more suitable in the Pacific Islands,' Edward had remarked to me without a trace of irony. 'It would make a very good flying yacht . . .'

*

'A privileged club': that was how Edward Hulton had thought of the wartime Sunderland crews, bonded together into a small family by their arduously long patrols. 'We were jokingly known as the RAF's four-engined yacht club,' Dick Stratton told me – he'd also been with Coastal Command during the war – 'because we pottered about on the sea with marine craft and refuellers and all sorts of wonderful things that kept you busy. Glorious fun – and I always used to say, gloriously inefficient!' It doesn't seem a coincidence to me that J. L. Carr had managed to get flying boats and cricket into the same novel. Membership of the MCC, self-appointed custodians of a rulebook both recondite and irrelevant to anyone but *aficionados*, is a matter of waiting years for the privilege of wearing a hideous tie.

Ken Emmott had flown Edward Hulton's Sunderland for him. (Hulton, naturally, wasn't even a qualified pilot – had given up on lessons years before.) Four years after flying a plane for the last time at the age of seventy-two, he still ran a rental business out in Florida from his home in Surrey. He was certainly not a clubby man in the blazer-wearing, blimpish sense – he gave me a caustic account of how, at some pilots' reunion he'd been persuaded to go to, one of these old codgers (I think that was actually the word he used), curious about the jumbo jets he'd been flying, had inquired, 'So what's it like, bringing in one of these big kites?' In a voice dry as sand Mr Emmott was compelled to dwell on the memory: '"*Bringing in* one of these *big kites* . . ."' He looked at me at a loss. But though he reflected with wonder on the latest satellite positioning systems in modern airliners that would flash up a new bearing of your place on earth even as you steered the nose-wheel 10 feet to the left, it was a painting of a white Coastal Command Sunderland unsticking from the sea that hung on his living-room wall.

By the late 1980s, when *Islander* was finally ready to fly again, Ken Emmott was the only man left in Britain still possessing a current Airline Transport Licence of the kind CAA bureaucracy required for the largely uncalled for assignment of piloting a civilian flying boat. He'd flown RAF Catalinas in the Middle East during the war, and then, like Vic Hodgkinson, BOAC Sandringhams and Solents afterwards, before transferring to the Comet development unit to prepare for the introduction of the world's first jetliner. By the time he retired from British Airways, as it had become, he was on 747s: one thirty-year civil flying career since the war registering aviation's astonishing technological advance. When G-BJHS *Islander* was rolled gingerly down the slipway into the water, he'd been at the controls of a flying boat for the first time since 1950. 'I remember the sensation I had, sitting up in the cockpit, which I hadn't had for thirty years,' he recalled. 'The gentle rocking, bouncing over the waves towards the buoy. It wants to go with the tide, with the wind . . .'

Even now this composed, precise man was not indulging in limpid nostalgia. Now slightly stooped, with crinkly grey hair, hands folded and at ease with themselves, he was going to continue the instruction from where Vic Hodgkinson had left it as we'd gazed across the River Test: the exact art of flying a flying boat. Mr Emmott told me of a test pilot on the Bristol Britannia airliner who'd quipped, 'I fly this bit' – the cockpit end – 'the rest follows on behind.' Landplanes were much easier to fly, he said: with a flying boat you had to fly all 85 feet of it.

For a take-off, once you were out on the water, everything was variable. 'It won't just sit on the runway – it'll roll – so the wings won't stay level: you have to use the ailerons. Then, because of the torque of the engines, it'll swing: you have to use the rudder to keep it straight.' Because the swing was habitually to port, you opened up the port engines first, and built up speed to 50, 60 knots until the flying boat's 5-foot draught was out of the water and the craft was 'planing' on its step – skating on top of the water, so that the kink half-way along the hull broke the surface tension preventing it 'unsticking'. '*Then*', said Mr Emmott, 'you can open up the starboard. And then it'll porpoise – so you have to have the control column pulled all the way back.' Porpoising was what happened if the craft became airborne at too low a speed; because its nose was too high. 'You *must* take off at the correct speed, and fly level. I remember the words in the BOAC manual,' he warned: if you didn't, '"It will crash back on to the water with a force capable of breaking an engine."'

J. L. Carr's *A Season in Sinji* finds good words for a flying boat's take-off run: the water rumbling underneath, 'followed by that ghastly scraping din under her keel, like a rake being dragged across a corrugated tin roof'. Mr Emmott translated that from the pilot's point of view. You'd had 'your left hand on the ailerons, right hand on the throttle' (he was counting them all off), 'feet on the pedals', control column pushed right back to keep the nose down until the flying boat was planing – and now, 'all these controls have to be brought off, because at low speed they're very ineffective, but at high speed increasingly effective.' At which point, with all the controls now turned round, a spectator on the shore beholding a majestic ascent from the waves, 'you take off,' concluded Mr Emmott, 'like a one-armed paper-hanger.'

Imagine trying to do all that on the narrow River Dungu, with rocks beneath the surface, a current flowing, and a bend to port ahead! I was coming to appreciate the fix Empire boat *Corsair* had got itself into in 1939 by coming down in the Belgian Congo. But also you could see how the flying-boat fraternity would seem bafflingly esoteric to aviation's rank and file. They chose to spend their time on one-armed paper-hanging! It was a perversely demanding art, straddling three elements rather than just two. Ken Emmott had once had to swim for it himself in Southampton Water when his BOAC captain had landed too fast, bounced their Sunderland off the water and cut away a large section of the nose before they sank to the bottom. Struggling out had not been made easier, he reflected, by the heavy overcoat, boots and gloves he'd been wearing, like most flying-boat crew, against the cold in those unpressurized, unheated cockpits.

Even right at the end of your flight, once you'd touched down, mooring the craft required a last finesse, when the radio operator had to lean out of the front hatch and hook the buoy with a grommet. 'A lot of flying-boat captains had a great pride in getting on to the buoy,' Mr Emmott observed, 'which was quite tricky in some places. And if you missed the buoy, that was *ignominious*! The whole fleet knew about it! Some of them would have to take a tow out to the buoy, but that wasn't quite the done thing.'

This was why only an Englishman could write a novel that so naturally juxtaposed flying boats and cricket. Even Dick Stratton, reflecting on the reasons for the Princess's obsolescence, had talked of how they'd been 'batting on BOAC's wicket'. It was a question of a cover drive against a hoick to cow corner, never mind that you might get a four for each. When you made a game that difficult the only point in playing it was for itself – as a craft, a dream of perfection. The unnecessary difficulty of being an air mariner perversely made bodging it not good enough. No wonder the impatient Americans had got cracking on the Boeing 707.

5

Windermere

One of the very few longer flights Ken Emmott had made in Edward Hulton's Sunderland before delivering it to Oshkosh, Wisconsin, on his seventy-second birthday for its new owner, was in 1990, to land on Windermere. The Lake District! – the most beautiful mountain region in England: a tranquil refuge mythologized and celebrated in the poetry of Wordsworth, the stories of Beatrix Potter and Arthur Ransome's Swallows and Amazons, and the fastidious hand-calligraphed and hand-cartographed walking guides of A. Wainwright. What in the slightest – apart from the obvious water – did the Lakes have to do with flying boats?

But I'd preceded G-BJHS *Islander* to Windermere. The trail had been sparked by another innocuous reference in C. H. Barnes's *Shorts Aircraft since 1919*: page 368. No drybones statistician – the Corsairville story had fired his imagination – Barnes was still an encyclopaedic chronicler of flying-boat production schedules and serial numbers. Above plan drawings of a Sunderland in profile, head-on and bird's-eye view, and details of all-up weight (Mk I) and max range with overload fuel (Mk V), he totted up where all 749 Sunderland flying boats had been built: '341 at Rochester, 240 at Dumbarton, 133 at Belfast and 35 at Windermere.' There it was: during the war 20-ton flying boats had been built in the middle of the Lake District. Who could not want to know more?

The moment I sat down in the Kendal offices of the Friends of the Lake District, the pressure group with a distinguished century-long record of conserving the region's unspoiled beauty, and opened their old file on the subject, I came upon a fascinating and quirky story. For all their apparent discreteness, thousands of miles, whole climates apart, it eventually made me see a more than coincidental link between the Lakes and that backwater of Central Africa. In taking me to Windermere, flying boats were also helping to explain the allure of Corsairville.

No matter that there was a war on: the Friends were appalled. What had been decided on was nothing short of an 'abomination', wrote their Secretary, the Reverend H. H. Symonds, in the Annual Report for 1940: an abomination 'which profanes the sanctuary and makes desolate a famous and frequented part of it'.

Confirmation had come in a secret letter from the office of Lord Beaverbrook, the Minister for Aircraft Production, to the local MP:

> My dear Keeling,
> You will remember coming to see me on a deputation to ask that this Ministry should not erect a factory on the shores of Lake Windermere . . .
>
> The product is a flying boat. A site on the edge of deep water is essential. We had a thorough search made and, indeed, that was resumed after I saw you . . . We sent a man to investigate at Lytham St Anne's. The mud-flats were our difficulty there.
>
> We have, therefore, had to decide on Windermere. I am sorry. Time, however, is all important . . .

By the end of 1940, when this letter was sent, the German navy had concentrated its resources on its U-boat fleet, Italy's submarines had also entered the war, and Allied shipping was being sunk everywhere from the coast of Norway to the Bay of Biscay. RAF Coastal Command could call on only one aircraft with a range sufficient to track the U-boats effectively – and even sink them with depth-charges: the Short Sunderland flying boat. As we have already seen, Imperial Airways stood no chance of any more civilian Empire boat deliveries to replace stranded accident victims like *Corsair*: not only had Shorts turned over their production entirely to the Sunderland – they'd set up extra lines on the Clyde and in Belfast to try and meet demand. Then its main factory at Rochester on the Medway was bombed.

The Lake District: quiet, sparsely populated – and miles from the Blitz on the big cities – and containing the longest stretch of inland water in England. Where more remote and unexpected and safe for a secret shadow-factory to build and repair the RAF's largest seaplanes? But if the scenario of Sunderlands alighting on Windermere was alarming to the Friends of the Lake District, it was not quite unprecedented. An esoteric tradition of seaplanes on the lake had gone before, right back to before the first war. Back in 1909 a Mr Wakefield of Blackpool had concluded that the problem of flimsy flying-machines sustaining damage when they landed heavily on uneven ground could be solved by a water-landing. Derision greeted his proposal, but two years later, in 1911 on Windermere, his *Water Hen* achieved the first successful take-off ever by a 'Hydro-aeroplane'. Its pilot, Captain Stanley Adams, went on to run Wakefield's Lakes Flying School, offering tuition in flying seaplanes at £50 a time, and passenger flights – another world first – at £12 each. Another pioneer inventor, who lived at Hawkshead, was Oscar Gnosspelius. After the war Gnosspelius became a mining surveyor in South Africa, and married Barbara Collingwood, a childhood friend of Arthur Ransome. His learned knowledge about veins, reef, pyrites and methods of panning and washing during Ransome's research for *Pigeon Post* subsequently earned him the book's dedication. But before the war Gnosspelius, finding in the Lakeland landscape precious little flat ground for his aeroplane experiments, had lighted upon an 1873 book by the Rev. Charles

Ramus entitled *The Polysphenic Ship*, in which its author developed the notion of the *stepped pontoon*. The notion led, in 1912, to Gnosspelius's successful take-off from Windermere in his 40 hp 'hydroplane', further variants of which he built until war broke out. When hostilities ceased he was snapped up as a designer by Shorts. Presumably Arthur Ransome must have known of his good friend's erstwhile contribution to marine aviation, though the authorized biography gives no clue. Imagine a thirteenth Swallows and Amazons novel in which the Blackett children construct their own primitive hydroplane on Windermere and try to take off and clear Orrest Head!

The Air Ministry settled on Whitecross Bay, at the northern end of Windermere, for the seaplanes' slipway into the water, and built the new factory on 28 acres of wood and farmland in the adjoining Calgarth Park. The new hangar's distinction of being the biggest unsupported span in the country is unlikely to have impressed the Friends of the Lake District; they consoled themselves with the promise they had extracted from Beaverbrook to close down and demolish the works as soon as the war ended, and return the land to its former agricultural use. Back along the main road at Troutbeck Bridge a prefabricated village of 243 bungalows and hostels also went up, ready for the skilled aircraft workers who were to be transferred from other plants to get production going and train the local workforce.

The Lake District has England's highest annual rainfall, but on my visit I found brilliant sunshine. Norman Parker now lived on the Droomer housing estate above Windermere at the foot of School Knott. In the early years of the war, he told me over large slices of the fruit cake he'd baked that day himself, he'd been working at Fairey's near Stockport, when he found himself among a group of fitters being counted out into two queues. 'I got put in Barrow – that was to go and work on submarines at Vickers. Next to me in the other line was a man called Jim Brotherton. "Windermere!" he said to me. "Out in the bloody wilderness!" I said, "Quick – get in here, man," and we changed places. So he went to Barrow, and I came here.' Les Hills, a joiner, was sent up with a contingent from Shorts at Rochester, and put on making jigs and tools for the new factory. 'Well, I was highly delighted. The Lake District! Who wouldn't be! And coming from Kent, where we'd had air raids daily – if not hourly – and a direct hit on the works.'

'Talk about a garden factory,' Norman Parker reflected. 'I arrived on a beautiful clear autumn day – the pale sunlight through the beech trees, the reds, browns, russets – and I wrote straight back to my wife, "Come at once, I'm now in heaven."' It was the kind of weather I was seeing around me now. So here was a brand-new factory amongst trees and rhododendron bushes, at the edge of a vast lake, where you could cycle to work in the mornings, and the fells rising on all sides for your free days. Mr Parker took up hound-trailing and played football against the prison guards at Grizedale Hall, where top-ranking German officers were interned as prisoners of war. 'And I'd look through the factory window out at Wansfell and say to myself, I'm going up that.'

Some of Les Hills's Rochester colleagues, however, didn't like the seclusion at all and retreated to the Medway as soon as possible – and even for those who did stay on, the transition from a metropolis to a rural lakeside works took some getting used to – just a single shop, and that a long haul from the factory back to Troutbeck Bridge, and an edgy reception from the local people. But local suspicion evaporated as soon as jobs became available at the factory. Hitherto, opportunities around Windermere had mostly been limited to hill farming, or chauffeuring and gardening for the many large houses in the area. Now here was the chance to learn skilled, well-paid crafts. Buses brought workers in from Hawkshead, Coniston, even as far as Kendal. Norman Parker estimated that at its height the Shorts works was employing some 2,000 people.

All this, and far away from the uncertainty and terror of nightly aerial bombardment. Every so often the Hawkshead Home Guard would take to their boats under cover of darkness and test the Shorts security with a floundering beach-landing. A solitary bomb – probably jettisoned by a German bomber unable to reach Barrow – fell near Troutbeck and killed a sheep. I went to see Joan Hewitt and Marjorie Parrington, now living in a beautiful house in Bowness with a view across Windermere: back then, as the Mossman sisters, they'd been sent home from aircraft-production training in Preston to rivet portholes for flying boats at Whitecross Bay. For teenage girls there was a good social life around the works – dances, fairs, sports days, and a cinema at the production village. 'It was hardly as if there was a war on,' Joan Hewitt recalled as we sat out in their conservatory. 'We had quite a gay time, really.' Kendal Library's local-studies section didn't have any material on the factory, but the librarian had an idea her mother knew of someone who'd worked there. She came off the phone in amused confusion: the person she'd been thinking of turned out to be a woman who'd given birth to a baby in the works toilets.

There were reminders of the world at war beyond the Lakeland fells. Some of the pilots who came to fly the newly completed Sunderlands out were Australian – possibly from Vic Hodgkinson's 10 Squadron. One former employee, Madge Wilson, who'd worked in the typing pool at Whitecross Bay, remembered a Sunderland that had come in from Norway for repair, its rear gun-turret shot to bits and full of blood. But overwhelmingly the former workforce had picturesque, treasurable memories. Marjorie Parrington told me how she'd find herself holding her breath when a Sunderland set off down Windermere on its 80 m.p.h. take-off run. Norman Parker remembered how the burr of its engines came up off the water and reverberated around the hills. On one occasion he was taken up on a test flight out over the Isle of Man, and able to look down on where his wife had been born. The flying-boat factory sounded just like the kind of Utopian, bucolic industrial community that the Lakeland sage John Ruskin had tried unavailingly to establish in the previous century from nearby Coniston. The people at Whitecross Bay had been privileged with a peaceful, rather paradisal war. But war memorials aren't erected to commemorate idyll and sanctuary.

By the time the war ended Windermere had built thirty-five Sunderlands – in effect one a month. Small-scale production compared to other Shorts factories, but it had also repaired as many battle-damaged planes. If the lake itself, surrounded by mountains liable to disappear in a sudden Lakeland mist, might seem a dangerous place from which to try and fly a 20-ton flying boat, in fact the reverse was true. A north–south wind blew straight up and down to take off into, and for landing there was a sheet of water so calm that often a motor boat had to go out beforehand and furrow a wake so the pilot could judge his height above the surface. Indeed, the few fuzzy contemporary photographs I was shown of these rotund machines wallowing in the lake only confirmed the sheer size of Windermere itself: a mile across, and 10 miles from end to end. I heard one tale of a pilot who'd taken it into his head to take off *across* the lake, and got the plane into the air just in time to gain enough height to skim the summit of Coniston Old Man.

Towards the end of the war an even bigger flying boat touched down on Windermere – the enormous Shetland, nearly twice as big as the Sunderland, not that much smaller than the Princess, and the biggest seaplane Shorts ever built. All nine Sunderlands had to be taken out of the hangar to fit it in to be weighed. The idea was that such monster craft would go into post-war production at Windermere and safeguard the future of the works. But by the time the war was over neither the RAF nor BOAC wanted any saurian Shetlands, and Shorts soon stopped building flying boats. Meanwhile, the Friends of the Lake District were reminding the Air Ministry of its undertaking five years before.

To many, that promise of demolition now seemed an anachronism. The local council found it needed to retain the workers' prefabs to house those returning from distant war service. A proposal to convert the works into a textiles factory attracted considerable support from a community for whom the summary elimination of so many well-paid jobs was a heavy blow. Moreover, as one letter to the *Westmorland Gazette* maintained, for the Friends to assert that the tree-shrouded works defiled the area was 'quite absurd. I will go so far as to say that seven out of every ten visitors to Windermere would be totally unaware of its existence.'

At the beginning of the fifties, to not inconsiderable local disappointment, the factory buildings did come down. But they'd been built on foundations sunk 15 feet deep into the marsh by the lakeside, and now the Ministry of Agriculture refused to write the cheque for the massive excavations needed to return the land to agriculture. A local councillor suggested that 'the Friends of the Lake District should erect a monument to themselves' on the site of the factory, 'to let all people know that the disgraceful eyesore of acres of concrete in the National Park was the result of the work of the Friends.' Ruefully, all parties agreed that these acres of concrete could at least make a good caravan park. When it opened, Norman Parker took up a job there. Les Hills went back to joinery and cabinet-making. The prefabricated workers' village gave way in time to a new school and swimming pool.

I found the Whitecross Bay caravan site almost as invisible from the main road behind its screen of trees as it must have been during the war. You could easily miss the concealed gateway as you sped round the bend towards Ambleside. Inside, it wasn't the most picturesque mobile-home setting I'd ever seen. The barrier and gatehouse at the entrance, the straight concrete roadways, all harked back to the wartime use, had the feel of a military camp. There were long grooves in the ground where the hangar doors had slid on runners – and these unsightly acres of concrete hardstanding. Yachts and motor boats now made use of the slipway, which had also come in useful the previous year for launching a new Windermere pleasure steamer. Just two of the original buildings remained: the generator room, now the caravanners' launderette, and the engineering sheds which the site manager had 'themed up', as he casually put it, with old photographs of the wartime factory, as the rather gloomy 'Flying Boat Bar'. I have to say that that was just how it looked: like one of those post-war pubs half-timbered to look medieval: themed-up.

The arrival of Edward Hulton's Sunderland for the 1990 Windermere Festival confirmed the flying boats' presence hadn't been a myth – though his plane, gleaming white unlike the camou-flaged wartime craft, hadn't been built in the Lakes. The caravan site printed up a facsimile edition of the wartime Christmas card the Shorts workers had sent each other, a photograph of the first plane built at Windermere. Boatmen ferried people out to *Islander* for a peek inside to raise money for charity. And yet – I'd been unable to revisit the Lakes for the flying boat's visit, though I spoke to Les Hills and others on the phone – what struck me was the low-key reception from the local people who'd worked on the Sunderlands at Whitecross Bay. None were getting any younger, but even those, I was surprised to find, uprooted during the war and then finding the Lakes had become home so completely they'd never gone back, hadn't bothered to go down to the lake to greet the nostalgic arrival.

Why? Partly, I think, because the flying boats on Windermere were a wartime aberration, a historical interstice: brought about by the kind of expediency, the overturning of all the normal ways of doing things, that would otherwise have prevented it – like the *QE2* in Falkland Sound while British troops fought for Port Stanley; like a dam, a lake, a cluster of grass huts and a flying boat tied to a tree in the heart of Central Africa. In that respect the retrospective magic of such a brief episode is that it connects nothing with nothing, came out of nowhere. For those who'd been part of that garden factory, fifty years ago, it had finished.

But also, as I'd learnt, flying boats could land anywhere. They didn't need the landscape remodelled in order to do so. Lincolnshire remains Bomber County – still covered with, and therefore memorializing, dozens of old wartime heavy bomber bases. In *The Making of the English Landscape* W. G. Hoskins rails at how 'Airfields have flayed it bare' – but flying boats had been able to come, stay, and then leave with scarcely a trace. I stood on the top of Orrest Head looking west over the long sweep of the lake: down to the right was the clump of green that hid the slipway and a few patches of concrete. 'Seven out of ten visitors to Windermere would be totally unaware of its existence' – more like all ten. Magically, flying boats left the Lake District as they found it. To say they'd been written out of the Lakes' history would not quite be true. They were never in it. The official image of the Lake District – from its representation in the poetry of Wordsworth, through Canon Rawnsley's foundation of the National Trust there at the end of the last century, to current national-park planning policy – is, and rightly, of an unspoilt natural wilderness. Heavy industry was never meant to be part of the picture. But though the activities of lead- and slate-mining, and gunpowder production, have left obtrusive and ineradicable scars, 2,000 people building Sunderland flying boats hasn't. There is not one reference to them in Wainwright's *Pictorial Guide to the Lakeland Fells* (7 vols.), or in Frank Welsh's standard *Companion Guide to the Lake District*, or in all the other guidebooks I consulted.

So here was the secret history of a secret place; a serendipitous rediscovery of a part of the English landscape one thought one knew – revealed to have been wearing clothes that oughtn't to have fitted;

a kind of fairy-tale. It is the sort of flying-boat story that begins to show how Robert Jackson, in *The Sky Their Frontier*, confidently evoking the salvage crews who 'literally hacked their way through the jungle', can imagine Corsairville in terms that would be more appropriate to Walter de la Mare's 'The Traveller'.

Most exactly, perhaps the significance was this: landplanes, especially airliners, are urban phenomena – they fly to and from cities. Even the airport they leave from is a small town. They stand for, and bring with them, modernity, change. Whereas flying boats, leaving their landscape untouched, highlight continuity, timelessness. They're visitors, not conquerors. Ralph Lawes had been a flight engineer on BOAC's wartime 'No. 4 Line', flying converted Sunderlands from Poole, once North Africa had been liberated, as far as Cairo, where they'd meet other British flying boats arriving from Calcutta in the east, Khartoum in the south and Lagos in the west – perhaps five or six a day, he told me when I went to see him, 'like birds coming in to roost for the night'. Time and again in my travels I was to hear, in the reminiscences of those who had flown, flown in, or simply watched, flying boats, them likened to birds. I've used such metaphors myself already. Flying boats make me think of the final stanza of Yeats's poem, 'The Wild Swans at Coole':

> But now they drift on the still water,
> Mysterious, beautiful;
> Among what rushes will they build,
> By what lake's edge or pool
> Delight men's eyes when I awake some day
> To find they have flown away?

I wonder if at least the poet John Pudney might have read these lines, too, and thought of the Empire boat *Corsair*, a silver speck disappearing into the African sky.

'One notices and remembers what has been "coded" – usually by literature or its popular equivalent – to notice and remember,' writes Paul Fussell in *The Great War and Modern Memory*, his study of the literature of the First World War. The fields of Flanders were as thickly seeded with powder-blue cornflowers as they were with red poppies – but it was poppies that had been a staple motif of English poetry since the time of Chaucer and, by the time the British Legion came to 'choose' its symbol of remembrance, poppies' literary preponderance in the poetry of the Great War had effectively made the choice already. They were what those in the trenches had been, as it were, trained to notice.

In this light consider Fussell's further assertion that 'English writing from the beginning has been steeped in both a highly sophisticated literary pastoralism and what we can call a unique actual ruralism.' Here is the final ray of light the Lake District's flying boats shed for me on the legend of Corsairville. The story of the garden factory is a true pastoral, a genre that everyone in England knows, though they might be unaware. A small, bucolic community; a calm stretch of water; life simplified, benign – the tiny particulars of a landscape celebrated as though it stands for all England. Dudley Barker, John Pudney – all those other British historians: pastoral is the genre that, if you like, would have written them. Home is the country, not the city; the seat of real values is the small village, not the sprawling metropolis; permanence is found in isolation, off the beaten track, by going back to the land. This was the way of seeing flying boats gave you – even if the Lake District to the River Dungu does seem to require, and in more than one sense, an especially extended flight.

6

Florida

I missed what I'd been so looking forward to: seeing it land.

There were half a dozen of us waiting in the small terminal building on Watson's Island, a sprawl of scruffy boat-yards and car repair shops across the bay from the skyscrapers of downtown Miami. It was a long wait: check-in an aimless hour and a half before for an early morning departure, and only a few *Southern Boating* magazines scattered about to read. Just like the old days: a start before dawn.

Gerry Bailey was bound for Bimini, where he was setting up a diving charter business and had recently bought a 50-foot boat. Chatting as we gazed out across the water, the pale sun gilding the mirror-glass sides of the office blocks opposite, we discovered a mutual interest in the Spruce Goose, the extraordinary eight-engined all-wood flying boat built by Howard Hughes in the forties. Bigger even than the Princess, in some dimensions it was still the biggest aeroplane ever made. Only one of the world's most maverick and singular (and richest) men could have taken on a wartime military commission to build the prototype for a fleet of massive merchant ships of the air, to counter the German U-boats' predation on the crucial Atlantic convoys – and furthermore, once the Pentagon had refused the diversion of any metal stocks for the project, *to construct the whole thing out of plywood*. It had taken ten years to build, and by the time it first taxied out on to the water Hughes was being sued by the US government for the development funds he'd been given; it was also utterly obsolete. But it *flew*, or at least lifted off the water just once, and stayed 60 feet aloft for four minutes before Hughes brought it down again. Nobody knew whether he'd meant to fly it, or whether it had lifted off of its own accord: its enigmatic pilot had merely conceded that 'I like to make surprises.' Then Hughes had put it back in its hangar and never flew it again.

We'd each been to see the Spruce Goose at Long Beach in California, housed in a magnificent dome. You bought your ticket and shuffled into a dark ante-room adorned with Kodak sponsorship logos, and then, in a genuine and awesome *coup de théâtre*, the black wall in front of you turned out to be a partition that rose with a fanfare to reveal, floodlit and Pharaonic, this beautiful, silver, giant seaplane. But the exhibition had been no more viable than the flying boat itself and now, said Mr Bailey, the Spruce Goose was there no more. It had been dismantled and placed in storage in a warehouse in Washington. 'And usually,' he went on, 'when they cut an airplane into pieces, they never put them back together again.'

Suddenly, as he spoke, like an inquisitive dolphin it was nosing through the water towards us. The skidding, pluming touchdown: not landing, but that lovely word, with its hints of buoyancy and weightlessness, that could have been coined for a flying boat: *alighting*. After all the wait, I was too late. The amphibian bumped up the slipway on its wheels and came to a roaring halt. You almost expected a shiver of its wings to dry itself in the sun.

Quite simply, I wanted to fly on a flying boat. At that time there were none in Britain going anywhere near water, and none in Africa. But in the United States there was still one place, I discovered, where you could turn up, buy a ticket, and catch a scheduled flying-boat service. That was why I'd come to Florida, and here it was.

Florida had always been good seaplane country. British pilots like Ken Emmott had done their wartime training on Catalinas at

Pensacola. Florida had even boasted the world's very first air-passenger service – by seaplane, of course. As far back as 1914 a rickety 'hydroplane' had hopped across the water from Tampa to St Petersburg, carrying one passenger a time for five dollars, before the venture, portentously, went bust after four months. And here in Miami, above all, built around its cays: down in trendy Coconut Grove I found the fine art deco City Hall, its frontage still encircled by golden globe logos. The adjacent yacht marina was dominated by two huge gaunt hangars. Back in the thirties this had been built as the Dinner Key terminal for Pan-American's flying-boat services to Latin America: 'Over 100,000 visitors a month came to see the giant Flying Clippers,' recorded a historic plaque posted in the small garden outside the City Hall.

Remarkably, too, the plane I was about to catch was run by the world's oldest airline. Flying Boat Incorporated, trading until recently as Chalk's International Airline, had been serving this route out to the Bahamas almost continuously since 1919. But the difficulties of sustaining a viable operation using flying boats seemed evident in Chalk's recent history. Back in the seventies it had been flying twelve times a day from Florida out to the Bahamas. Now there was little more than one daily round-trip. A couple of years back the company had ceased operations altogether for several months. For the last year and a half it had been flying, appropriately, under the name Pan-Am Air Bridge – the famous airline that died with deregulation in the eighties had been reborn as a Florida discount airline, and taken a 30 per cent stake in the flying-boat company. Even so, Chalk's was apparently about to be sold yet again.

But no one on the Pan-Am staff here at Watson's Island seemed aware that they were participating in a fascinating historical anachronism. When I bought my ticket the service was glumly taciturn even by the standards of low-margin short-haul aviation. (I heard later elsewhere that wages were insanely low – $14,000 a year for a flying-boat pilot.) The terminal walls were hung with some nice sepia-effect period photographs of classic flying boats; a glass cabinet held a clutter of uncollectable aftershave-type gewgaws. You couldn't buy any kind of souvenir brochure. My return ticket from Miami to Paradise Island via Bimini, a round trip of more than three hours' flying, cost less than $200 (£130). Touchingly, if hardly invitingly, this was not being run as a living museum like a steam railway, a branch of the heritage industry. Chalk's was just getting on unsentimentally, as it had done since after the Great War, with its chosen and difficult way of making a living. Nothing else, for sure, could explain how this rare, historic, fifty-year-old Grumman Mallard flying boat, only forty-seven ever built, that was now ready for us to board had been covered in a lurid blue, yellow and white all-over advertisement for Corona Extra beer.

The Mallard came from a fair-sized family of flying boats, all amphibious, with wheels that enabled them to haul themselves up on to the beach and save passengers having to bob about in launches or second officers throw ropes at buoys. The Goose was a smaller model; the Widgeon was the baby; big brother was the Grumman Albatross, a military flying boat. Our variant had been designed for corporate use – the forties equivalent of an executive jet. Inside the small cabin were seventeen narrow seats, and exceedingly grubby batik-pattern curtains fringing the windows. A distant soundtrack was playing on the headsets – a ticking disco-beat giving way to steel band and then declamatory reggae – but as soon as the two engines began to thresh it was virtually inaudible. There was no bulkhead between cockpit and passenger cabin, so I took the front seat for the view ahead through the windscreen. In front of me was a small sign. I'd read or heard its exhortation on every single flight I'd ever taken, precaution against unspeakable calamity, but for the first time there was a queer context:

IN THE EVENT OF A WATER LANDING
SEAT CUSHION MAY BE USED FOR FLOTATION.

Wasn't that the idea? Weren't we aiming to make a water-landing?

We bumped down the slipway, made a fast 90° turn on the water with the manoeuvrability of an outboard inflatable, and as the pilots opened the throttles the noise was deafening. It was the speed that surprised me: you see the Movietone newsreel snippets of the Empire boats pushing their bow-wave like a slow-motion snowplough – but this small Grumman, less than half full, was as nippy as a speedboat, and it seemed only seconds before the pummelling of the water under the hull and the spray flecking the windows fell away and there was air beneath us. Was that all there was to it?

At Bimini, reached quite quickly, we dashed through a torrential shower to take cover in the poky customs hut. 'Such a beautiful island,' said Gerry Bailey, 'no other way to get to north Bimini.' All I could see was a wall of rain, but the view was still interesting enough. From out of a hatch in the Mallard's nose were being hauled shrink-packs of toilet rolls, shower rails, polythene-wrapped duvets and pillows, and a ventilation grille. The flying boat also seemed to be the local delivery truck.

We gained height again from Bimini over soupy white sloughs, and then shallows of bright aquamarine – flying at only a few thousand feet, the pilots changing course frequently to avoid the ominous bruised sky of storms. The noise was enveloping, a crazy din that drowned all speech. Fifty years ago plane-makers didn't bother much with soundproofing. Ahead through the windscreen was gunmetal sea, and more sea; with our circuitous course around the bad weather we were already late. Just flying out, and on, creeping above the ocean, I had a first sense of what those endless Coastal Command sorties must have been like in a drumming Sunderland.

On a propeller-driven plane there is an exact, delicious moment that announces: we're going in. On a vast wide-bodied jet the captain has to click on the intercom and tell you that *we shall shortly be starting our descent*, but on a prop you can hear it and feel it, a sudden sag in pitch, an audible tailing-off, like an exhalation. The nose dipped: through the windscreen there was just water. That was where we were aimed. It was a baffling, thrilling feeling, to be set on a trajectory to plunge in head first like a guillemot. A pleasure steamer and a yacht also seemed to be right in the path of our landing-run, but still we nosed down towards the blue.

Touchdown in a flying boat has to be the most exciting. Levelling out alongside the steamer we hit the water with a thump. Water, that fluid, lapping element: when you meet it flat-on it is hard and granular as granite. We clattered through the surface, spray thrown all over the screen, as though skidding and grating over rubble. For a few instants foam and froth clutched up the window glass like wild foliage, it seemed we were a submarine about to duck under, and then the engines were dinning again to taxi us in.

Paradise Island, where we'd come down next to the airport runway, was separated from Nassau across a half-mile of water. The one road from the airport passed a golf-course on its way to the resort complex. This was a holiday isle: towering pink hotel blocks and a casino gave on to a pale sandy shore – and the building site adjoining the biggest resort, Atlantis, looked set to double it in size. All this new business! – but at the airport (built, according to my cab driver, about twelve years ago), it was Paradise Island Airlines whose Fokker airliners were flying four times a day to Miami and four more to Fort Lauderdale, with a flight time of under an hour when the flying boat would take nearer two, and at Miami Airport you could walk from one gate to another to connect with anywhere in the world, while the nearest onward link from Watson's Island was a lonely bus stop up on Macarthur Causeway. Holiday-makers in search of sun and sleep on a beach didn't want to travel fascinatingly, any more than commuters wanted a steam locomotive to pull them to work. They just wanted to get there.

After dropping us the Mallard had been supposed to fly on to Walker's Cay to pick up a cruise-ship party for a private charter, but the bad weather that was flinging rain, gusting winds around the island and driving the band at Atlantis off the bandstand meant it was now staying put. So 'the flying beer bottle', as one of my fellow Miami passengers had fondly called it, was parked over the far side of the apron and the young pilot, Sean Smith, now had plenty of time to sit down in the terminal and chat to me after all.

'Well, that's a good question,' he said when I asked how he'd come to be on flying boats. 'It was just something that happened by chance.' No romantic yearnings after seeing pictures of Pan-Am Clippers in *The Boy's Bumper Book of Aeroplanes*? No: he'd been a commercial pilot on landplanes, put in a CV when the Chalk's job had come up, and that was three years ago. But how about all the esoteric skills? I wondered. What about the tide tables? The phases of the moon? The hooking of grommets on buoys, the one-armed paper-hanging? 'Oh, you can go to any FAA agency and you can get an add-on rating in two days,' said Sean. Chalk's did, he conceded, then give you some training to 'acclimate' to the aircraft, and, yeah, you did need to know about tides and all that – but his smile said, we're not talking about taking holy orders.

But though flying boats were not for this quietly confident young American the Latin Mass they often seemed to be mythologized into back in England, neither were they just another rung on Sean Smith's career ladder. If he could snap his fingers tomorrow, I asked him, and find himself the captain of a brand-new Airbus . . . ? I was surprised by the relaxed conviction with which he shook his head. 'You can never get the salt water out of your veins,' he declared. Of all the Grummans, he explained, the Mallard was the most powerful. 'It's 1947 vintage – you do the maths – but it doesn't move like an old tanker. It's built like a Mack truck but it moves like a sports car. Consider water-skiing,' he said (occasionally even he slipped into the kind of pedagogic tone I now recognized in flying-boat authorities), 'and then consider this aeroplane. Throw in the aspect of the water and you can do so many things.' They took Norwegian cruise-ship passengers on tours out to pretty places like the Berry Islands. They did air tours down the Miami coast on Saturday mornings, flying low alongside the art deco district, past the weekend kite-flying contests at Holover's Inlet and the old lighthouses at Key Biscayne, and playing big-band music over the headphones. He got to go to Stirrup Key, tiny cays in the Exhumus and Andros – all kinds of 'laid-back, fishing and diving places' you couldn't get to any other way. 'It's the most fun flying you can ever experience.'

But it all came at a price. Two out of Pan-Am Air Bridge's five Mallards were out of service needing work, and when Sean said these fifty-year-old vintage airplanes required 'intense maintenance' he wasn't exaggerating. That insinuating, continuously destructive salt again: every day they had to run fresh water through the airframes, wash down the hull, apply all kinds of preservatives, coat rivet lines and joins with grease. 'For every hour we fly,' said Sean, 'you're going to take three to four hours on maintenance.' It seemed miraculous and heroic that this little airline had made it through eighty years.

When it was time for Sean to fly us back to Miami I saw one reason why the flying boats endured. I checked in as the irritable A-to-B traveller another full hour before departure – for a seventeen-seater! when half of us had tickets anyway! – and when American had let me show up only an hour and a quarter before to catch a 767 across the Atlantic, Heathrow security checks and all! Why couldn't they just *get a move on*?

But the clerk was kept busy for an hour, for as well as the teenage mums toting babies, and the boisterous young men with mobile phones who had to be calmly relieved of full pints of beer at the gate (this flight was going to be pretty full), a mountain of cargo was piling up in front of the desk. There were bundles of newspapers, boxes labelled 'Fresh Vegetables', mesh bags of oranges, and blister-packed litre bottles of mineral water. There was a simple polarized tableau here in the terminal. Turning up for the next Paradise Island Airlines flight, the white faces; checking in for the flying boat – myself and an elderly woman excepted – black. The tourists, in their lucrative thousands, with their Samsonite cases and their luggage trolleys, caught the quick airliner. But Chalk's was the local service, a need hereabouts that hadn't changed, I figured, since Grumman Mallards were brand-new.

This time, so heavily laden you could feel the flying boat sitting low in the water, the water thrilled up the windows on our take-off run. We left behind gruel-swirled reefs and puckered half-submerged sandbanks as we climbed away from Paradise Island. Soon the sun was shining between the clouds to silver patches of the sea in saucers of light. Further off, the water was undulating foil. I had a hollered conversation with a big guy opposite who called himself J R. 'Like, I haven't seen my mother this year,' he told me, the reggae soundtrack skittering out of his headphones. 'And yesterday I surprise her, I come on Chalk's. Before I was a baby – before I was born! – this Chalk's, this is a legend! It's like a, like a fun thing. It's like a jet-ski! I could be wrong,' he said, 'but I feel more secure on Chalk's. If you have a problem with an engine, or two engines, you can come down, just like a yacht!' My straining questions out of the way, he shut his eyes and grooved and jived in his seat to the reggae. 'Show respect, man,' he called to Sean Smith as he clambered out at Bimini, and the pilot replied, 'Take it easy.'

At Bimini another Mallard was waiting for us to connect for Fort Lauderdale, painted a gleaming sleek white and christened *Cuba Libre* on the nose, rakish as a barfly in an ice-cream suit, its pilot poking a Victory V up at us as we nosed down the slipway. I moved to a seat under the wing, and here was the best vantage point of all. You felt the sudden lilt as the water lifted the hull off the wheels, and then the undercarriage retract into the hull. Low in the water, we thumped along the waves – it was like a car hitting sleeping policemen.

We soared in low over downtown Miami on our approach run, curving around the side of the tall Doubletree Hotel to skim the top of the *Miami Herald* building and head for the water. Each time touchdown made you feel so many things. We were a toboggan juddering over rutted ice. The water frothing up the window glass – like something catching you, breaking your fall. The word NASA always uses of space capsules hurtling back into the earth's atmosphere: re-entry. Such a *visceral* form of flight: the magical passage from one element into another registered in every rivet of your craft and every one of your senses. The throttles open for the taxi to the slipway, as though the Mallard is bellowing, 'What about that, then?'

Simple topography had kept this part of the world at least partly the preserve of seaplanes. So many of these Caribbean islands were too small or too hilly for anything much bigger than a light plane. The easiest option of all was for the plane to use the harbour like the millionaires' yachts did. Until only a few years earlier they'd still had flying boats in the American Virgin Islands – Antilles Air Boats having previously, of course, operated *Islander* and *Beachcomber*, the last two Sandringhams that were now preserved. But though that airline's demise had been sealed when Hurricane Andrew had wrecked its fleet of Grumman Gooses, another of aviation's rare water-dwelling species was now a regular sight, and it would be possible for me to continue travelling as – the wonderful title of the book Don Bennett had written during his brief Brindisi layover – an *Air Mariner*. I caught an American Airlines 757 from Miami to the island of St Thomas and, to follow the Mallard, went looking for an Otter.

St Thomas, I soon found, was a kind of conservation reserve for all sorts of unusual or vintage aircraft – the sort you usually glimpse around the periphery of airfields as your jet taxis to the far end of the runway. My hotel was right next to the airport: a lounger on its little private beach was the best possible location for idle plane-spotting. Between the screaming Delta 757s and the little top-winged Pipers see-sawing aloft, elderly Dakotas droned slowly over the hillside like bumble-bees, and I even saw an old Lockheed Electra, such as Amelia Earhart flew on her last flight, trundling down the runway in the twilight. But Seaborne Aviation's address in the *World Airline Guide* was in Juneau: how on earth had an airline from Alaska strayed so far off course to be flying a seaplane run down in the Caribbean?

The smart white De Havilland Twin Otter rocked on the water at the yacht marina, dwarfed by P&O's *Dawn Princess* and the *Rhapsody of the Seas*, mighty cruise ships nine storeys high, a cliff face of windows. It was these liners, at least one a day docking in St Thomas's capital, Charlotte Amalie, that had brought the floatplanes down from Alaska. 'We all started flying between the logging camps,' Phil, one of the pilots, told me. 'A floatplane's the only practical transportation. It's the same sort of country up there, except for the temperature.' The cruise ships all called in at Ketchikan, Alaska, too, and Seaborne took their passengers on charter trips just as Pan-Am Air Bridge did in the Bahamas. Now the shipping lines wanted the seaplanes to take their vacationers pond-hopping in the Caribbean, too, so when the liners left Alaska in the fall Seaborne's pilots flew their Twin Otters down the length of the States via Minneapolis and Las Vegas and spent the bitter Alaska winters in the balmy Virgin Islands. 'And we see the same ships again now,' said Phil. I liked the way that ships led to seaplanes, all out of the same element.

Phil said flying this local service between St Thomas and the neighbouring island of St Croix, twenty minutes away, was 'pretty much a no-brainer'. 'The weather's nice,' he conceded, 'but Alaska's much more challenging.' Maybe it was, compared with this shuttling to and fro half a dozen times a day. But our Twin Otter flew at just a thousand feet above the waves – it was a blazing, 90° day – and, that close, the swell was like stretch marks on the sea, almost a phosphorescent glitter, like a million entwining snail's traces, or as though innumerable children had ridden their bicycles across a dewy lawn. I couldn't take my eyes off it. Airliners fly too high, literally miles up, sealed above a floor of cotton wool. The author Samuel Hyncs once wrote that every landscape is beautiful from the air: he might have added, the sea, too, if you can get close enough. I wanted to shake these other passengers snoozing or perusing the real-estate ads in glossy magazines: *look*, will you? Those white breakers where the reef shelves – they really are like frayed lace!

Already the routine pandemonium of the American Airlines flight from Miami seemed bafflingly distant. The dodgems in the drop-off lane; the immense check-in queue, revealing that even on internal flights Americans travel with a baggage train voluminous enough to have sustained Dr Livingstone for several years (who needs to take ceiling tiles to Denver?); the cabin crew ducking cases too big for overhead bins and pleading with passengers to take any free seat – even a grizzled man in front of me (one could only assume some lower-back problem) who passed the whole flight seated on a plastic meal-tray: that was modern mass-market flying. But right now we were sailing down over translucent light-green shallows – surely we couldn't land on water mere inches deep? But when we skimmed a jetty and touched down like a ski-jumper the water was plenty deep enough, just impossibly and beguilingly clear. *Whomph*: a floatplane came down in a crisp skid. There was a pleasant poise to it, but none of the full-tilt, head-on buffet of a flying boat dissipating the muscled resistance of water. The Twin Otter docked right outside the King's Landing Yacht Club. A minute later I was sitting on its terrace in the sun with a coffee. Mass air travel took you away from the world, confined you within its own closed, codified frenzies. But here on St Croix, the narrow alleys of Christiansted leading away up to its main street, you set down your glass, strolled along the landing stage, and then you were bumping and surging across the water. This serene seaplane run, slow and low enough for you to take in every inch of the way, to let the journey travel you, connected flying back to the rest of the world.

'What I particularly like,' Pan-Am's Sean Smith had told me, 'is, you're able to go to certain destinations that are almost . . . remote. You'd almost have to get there by boat.' He'd been thinking of places like Stirrup Key in the Bahamas – but until recently Pan-Am's Mallards had also been flying out to the most remote of all island destinations in the United States. Though the vintage flying boats had now pulled out of Key West – even fifty years after their great demise, here I was still just missing them – a seaplane was going out to the Dry Tortugas.

The Fort Jefferson National Monument stands on Garden Key, an uninhabited island in an archipelago 70 miles off the southern tip of the Florida Keys. The first of what were to be more than 16 million bricks was laid in 1846, the plan being to erect a huge fort that would secure free passage to the Gulf of Mexico for Atlantic-bound ships coming down from the Mississippi. Construction continued for thirty years, and never finished. During the Civil War the fort remained under Union control – the only place where you could go north to fight the South – though the different colour bricks along the top of the fort are evidence of how alternative shipments had to be brought all the way down from Maine when the South put a stop on supply. Never used in military conflict, the giant defence folly had for a while served as a jail, but now dominated a National Park and wildlife refuge that teemed with seabird colonies.

I flew down to Key West in a little Continental Airlines Beech twenty-seater: this'll be a fine view, I thought – tracing the line of the Keys all the way down. But you forget: planes fly as the crow flies, and the direct route from Miami to Key West was due south-west across the Everglades, on this overcast day a drab grey-brown like tundra, at least when you could see anything beyond the cloud moisture crazing the window. At Key West the weather was worse: determined, vertical rain, and a sky congealed like milk skin. Eleven in the morning, and at Seaplanes of Key West all passenger-flying was already off for the day. 'This is about as bad as it gets,' said the manager, a Yorkshireman called Pete Green who'd come to Florida one year for a holiday, and never left. He rolled up his sweater sleeve ruefully: no tan yet this winter ... On his latest computerized weather map was a comprehensive splurge of green between Key West and the Dry Tortugas: rain. 'We can fly through that,' he said, 'but it's the yellow and orange, here, we don't wanna go anywhere near. That's bad thunderstorms.' There was just one remaining chance that I could get out to the fort. Later in the day the Cessna floatplane was booked to fly two National Park rangers out to start a work assignment on the island. The sea would be too turbid for the usual sightings of sharks and rays, there'd be no time for bird-watching, let alone snorkelling, at the fort, but if the weather had eased enough by two, I could hitch a ride. 'It'll be like going to Brighton on a filthy day,' said Pete.

Key West, an island itself, still retained hints of its former flying-boat days. On the wall of the Conch Flyer restaurant in the airport terminal where I killed some time, the local Conch Republic Rum Company's plaques featured a big white four-engine flying boat as its logo. There was a blow-up Pan-Am Mallard in Corona-beer livery hanging above the bar. But back in the little office of Seaplanes of Key West, waiting for the park wardens to show, Peter Green filled me in on present-day realities. Several firms had gone bust trying to run seaplanes out to the Dry Tortugas, he said. 'Runway to runway would be about a third of the price. Put it on the water,' said Pete, 'and your insurance trebles.' Weird: I recalled J R telling me how he felt safer on a plane that could become a yacht. Why not a lower premium for airlines flying over water if your plane was specifically equipped to come down in it? But the problem was airworthiness: Pete pointed over to a white floatplane tucked away behind a hangar. Looked neat enough: his firm had inquired about buying it for the Fort Jefferson run. The federal aviation inspector had said the corrosion caused by parking it outdoors was too bad ever to put it in the air again. 'Just the salt in the atmosphere is a nightmare on this island,' said Pete. 'People who come down from Alaska in their amphibians, they won't land on salt water down here – not even once.' A floatplane did little more than dip its toes in on each landing, but at the end of every day, Seaplanes' Cessna had the hose turned on it for a full hour and a half. The brand-new plane they had on order was going to be epoxy-coated in the factory – it was no good trying to protect it any later. But Seaplanes of Key West also had a uniquely handy insurance against the hazards of marine aviation. Their company also owned Key West airport here, and on days like today the airlines had to carry more fuel in case the bad weather forced them to hold until it was safe to land. 'So when it rains,' said Peter, 'although we can't fly, we sell more fuel.'

The seaplane pilot, John Wagner, looked in, a stocky guy in T-shirt, shorts and flip-flops. Still no park wardens, so he sat down at the computer to take on Pete's Apache helicopter simulation game. Jerky cut-outs of enemy planes loomed into the cockpit gunsight and dissolved in flowers of flame. 'I'm just blastin' away at everything,' said John. He was the kind of person who finds one sentence will usually serve, whatever there is to say.

The rangers eventually swanned in an hour late with a giant pink cool-box, no apology and a blithe 'Hi, we're ready to go!' Strapped into the yellow and white Cessna, one of them, a finicking guy with a greying bi-level haircut, who'd been fussing about the emergency-exit door, leaned forward and said to John, 'Could I see your OAR licence?'

In that cabin winter set in. How did he expect to get to work if none was forthcoming? Swim?

'I've been flyin' seaplanes for twenty-seven years and this is the first time anyone's ever asked to see my licence,' said the pilot in a voice that seemed to come from a distance, extracting the small white card as though it was one of his own teeth. The flight out was a half-hour of frosty silence. We flew just 450 feet above the water. Today it looked hard, igneous, basalt. Here and there pinkish sea-turtles were splayed on the surface. Beneath us the Fort Jefferson tour boat was bouncing through the waves on its way back to Key West. The chunky hexagon of the fort was suddenly ahead: we wheeled in and swooped on to the water like a gull – that single descending parabola, air into sea. The rangers tottered off up the beach with their big pink cooler. Just one couple with a small motorcruiser stood watching John wade into the shallows and release the Cessna's tie-rope; otherwise on this hooded day the fort really was abandoned to the circling frigate birds and skimmers. 'Clever plane,' announced John, standing in the shallows watching it turn itself round on the tide. 'Had to do a lot of flying before I found somewhere I could fly barefoot.'

Back in the cockpit John fired the engine again. 'That guy kind of pissed me off a bit,' he growled – as though I hadn't noticed. A government parks employee! 'Guy asks me a question like that, I see a lot of my tax dollars.' But now he was liberated: just him and me in the front seats of this tiny five-seat Cessna 206, a Ford Escort on floats. The huge brick ramparts were already receding: I'd had no time to explore inside, but no matter. This visit brief as a bird's: it was like flying 70 miles and finding Battersea Power Station in the middle of the sea. 'Now it's a fast boat ride,' said John, 'and then we'll go looking for some dolphin.'

We had to yell at each other over the racket of the engine. John had grown up in Ontario, Canada, flying his father's plane, and then gone on to be a bush pilot flying hunters out to their lodges. 'Our house was at the end of the road,' he called. 'Beyond that, it was the seaplane.' We peeled off and dived low for him to show me two of the many wrecks littering these treacherous shallows and reefs: the broken mast of the *Arbutus*, used by the treasure-diver Mel Fisher, and the rusty hulk of the US destroyer *Patricia*, sunk for target practice. He pointed out the circles of lobster-trap booms, the brown blobs of seaweed, the black shreds that were flocks of skimmers. Just above the waves the long slow-flapping wing-span with a blazon of white was a pelican. Out here, as on St Croix in the Virgin Islands, there were birds everywhere – we looked down on them as an airliner looks down on small Cessnas. At St Croix the pelicans had banked around yachts' masts and dropped like parachutists. A small blue heron had cranked itself straight and single-minded across the harbour. There, and now here, too, huge forked-tailed magnificent frigate birds soared and circled. And then there was us, above the pelican as though in a higher holding pattern, and beyond the frigate birds had been the Twin Otter booming down its white furrow. With its vast treeless airports and its bird scarers to prevent the vast and dangerous expense of a bird strike on titanium-bladed turbofans, jet aviation utterly excludes the aerial creatures who first gave us the idea: if *they* can fly . . . ? But here, amongst all this flying, the ubiquity of the oblivious birds reminded me that I was doing the same as them. 'They're always white, aren't they?' my friend Mathew had said to me back in London, answering his own question, *Why flying boats?* 'They *should* be white – they're painted the same colour as gulls. That chest, that great breastbone . . .' Airbus 300, 320; Boeing 737, 47, 57, 67: our airliners are mere numbers, machine specs. Fifty years ago you could christen a plane a Mallard, a Widgeon, an Albatross, and mean it.

We overtook the churning ferry-boat again, still battling back towards Key West. John exchanged a glance and filled his cheeks with imaginary vomit. '*This* is the only way to travel,' he bawled, jabbing the control panel. 'That won't be back till seven o'clock tonight!' He was craning his gaze to peer into the waters as we approached the Marquesas, a verdant atoll among lazy shallows. 'Usually you find some around here . . .' Suddenly the seaplane was dropping in an exhilarating seaward swerve, and there, tremulous under the surface, maybe a hundred feet below us as we swung down the sky, was a school of a dozen dolphin.

Starting from water made flying different. Take-off in a landplane was the land falling away; in a seaplane you always had to climb out into the sky. Water was an element that held you, not just with gravity but also its own surface tension – until you got a flying boat planing on its step and broke the suction it wouldn't let you go. But also water to air to water made the flight seem more uncertain – not more dangerous, but you could never get away from the awareness that you were up in the air. In a big airliner you could easily imagine it was just a train rocking along on rails of air; close your eyes and the ravelling rumble could be a tube train hurtling through a tunnel. Sir Norman Foster, in one of a series of programmes about classic buildings, chose as his favourite the Boeing 747: a steady office-block in the air. On a seaplane you couldn't take the square solidity of your feet on the floor of the departure lounge up with you. Partly it was going to the water's edge to catch your plane: that was where a kind of certainty ran out – you'd come to the end of the land. Also it was a sense that a seaplane had only temporarily come inshore, like the rare landfall of a petrel, or a beached whale. Its natural habitat was out there, out at sea: it beckoned from the infinite. Flight felt provisional: it sustained itself minute by minute. The *Air Mariner*: it was such a mysterious phrase (though I doubt the pragmatic D. C. T. Bennett would have been alive to its poetry) – for it captured the feeling I'd had on every seaplane flight, that even in the air you never lost touch with the other element: that every flight was also a kind of voyage.

I had one final homage to pay. How could I leave Florida without going to see the last airworthy Sunderland? Since Edward Hulton had sold it and Ken Emmott had flown it across the Atlantic, *Islander* had been residing at Polk City, 40 miles east of Tampa in the north of the state, at the new Fantasy of Flight attraction. I was pretty certain it wouldn't be flying – indeed, that it hadn't taken to the air in a while – and I knew well enough what it looked like. But I was curious nevertheless. Who were the new flying-boat people who'd been drawn to this elderly itinerant? What was the next chapter in its long story? There was always anticipation in going to seek out a seaplane. There were not many of them, and they were scattered to the winds.

I arrived at the Fantasy of Flight airfield just as a Stampe biplane had touched down. It came to a halt outside one of the hangars, the long-haired man in the rear clapping the sides of the cockpit and exclaiming, 'I want one! I want one! I want one!' Regarding the scene with interest was an elderly gentleman in a baseball cap who turned to me and said, soft and quizzical, 'I guess he feels strongly about it.' In the pilot's seat was a lanky bearded man with a long plaited pony-tail and sunglasses, revealed when he'd jumped to the ground to be clad in jeans, a denim jacket and sneakers. I was in luck. This was the great Kermit Weeks. I'd faxed him before leaving

England to see if he could spare time to talk to me, and not heard back. Too busy acquiring more vintage planes, no doubt.

This man had the biggest private collection in the world, and it was growing fast. In earlier life he'd been a champion gymnast, which in turn had led to the aerial tumbling of a six-times national aerobatics champion. He'd already amassed one substantial plane collection on an airfield south of Miami, including what was now the only flyable Mosquito, then donated the lot to a charitable foundation and started up again here. He'd since accumulated over a hundred aircraft, and was in the process of building an entire thirties-pastiche airport amidst this bland pastureland – an art deco terminal building and two hangars had already gone up. He'd just brought in an Avro Tudor from Australia, he was about to ferry back the last flying B-26 Marauder bomber, there were various planes in England waiting to come out – and that was just the beginning!

Kermit Weeks threw out expansive, clattering bursts of sentences while making rapid progress through a packet of cigarettes. I matched his strides around the airfield, his loud, fruity baritone ranging over the indignities that people inflicted these days on Catalinas: 'They wanna cut holes in 'em, convert them into Winnebagos!'; through the succulence of the stone-crab legs served up by a Coconut Grove restaurant I really should check out if I was interested in the old Clipper base: 'They tear the leg off and throw it back and it grows a new one'; to the uniquely fearsome stallion that was the De Havilland Mosquito: 'It's got about *that* much throttle' (his fingers enclosed an inch and a half) 'for seventeen hundred horsepower – and we never did get the brakes to work properly on it. If ever there was a plane that was gonna bite you it was that one.'

He took me up in his newest attraction, a hot-air balloon that from next week would give visitors a 400-foot-high view over Florida to Disneyworld silhouetted on the eastern horizon. Kermit pointed down at the airfield's entrance gate. 'You know, one of my friends said to me the other day, "You should get a ten-foot-high *frog* put up just down there by the road!"' Beyond the grass runway was a lake, and here the collector had the biggest plans. 'When you see that Miami City Hall? Think of that down here.' After two and a half years he was still waiting for the development permits, and he'd have to, er, mitigate some wetlands, but right there, on 8 acres at the lakeside, he was going to build his very own Pan-Am Clipper seaplane base.

He'd never have a Boeing Clipper, of course, but far below and prominent white, with its Desperate Dan jutting jaw, dwarfing the other planes and the ant-visitors, he already had his Sunderland. Bringing it across the north Atlantic via Reykjavík in Iceland – another wartime flying-boat base – he and Ken Emmott hadn't gone higher than 2,500 feet the whole way, the same altitude as the Mallard. They'd coasted the southern tip of Greenland, the ice-packs and the mountains, at just a thousand feet, said Kermit: an unbeliev-able experience. It was a couple of summers since he'd last flown it, ferrying the Olympic torch for the 1996 Atlanta Games on a leg from Sarasota to Miami, where he'd touched down at Dinner Key. 'We kind of think of it as our signature aircraft,' he said. 'It's a neat thing and I can't say enough about it, and I wish we could give rides in it.' He planned a Florida coastline tour in it next, visiting all the old seaplane sites: Pensacola, where the navy trained; Tampa Bay, where those primitive Benoist hydroplanes had flown in 1919; Key West, Coconut Grove in Miami, and the wartime base at Jack-sonville. In the mean time, Kermit told me proudly, every Christmas they parked the Sunderland at the south end of the runway next to the Interstate, and covered it in fairy lights.

Had it taken him long to learn how to fly it? Kermit shook his head confidently. He rattled off how he'd upgraded his seaplane rating when he knew the Sunderland was his – he made it sound more like getting your car tax – and how he'd already flown on four-engines with planes like his Liberator: flying it had not been, as he put it, 'a significant learning curve. Ken Emmott did the first two test flights,' he said, 'then he threw me in the left seat and I did the rest.' He did concede that 'the immensity of operating something that large on the water was a real challenge', and that 'the whole water aspect was a fascinating deal' but, as with Sean Smith, I'd got an American answer to what now seemed somehow a British question and, here in Florida at least, a lame one at that. When I told Kermit how the old Imperial Airways flying-boat captains, immaculate in their white linen suits, would have their crews salute them aboard, a cut above all other benighted aviators, he chuckled, genuinely amused. Sure, seaplanes were different, he said. You had to be careful flying helicopters, too.

The balloon brought us back to earth. It was time for Kermit to go: a Discovery Channel film crew was waiting to film him flying his Duck, a remarkable amphibious Grumman biplane whose single float protruded like Mr Punch's chin. Kermit, of course, had the only example left. In the cafeteria I chatted to the veteran gentleman who'd watched the Stampe land. His name was James Scrivener, from nearby Zephyr Hills, and he and his friend Roland Mosher came over regularly to see how Kermit was getting on with his restoration of a PBY Catalina flying boat. 'He told us it's not good enough to fly, but too good to throw away,' said Mr Scrivener. He'd flown on Catalinas during the war on air-sea rescue duties, patrolling the bomber routes looking for ditched survivors. Had he enjoyed those times? 'It was a little dangerous in those days,' he said in his soft, quizzical way.

'There were people shooting at you!' said Mr Mosher, who'd flown Liberator tankers over 'the Hump' between India and China.

Mr Scrivener said they'd flown almost on the water most of the time, and he had one story to tell – you could see him wondering at it as he went. Just off Midang in New Guinea, he said, there was an old volcano, about 1,100 feet high, with a lake inside the crater, and one day they were passing it on a routine operation. 'And we thought, *why don't we land on that?* So we set that PBY down in that old volcano. And then we had to circle around,' said Mr Scrivener, 'to try and be able to take off again!'

Mr Mosher gave me a sidling glance and said, 'Short runway.'

Well, they got it off again, said Mr Scrivener, 'but that was about as foolish a thing as we ever did.'

Outside the hangar Kermit was climbing into the cockpit of the Duck. 'I should pre-warn the guy down in the basement,' he was calling out to the Discovery Channel sound man, who'd drawn the short straw and got to travel in the enclosed lower compartment, 'the original brakes on this thing were so weak they put new ones in on wheels I have to crank up. After take-off I'll lower the nose to take the weight off it to crank the last couple times, so if you feel the plane *dip*, that's what it is. Hey, can you get my hat?' A maroon baseball cap was brought, the Grumman's engine exploded into life in a frenzy of white smoke, and with tank-like sound effects the brutish Duck was off down the runway.

A serene peace returned to the airfield. Kermit had said I could take a look inside the Sunderland, so I went to find Chris, the young Dutchman who'd managed to wangle his engineering-studies work experience into a six-month placement grinding the corrosion off a wartime flying boat. Around the windows he'd taken the skin down to the metal – but the whole airframe needed going over, he said. Salt against metal: the battle never stopped. 'He's had a request from Germany to take it over there at the end of the year,' Chris said, 'for the anniversary of the Berlin airlift. But I don't think he's going to.' It would be yet another vast creeping haul for a modern Flying Dutchman. Imagine the sight of a Sunderland – like those that had flown in ten times a day to bring meat, cigarettes, sanitary towels and even, perversely, salt – alighting again on the Havel lake fifty years later!

We ducked in through the side hatch into a foetor of sour air and perhaps stale water. I hadn't expected the first-class luxury of BOAC's Springbok Class, but here was an odd anticlimax nevertheless. In the main passenger cabin were shabby brown carpets and faded seventies airline seats. The walls were covered with ghastly swirling-pattern Fablon out of a seventies kitchen nightmare. I felt like I'd wandered into a grim bedsit let by an absentee landlord. The rear upper cabin was even worse. 'Ugly, huh?' said Chris, as we beheld a pink-veneered fake-wood bar, brown quilted leatherette padding, and sofa-cots in biscuit-wove that a Volkswagen Microbus dormobile owner would have been proud of.

This was how it had arrived from England. Amazing that you could spend over £2 million and achieve something this tacky, this cheap. Perhaps such shabbiness testified to the effect on even the deepest pocket of such heroic caprice: keeping a white elephant like this flying in the late twentieth century. But I couldn't help it: here in Florida this British flying boat reminded me of other things: of being invited to the Garrick Club and finding it served school-dinners food; of looking forward to visiting famous county cricket grounds like Hove and Southampton and finding peeling gimcrack stands, luminous blue plastic seats and sploshed whitewash; of my summer's work for one of London's most distinguished publishing houses, in offices of echoing linoleum, manual typewriters and matchwood chairs. It reminds me now of my American friend Todd remarking how un-English he found the All-England Club's Wimbledon tennis tournament – 'because it's so *perfect*!'

It was a small hint: a corrective glimpse of the threadbare. It was no good just reading a British myth about Britain to your British self. Myths don't mean just what their authors think they mean. And sometimes myths, like wines or cask ales, don't travel. I'm trying to account for why I felt so embarrassed inside that Sunderland, in front of the unassuming young Dutchman – unreasonably shamed. I think it was not only because I acknowledged it as my own – the poverty of it! – but also because I recognized it so readily. It wasn't just a matter of crappy taste, the way I could always pick out a middle-aged Englishman in America by the poor haircut and the zip-up windcheater. It was deeper, more obscure: something to do with the intensity the English bring – and I'd brought – to nostalgia, and at the same time the vagueness of its regard; with how often that nostalgia depended on not looking too closely, on ignoring moribundity.

Anyway: so rip it all out, gut it, that whole shabby interior, for that's all it was – a pile of old seats. Kermit Weeks had had the thing for three, four years already and hadn't yet got round to it either. Treat the corrosion so you could fly the thing to Pensacola! Let it take you to more places where only flying boats could go. 'This is an *attraction*,' he'd corrected me; 'not a museum. Not everyone likes airplanes, but *everyone* has a fascination with flight – it's a universal thing. The airplanes are just a means to an end.'

Centaurus

7

The Empire Boats

Who, nowadays, would write home to their relatives a detailed account of their airline flight? More to the point, who would bother to read it? These days travel is supposed to begin only when the air journey has ended. But in 1938, from the Continental Savoy Hotel in Cairo, Ian Henderson did just that. Two years earlier he'd sailed up the Nile from Khartoum to Juba in southern Sudan, to take up the position of District Engineer with the Public Works Department – the 700 miles by 'fast mail steamer' taking fourteen days. (General Gordon had once managed the trip in a day less.) And now, having come home on leave by boat, he was flying back to Africa. Roused at 4.45 a.m., he'd wandered down the silent corridors of the South-Western Hotel, been driven along Southampton's dark streets past the liner *Empress of Britain* – and there, rocking inside the pontoon landing-stage, was his conveyance. Not so big as he'd expected; an interior surprisingly similar to a comfortable Pullman car; just one other passenger beside himself, but the steward still anxious to seat them aft to balance the mail freight:

Dawn was now showing, and the men on the pontoon gave a shout to the ship and she glided out of the dock. One by one the engines started up with a roar and flames from the exhausts. Vibration was not excessive – little more than a London bus. Everything was dead calm, and we slowly taxied over the water. Then the pilot opened up the engines and we went a long way like a speedboat, and turned several complete circles whilst he warmed up his engines. Then he . . . straightened up the plane for the open sea, and then pressed the accelerator to the limit, and the noise was considerable . . . I was pressed back into my chair by the acceleration, and a great wave of water could be seen rushing past the windows . . . suddenly we were airborne. It's hard to describe the feeling, but the noise of the water ceases, the vibration almost stops, and the plane seems to give a little pitch and toss as she gets into her own element.

It was 16 September 1938. The flying boat's name was *Corsair*.

Such absorbed curiosity – and a touching uncertainty as to what kind of beast it was! Mr Henderson, a jolly, bright-eyed man, had kept his letter all this time and, sixty years later, in his upstairs study in a quiet cul-de-sac in Egham, was proud to read it out to me now – the account, in personal terms, of a small historical event. He laughed when he read out the bit about the pilot pressing the accelerator – 'You see, you don't know!' A ship! A speedboat? A plane? A kind of luxury train or bus? Only a year old, the new Empire Air Mail services linking the UK with her furthest-flung dominions in Africa, India and Australia were still a considerable novelty, and Imperial Airways' fleet of state-of-the-art 'C-Class' flying boats as alluring as Concorde or the first Jumbos. Underneath the young Henderson's evocation you can hear the unspoken exclamation, *So this is what it's like* . . .

We have to adjust our modern sense of proportion. We look back from a time when, in a recent television commercial, the actress Helen Mirren extols the virtues of Virgin's new overnight non-stop service to Johannesburg: just close your eyes, curl up those slinky legs on the foot-rest and – wake up there! 'I was in Africa one day,' reflects the narrator of V. S. Naipaul's 1979 novel, *A Bend in the River*, 'I was in Europe the next morning':

It was more than travelling fast. It was like being in two places at once. I woke up in London with little bits of Africa on me – like the airport tax ticket, given me by an official I knew, in the middle of another kind of crowd, in another kind of building, in another climate. Both places were real; both places were unreal. You could play off one against the other; and you had no feeling of having made a final decision, a great last journey.

But we have to imagine 1937 as a great speeding-up and streamlining. The traveller's normal route to Africa, of course, was the sea passage: the Union Castle line's weekly mail steamer from Southampton, a full two weeks to the Cape, and longer still if you were bound for the east coast. It was both time-consuming and featureless – fourteen dreary days dragging by out at sea, to be filled either with a lot of reading or, recalls one former seafarer, 'trying to avoid a lot of hearty holiday-camp-like communal activities'. It was the same kind of A-to-B translation as modern jetliner flight, albeit infinitely prolonged: you didn't go *through* anywhere, except an eventual boredom threshold.

We have almost lost the sense of haste in the verb 'to fly'. 'I must fly,' we can still say, and mean: *got to dash*. But flying itself – what aeroplanes do – was in the inter-war era a constant process of time-shrinking. The race between nautical and aeronautical was joined on 26 February 1926, when the Union Castle ship *Windsor Castle* steamed out of Cape Town, Southampton-bound, on the same day as the pioneering aviator Alan Cobham took off from there in his De Havilland biplane. Cobham was on his way home after having completed a survey flight from London, undertaken as 'sound propaganda for British aviation'. The simultaneity was coincidental but, once realized, the challenge was on for an aeroplane to be the first home. The ship could steam on round the clock, but at a mere twelve knots; the plane could only fly for around eight hours in every twenty-four, but at 95 miles an hour. Having to fly over land the whole way, in order to descend frequently for refuelling, also meant Cobham's total route of 8,500 miles was almost 60 per cent longer than the ship's.

Cobham and his two colleagues, a De Havilland engineer and a film cameraman shooting a film of their flight for Gaumont, lost a day in Ndola, in the then Northern Rhodesia, when a storm turned the mud runway to quagmire, and needed the help of hundreds of villagers the next morning to stomp it down smooth enough for take-off. At Tabora in Tanganyika they could barely get airborne off another rain-drenched airfield. They hit sandstorms all the way up the Sudan, a gale in Cairo, another on the Mediterranean coast (two more days gone), and such violent turbulence rounding the cliffs of Cape Malea on the approach to Athens that the engine temporarily cut out as they plummeted, 'and the passengers and all the baggage were literally pressed tight against the roof of the cabin'. But they landed at Croydon on 13 March fifteen and a half days after leaving Cape Town. Cobham himself had flown the entire round trip to South Africa and back in an open cockpit. The *Windsor Castle* docked in Southampton two days later.

Without the delays, Cobham would have done it in just twelve days – but he was unconcerned to post his feat as any kind of stunt – indeed, he'd previously pronounced his aim as:

to knock the stunt out of flying – to try and make people realize that aviation was coming and that it was a practical proposition. That you could set out in an aeroplane, fly to Africa and you could fly back again, and all you wanted was improvement in aircraft and the making of airways.

For him the flight out had been the achievement – for one of his sponsors was the fledgling Imperial Airways, and by Kisumu in Kenya Cobham was already convinced his survey was about to open up 'one of the finest air transport routes of the age'. England, to the whole of Africa, by air.

If these days we don't even write letters home about airline flights, certainly we don't compose whole travel books about them. What you're reading is a sort of exception to prove the rule. The world is

1. Two Imperial Airways Empire flying boats over the Dead Sea in Palestine

2. Croydon Aerodrome and an Imperial Airways Handley–Page HP-42 outside the terminal building

3. Lady Cobham with her canary for company during her 20,000-mile flying-boat flight around Africa with Sir Alan Cobham 1927–8

4. Captain Dudley Travers (rear, wearing the flying helmet), with the boxer Primo Carnera, having flown in to Croydon on 9 March 1932

5. *Caledonia* over New
York, after her pioneering
Atlantic crossing in 1937

6. The Mayo-Composite, *Maia* and *Mercury*, in which Captains
Wilcockson and Bennett achieved the first transatlantic delivery
of freight by air in July 1938

7. Captain Arthur
Wilcockson in the
cockpit of *Caledonia*

8. *Cassiopeia* loading in Southampton Water, prior to departure on the first ever Empire Air Mail service to South Africa, June 1937

9. *Sylvanus*, *Scipio* and *Satyrus*, Imperial Airways' three Short Kent flying boats, moored at Alexandria

IMPERIAL
AIRWAYS
MAP
Southampton-Alexandria

10. Brochure advertising the
new Empire Air Mail service to
South Africa

11. The observation deck
inside an Empire flying boat

12. The flying boats' 'Clapham Junction':
Rod-el-Farag at Cairo on the Nile

13. Ringing the bell at Wadi Halfa in the Sudan to
announce the imminent departure of the flying boat

14. 'The canoe that goes for up': refuelling
Canopus at Olvengo on the Congo

15. Laropi, Uganda

16. Three Imperial Airways flying-boat captains survey the harbour at
Dar-es-Salaam from the wing of an Empire boat

17. 'Like gentle giants ...': *Cleopatra* circles over Durban

18. Coming in to touch down in the harbour at Durban

now full of airways, and airways have codified the world – our experience of Singapore a transit lounge on the way to Australia, two sides of the globe reduced to L H R and S D Y. Today's travel-writer often has to go to perverse lengths to make the journey worth writing about: over the Andes by mountain bike; round Ireland with a fridge. But before the war the flying travel-book was not uncommon – *Sky Gipsy*, *South By Thunderbird* – and Cobham himself wrote up his prodigious journey in *My Flight to the Cape and Back*.

The entire book runs to just seventy pages, including the Gaumont cameraman's plentiful photos, and if you want graphic description, self-revelation or whimsy, Cobham is not your man. He is a stolid writer, who sometimes sounds as though proposing the vote of thanks at a Rotary Club dinner – not the kind of person who sets out to let the journey travel him. But there are occasional moments that place the sheer oddity of his voyage at that time. There is the complete indifference of the Sudanese Shelluk tribe when the De Havilland lands at Malakal – who apparently dismissed flying, Cobham was told, as 'one of the mad things the white men do'; and the bafflement of their chief on being informed that Cobham's plane had just come the equivalent of a year's march from Cape Town, in six days. 'I shall never forget the expression on the poor old boy's face,' says the cheery aviator, 'as he put his hand to his forehead and shook his head.' And there is the woman at Kisumu, worried about how the crew would sleep, and disappointed to learn that they did come down at night. But *My Flight to the Cape and Back* is more than a unique historical record: its very brevity is what is startling. It traverses the entire length of the African continent, and links it in a single narrative to mainland Europe and Britain – in a comparative lightning-flash. The possibility of air travel is newly offering those wide, ironic perspectives that, by the time Naipaul was writing fifty years later, had stretched into absurd snapshots.

There are longer air routes. There is great variety, too, in, say, a passage to the Antipodes (assuming you do the journey as it would have been done pre-war, in short hops) – the Persian Gulf, the subcontinent, the Indian Ocean – but it is consecutive, not cumulative, unlike the itinerary of the Africa route. The Africa route, the slow transnavigation of a great land mass, the gravitational drop from north to south, top to bottom, has a unity. It is like a book: it builds, takes you to its centre, and by the end you have the whole picture. Think of David Livingstone, just sixty years before Cobham – those incredibly arduous explorations, years and years consumed on the march – and yet on a map of Africa his routes are the scratchings and circlings of an ant. Cecil Rhodes had articulated his Cape-to-Cairo dream soon after – of threading the north of the continent to its southern tip via a giant railway that would open up Africa's material riches to world trade – but a trans-Africa line would have been impossibly difficult and expensive. Between the wars the aviatrix Beryl Markham flew extensively in Africa, running emergency medical errands, taking big-game hunters up in search of their quarry and, of course, delivering the mail. In her autobiography, *West with the Night*, she recalls 'an impressive and beautiful signpost' that a British government road commission had erected near Naivasha in Kenya. Pointing north it blazoned:

TO JUBA – KHARTOUM – CAIRO

Even after a mild rainfall the intended road had, she writes, 'an adhesive quality equal to that of the most prized black treacle . . . [a] minor defect, coupled with the fact that thousands of miles of papyrus swamp and deep desert [had been] almost flippantly overlooked.' So much for overland: the sign endured, she concludes, 'like a beacon, daring all and sundry to proceed (not even with caution) towards what was almost sure to be neither Khartoum nor Cairo, but a Slough of Despond more tangible than, but at least as hopeless as, Mr Bunyan's'. Airliners, says Paul Theroux, 'are like seven-league boots': with his pioneer survey flight Alan Cobham established the first calibration of a mode of travel on the same scale as the continent.

There was a world of difference, of course, between a hardy aviator flying his small biplane the length of Africa for fun, landing where he could, and having facilities for refuelling and overnight accommodation, resident station staff, never mind sufficiently powerful and reliable aeroplanes, to permit a regular passenger-carrying service. In any case, Imperial Airways' priority in subsequent years was to blaze a trail across the Middle East to open a route to India. It wasn't until 1932 that the first HP-42 lumbered off the grass at Croydon to inaugurate a through service to South Africa. But by then Alan Cobham – now Sir Alan in recognition of his aerial exploits – had published another travel book . . .

Cobham's books tell you exactly and unadornedly what he did, and this one was called *Twenty Thousand Miles in a Flying Boat*. Shorts, the flying-boat makers on the Medway, wanted someone to test their new Singapore flying boat in tropical conditions: sponsored by them and Rolls-Royce, who'd built the engines, Cobham flew a complete circuit of the African continent. He made landfall from the Mediterranean at Benghazi, followed the Nile all the way south to Lake Victoria, the east coast down to the Cape, and then hugged the west coast all the way up to the Straits of Gibraltar.

At Kalafrana seaplane base in Malta on the way out, one of the Singapore's wing-floats – crucial to stabilize the craft on water – was torn off in a high swell, and Cobham had a terrifying ordeal trying to beach the flying boat while watching fifteen-foot waves threaten to overwhelm them. Touching down at Cape Town, the Singapore became the first flying boat South Africa had ever seen. On the west coast Cobham had to put down with engine trouble on an isolated lagoon north of Abidjan in the Ivory Coast, and he and Lady Cobham (who'd come along for the ride this time) were conveyed by native dug-out canoe 'for hours and hours . . . through narrow canals bordered by dense jungle forests through which the sun could hardly penetrate' – to reach a small British trading-post and await the spare parts they'd ordered. They were there a month: a photographic plate of Lady Cobham sitting beside a birdcage with an expression of rather posed serenity is captioned OUR CANARY KEPT US CHEERFUL UNDER THE TRYING CIRCUMSTANCES. The twenty thousand miles took the best part of six months, and at the end of the book, recounting their eventual return home, Cobham confides – it is hard to decide whether he was capable of a deadpan wit – that his wife 'had looked forward to this day so long that when it at last came she had no sensations on the subject whatsoever'.

But Cobham's new flight had pioneered sixty places around Africa where seaplanes could touch down and take off, including the obvious route from Cairo to South Africa – down the Nile, lake-hopping across to the eastern littoral, and down the coast. Even to establish the first basic facilities for landplanes to fly down through the continent as Cobham had done in 1926, the Air Ministry had, after the First World War, had to spend literally millions to prepare aerodromes in difficult country – carving landing strips out of dense jungle, draining swamps and demolishing anthills. 'For those unacquainted with this country it will come as a surprise to learn,' notes the official report in 1919, peering over its glasses, 'that anthills are often as high as 25 feet . . . and between 35 and 45 feet in diameter . . .' But come the rainy season and, as Cobham's difficulties had shown, landing grounds could become an impossible morass. Where better than Africa, with its huge rivers, vast lakes, and plentiful harbours and bays, for seaplanes? In his Singapore, Cobham had flown from Khartoum, at the junction of the White and Blue Niles in the Sudan, to Kisumu on Lake Victoria – Kenya's third city – and back, in just four days. By 1931 Imperial Airways had their own Calcutta flying boats running that leg on their Africa service.

But to account for the quantum leap forward of 1937, that the following year could see Ian Henderson boarding the Empire boat *Corsair* to take him all the way to Juba, we have to invert the telescope in another way. Just one fellow passenger to join him for a hearty cooked breakfast above the Isle of Wight that September morning – but still the steward had been concerned where they sat to achieve the best weight distribution for take-off. There would have been three tons of mail aboard. Even if the *Windsor Castle* competing with Cobham in 1926 hadn't had a single passenger booking, it would still have steamed out of Cape Town for Southampton: it was the mail steamer, and the mail had to go. With British colonial governments, civil servants and mercantile companies in dominions across the globe, there was plenty of it. The theory was rather like the little Scottish post-bus setting out every morning for the isolated crofts – on a rather larger scale. Human beings hitching a ride were a bonus.

These days, of course, the ethos is reversed. The advent of wide-bodied jets permitted the containerization of mail: the Royal Mail sends two 1,500-kg containers of letters to Johannesburg every day – some 49 tons of mail a month – on scheduled flights, and puts the carriage out to open tender. At the moment, South African Airways have the contract. Far from passengers getting bumped, or at least, seats not being sold on a plane, in order to make room for the mail, 'it's normally the other way round,' Andy Pickering told me at the headquarters of Royal Mail International. He was in charge of Britain's international mail for, quite simply, 'ROW': the Rest of the World. 'In adverse weather conditions, if the pilot wants to trim the aircraft differently or carry more fuel, it's usually the mail that gets thrown off.' Computerization monitors the volume of airmail to busy international destinations even as it builds up at Heathrow hour by hour during the night, and the Royal Mail can be proactive in farming out consignments to other airlines to ensure it arrives at its destination by the 'critical entry time' necessary to be processed on the following day. 'But what we used to do,' said Andy, 'sending mail down to Croydon and achieving same-day delivery in Paris: we can't do that now. In the past, if you'd got the one bag of mail there people could swoop on it and deal with it.'

But by the early 1930s airmail was not yet established as a way of communicating over long distances. Imperial Airways' transcontinental air services to places like South Africa and Australia were only just getting going, and frequently prey to mechanical and climatic vicissitudes. Sometimes passengers found themselves spending an unscheduled night under canvas along the way. The Post Office, with its long-established shipping contracts, took the opportunistic attitude that, once the airlines had taken all the commercial risk of setting up and running their new route, it might put the odd bag of mail their way. In 1934, however, even as the Postmaster-General was presenting Imperial Airways with the first royal airmail pennant, and the streamlined blue post-van was shuttling to and from Croydon Aerodrome to achieve such lightning expedition with the mail to Paris, Imperial Airways had come up with an audacious proposal.

It's a rare gift, to identify an enormous business opportunity by starting from an assumption of market dominance – and then envisioning how the world would have to change to effect it. Such self-prophetic vision – think of Rupert Murdoch and the satellite dish – will perhaps always have a seismic potential in the world of communications, because it is not an innovation in fashion (which can as easily change again), but causes a perceptual shift. It enshrines a new notion of how the world works.

The idea appears to have taken root in mid-air, as one of Imperial

Airways' Hannibal airliners throbbed towards South Africa. The 'flying banana' was on a promotional visit to Cape Town in 1933, which is why the airline's top brass were aboard: the chairman, Sir Eric Geddes, and the managing director, George Woods Humphrey. It was the company secretary, S. A. Dismore, who had floated his boldly simple thought. Supposing Imperial Airways were to carry *all* Britain's mail, to *all* its dominions, at a single 'all-up' rate no more expensive than it had cost to send it by sea? Throughout their flight to the Cape, the two men discussed if and how it could be done – and then, ironically, availed themselves of a slow sea-passage home to work out all the finer detail.

It was the moment when a fledgling company came of age – when it woke up to what it was doing, abandoned tactics for strategy, and decided to push the envelope. Imperial Airways was then nine years old. It had been formed in 1924 by amalgamating several of the penurious private airlines that had sprung up after the first war to pioneer passenger air travel from Britain – the government eventually realizing that it was often subsidizing two companies to compete against each other. The new creation was designated the government's 'chosen instrument' for a co-ordinated and purposeful development of Britain's airways. Imperial Airways – but the grand name originally bespoke no sweeping dream of girdling the world. The first choice had been the banal British Air Transport Services – until someone noticed the unflattering acronym. Though in receipt of substantial government subsidy, Imperial Airways was a private company whose major shareholders included the Southern Railway and Dunlop Tyres, and much of its culture was less than glamorous. As soon as it had been formed, all of its pilots went on strike in protest at the low pay. Five years later the company still sometimes had trouble meeting the weekly payroll, and thrift drove the accounts department so fiercely, recalled one early trainee, that 'if so much as two shillings was missing there was an inquest.' Even by 1939, when Sir John Reith briefly became its chairman, he was shocked, coming from the dignity of Broadcasting House, by the 'dark and narrow' passages and wooden partitions of the former furniture depository at Victoria that constituted Imperial Airways' head office.

Its fleet of aircraft, by the early thirties, still reflected a cautious conservatism: great underpowered biplanes with, quipped one American airline executive, 'a built-in headwind', usually ordered a few at a time – when competitors like KLM and Luft Hansa were already using much faster state-of-the-art new monoplanes like the Douglas DC-2 or the Junkers Ju-52. On a long-distance haul like the Cape an Imperial Airways passenger might be conveyed on four different kinds of plane. The Kent flying boats that crossed the Mediterranean to connect Europe with Africa – biplanes built as recently as 1930 – had toilet compartments with a flap that opened in the hull to evacuate the contents as on a train, startling the occupant with a vertiginous prospect of the ocean below. Despite their exceedingly high engine noise, they had windows you could open. The wreck of *Scipio*, the Kent that crashed on a heavy landing at Mirabella in Crete in 1936, remained visible thereafter to future passengers through the clear water.

And now this company was pitching to become the world's largest airmail carrier! It was an outstandingly bold and imaginative proposal – 'in postal history,' writes John Pudney in *The Seven Skies*, 'many regarded it as paralleled only by the introduction of the Penny Post in the nineteenth century.' The genius was in the simplicity: *all* the British Empire's mail, from the subcontinent's to Africa's and Australasia's, at a flat rate of a penny halfpenny per half-ounce. No surcharge on the shipping rate, no blue stickers, no more fortnight's delay for a letter to come back from the Cape or four weeks from India. Subtly, Imperial Airways' management decided to get the government on side before the traditionalist Royal Mail, and

Geddes memoed the Cabinet in March 1933. By the end of the following year the proposal had passed the Commons.

So much for the commercial coup; the logistics relied on another radical transformation. Everything was to go by flying boat. Proving flights like Cobham's had shown that seaplanes could go the whole way. Partly necessity was the mother of invention: even when Africa's dirt airstrips weren't out of action altogether during the rains, they were likely to be too small and soft for planes large enough to carry the new volume of mail. But the fiendish beauty of Imperial Airways' scheme was that other people would mostly pay for it. It would receive an annual subsidy of £750,000 from the government to run the scheme; a further £900,000 a year from the Post Office for the mail carried, and then £75,000 on top of that to cover the Christmas post. And by switching to flying boats, the company also got the Admiralty to agree to provide all the launches, refuelling tenders and mooring facilities at every stop for free. All Imperial Airways needed now was some new seaplanes.

What happened next is still remarkable even when one recognizes the uniquely favourable deal the company had pulled off. Imperial Airways ordered a fleet of twenty-eight new flying boats straight off the drawing-board. The total value of the contract given to Short Brothers at Rochester in 1934 was £1.75 million – five years earlier the airline's entire fleet had been valued at only half a million. There would be no prototype. They would be advertised as the fastest in the world. The company would officially dub them its Imperial Flying Boats – but very soon they'd become universally known as the Empire boats.

There are only photographs left now, and halcyon black-and-white films, but at least there are plenty of them. Sixty years on, the Empire boats still look magnificently modern. Set one alongside a 747 and in profile there is undeniable kinship. Technologically they were a huge advance: all-metal monoplanes, with four engines, capable of carrying up to twenty-four passengers (the Kents could manage just fifteen) at up to 200 m.p.h., and flying over 800 miles before descending to refuel. There was a smoking cabin up front (Brigadier Michael Biggs of the King's African Rifles remembered the excessive politeness – 'No, no, after you!' – with which embarking passengers jockeyed to reserve for themselves the smokers' berth) and an 'observation deck' along the side where travellers could stand and sight-see through the deep windows. The smell of leather – dark green leather, with which the seats were upholstered – pervaded the cabin. There was even sufficient space for a game of deck quoits. The crew's airy flight-deck was almost as spacious as the bridge of a ship. And yet, while the streamlined profile was of the utmost modernity, there is a softness about an Empire boat. A Junkers Ju-52, all corrugated surfaces and spiky motors, is like a tousled dog that has nuzzled a thistle. The DC-2: a bland flying lozenge. But the C-Class, with its deep hull and wide blunt nose, is a plump, docile dugong.

Nowadays we are used to the image rethink as one more routine tool in commerce – for a large company it is almost obligatory every few years, and airlines are the most profligate. When the product is everywhere essentially the same, it is a matter of needing to look different. But the Empire boats heralded a genuinely new era in British aviation, and the company responded with a sophisticated and alluring use of image to heighten reality. Imperial Airways mythologized them from the beginning.

It had always named its aeroplanes. The Handley–Page biplanes had all been *H*s, like *Hanno* and *Heracles* (classical nomenclature was favoured); the three Kent flying boats were *Scipio*, *Satyrus* and *Sylvanus*. But with the new C-Class fleet the company's tradition reached its apogee. Every one of the twenty-eight new craft was christened. Stellar associations were common: *Canopus*, *Castor*, *Cassiopeia*, *Capella*, *Capricornus*. Femininity was celebrated in classical heroines: *Camilla, Corinna, Circe, Calpurnia* and *Calypso*. Names like *Cavalier, Corsair* and *Challenger* intimated freebooting wanderlust. *Cambria, Caledonia* and *Cameronian* acknowledged the ancient geographical pull of the mother country. Postcards were printed depicting every plane. Each had its individual badge, adorning the headed stationery provided for passengers' use, accompanied by a poetic quotation to serve as the craft's epigraph. The Romantic poets were a particular source: Wordsworth supplied 'The Cavalier was eager to depart'; Byron, 'He left a Corsair's name to other times.' Even Lawrence of Arabia conferred his blessing on the Empire boat *Castor*. It all 'befitted their station,' remarks the historian Brian Cassidy, 'somewhere between an ocean-going passenger liner and first class hotel.'

This is true, as far as it goes – but it goes deeper than gradations of luxury. These *were* boats, and it was as though Britain had a new merchant fleet. Imperial Airways' senior captains, raised on HP-42s at Croydon, had to retrain in seamanship, semaphore and the intricacies of maritime law in order to fly them. They were now known as 'master' of their new craft, and tended to dress and deport themselves with the grandeur of a ship's captain. The cabin stewards and pursers were usually recruited from Cunard. A sea voyage was then the understood and accepted way of essaying a long journey: to market, if you like, these new Empire routes as plied by, literally, a flying boat, was reassuring and sensible. A voyage was what the Empire boats were offering: no more changes and transfers and odd train journeys in the middle and whatever variety of planes could be cobbled together. The same consoling echoes of a little bit of Britain out at sea that are evoked by the *QE2* or the *Canberra* – in this respect the new Empire boats spoke of mythical continuity.

But the new names seem to have stuck, as they never did with Imperial Airways' Atalantas or Calcuttas. Just as Concorde – the only other aeroplane since to be so familially cherished – is never *a*

Concorde or *the* Concorde, so from the start it was always *Canopus* and *Ceres*: your one was special, an individual host and travel companion. Perhaps for the first time in British aviation, mythology was appropriate. Seafaring has always had a rich mythical tradition, from Odysseus and Jason and the Argonauts onward, but now powered flight itself had found its historical moment. Hitherto, it had remained a slightly tenuous defiance of gravity, very much a case of winging it – wood held together by wires, pilot's hair streaming in the wind. As late as 1926 Imperial Airways captains still flew in open cockpits, windscreens spattered with oil. A biplane flying boat like the Singapore looks as though gravity will any moment see through the con-trick its untidy frame has pulled to achieve ascent. In 1921 an anonymous newspaper correspondent had hymned the opening of Croydon Airport's terminal building with fiery – and slightly misquoted – words from *Ezekiel*: 'The suburbs shall shake at the sound of the cry of the pilots.' Aviation was then, at most, worthy of the mock heroic. And any existential reverie of flight had been restricted to the solitary aviator, like Saint-Exupéry, whose *Southern Mail* appeared in translation in 1933 – the intensity of its speculation resting not least on a recognition of human frailty and vulnerability inside this tiny craft buffeted by dust-storms and cyclones.

An Empire boat, however, looks as though always made to fly, not Meccanoed. And by the mid-thirties the poets were starting to become air passengers, and passengers poets.

> More beautiful and soft than any moth

[wrote Stephen Spender in 1932 in 'The Landscape near an Aerodrome']

> With burring furred antennae feeling its huge path
> Through dusk, the air-liner with shut-off engines
> Glides over suburbs and the sleeves set trailing tall
> To point the wind.

Note Spender's hyphenation of a word now elided and utterly functional. *Air-liner*: back then it was two apparently contradictory worlds wondrously yoked – an ocean-going vessel of the skies. The ultra-modern plane is seen both as a militant futuristic symbol, and as soft and harmonious – 'In the last sweep of love' its passengers pass over the fields behind the aerodrome.

Spender was not unique during the thirties. Auden hymned airmen and airports; so did Cecil Day-Lewis. At the end of Graham Greene's 1935 novel, *England Made Me*, a formation of aeroplanes appears in the skies above the Swedish capital, Stockholm:

wheeling over the lake, zooming down towards the City Hall, rising and falling like a flight of swallows, the sun catching their aluminium wings as they turned . . .

It was a dream humankind had always wanted to come true: to fly like a bird. At last, after all the centuries of prophecy, from Icarus through to H. G. Wells, it had become civic reality. It was yet to become functional or homogenized.

Perhaps if Wordsworth had been able to watch a Short Sunderland, military sister to the C-Class, taking off from Windermere in the Lakes, he would have execrated it as he did the coming of the railways. But in obliviously composing the epigraphs for *Cavalier*, *Challenger* and *Cambria* he was confirming that, by the middle of the thirties, the historical moment had arrived when flight was a human phenomenon of great beauty, wonder and civility, and the advent of the Empire boats marked a kind of extension of the imagination, expressible only in poetry.

8

Nairobi

Ours would be an eight-hour flight, the captain told us. Bit longer than New York, I thought; bit shorter than Miami. A Kenya Airways Airbus to Nairobi: what else is there to tell you? No possible occasion for poetry: there are barely grounds for stretching prose beyond a sentence. There wasn't even a movie to watch.

The pilot did, however, talk us in some detail through our route. It lay across France, over the Swiss Alps, until we left the European land-mass at Rome. Then we'd cross the Mediterranean via Crete, and enter Egyptian airspace at Cairo. The Nile would take us all the way south through Egypt and on into the Sudan past Khartoum. It was exactly the old Empire flying-boat route – not that we'd be touching down at any of these places or, flying overnight and about six miles high, see anything of them.

But the Empire boats – unpressurized, and cruising at less than 150 m.p.h. – flew at just a few thousand feet, low and slow enough to afford superb views all the way (and to catch any bumpy air and bad weather). In those days the motion picture you watched to while away the hours was the landscape beneath you. To enable its passengers to take full advantage of their remarkable vantage-point, Imperial Airways even produced a little yellow booklet entitled *Through Africa by the Empire Flying Boat*. It is a comprehensive and eclectic document, running to some thirty pages in tracing the entire journey from Southampton to South Africa and back, and including all connecting legs to places like Accra and Lusaka. Nothing less than an aerial guidebook, like the aerial travel-book it's another lost literary genre. It points out the eagle's-eye view of the Governor-General's palace and the Mosque at Khartoum, and alerts the traveller to the sight of the big herd of elephants at Bor, a hundred miles north of Juba. Crossing the Victoria Nile at the Murchison Falls, it notes the likely glimpse of 'crocodiles basking in the sunshine along the river banks'. It previews the city of Kisumu on Lake Victoria with a digest of its principal geological resources (gold reefs and diamonds) and agricultural activity – rice, cotton and groundnuts. To do justice to the Great Rock Temple at Abu Simbel in Egypt it passes on the memorable description, by the Victorian traveller Amelia Edwards in *A Thousand Miles up the Nile*, of how its creators 'took a mountain and fell upon it like Titans; they hollowed and carved it as if it was a cherry stone, and left it for feebler men to marvel at forever.' Even had the Empire boats featured miniature TVs in the seat backs and a dozen music channels on the personal headsets, you feel, the passengers would have been too absorbed by the aerial safari they were on to notice.

'Years ago,' writes the Australian war correspondent Alan Moorehead in *No Room in the Ark*, 'the British used to run a flying boat service down through Africa, and although it was a slow and sometimes rather bumpy journey I can remember no flight that was quite so pleasant.' *No Room in the Ark* is actually a book about wildlife in Africa – but it is with an elegiac account of his flying-boat journey that Moorehead chooses to begin, and set the keynote for his appreciation of the continent:

There was no flying after dark, and the machine put down at some fascinating places on the way: Wadi Halfa in the midst of the Egyptian desert; Khartoum at the junction of the Blue and White Niles in the Sudan, Kisumu on Lake Victoria (the lake itself so big that you lost sight of the shore as you flew across it) and Livingstone, just a mile or two above the Victoria Falls.

Most of these stops were out-of-the-way places which had very little connection with the outside world, and so you were plunged at once into the authentic African scene. There were no familiar airport buildings, no advertisements, no other traffic of any kind; just this rush of muddy water as you lighted down on a river or a forest lake, and the boy who came out in a boat to take you to the shore was the genuine article, a coal-black African, sometimes naked to the waist. He looked as though he would have been really more at home in a thatched hut than in this strange world of flying monsters in the sky.

On the Zambezi river I recall they had to run a launch up and down the water a few minutes before the plane came in to clear the hippopotami away. I remember too, with particular vividness, a little place called Malakal on the White Nile in the Sudan, where the women of the Dinka tribe were six foot tall and as hipless as young boys. Their hair was thickly matted with grease and piled up in a marvellous coiffure high above their heads. They walked gravely along the riverbank and turned their heads away from the great flying boat on the water in the way that primitive people often do when they are confronted with something which they regard as quite miraculous and beyond all comprehension.

These scenes gave the passenger a brief but very potent whiff of Africa. He felt he was seeing the country as Livingstone and the other early explorers had seen it, and although I made this journey only once and as long ago as 1941 it filled me with an intense desire to come back one day.

For Moorehead the Empire boat had not just been an excitingly visceral experience of take-off and touchdown: it had been a way of seeing Africa. He felt it had taken him to the heart of something. It had given travel unforgettable meaning.

Such remembrance was far from unique. 'Oh, yes, people remember their flying-boat journeys,' confirmed Fred Huntley, one of the curators at the British Airways archive. On the occasion of the eightieth birthday of Enoch Powell, he told me, the *Daily Telegraph* had invited the politician to pick out the single most memorable experience of his long life for a feature in its colour magazine. The notorious 'Rivers of Blood' speech? His Cabinet service as Conservative Minister for Health? His return to Parliament as an Ulster Unionist? No: none of Powell's biographers had so much as mentioned in their voluminous chronicles of his career what he chose to reminisce about at great length: the flying-boat journey that brought him home from war service in India.

And the truth of Mr Huntley's matter-of-fact observation was overwhelmingly demonstrated to me. I placed a tiny advertisement in the Personal column of the *Daily Telegraph* – no more than a couple of square centimetres of microscopic type – appealing for memories of the African flying boats, and several similar announcements in pensioners' association newsletters. I was deluged with letters from all over the world. My answerphone tape was full in days. It was almost as though the respondents had been waiting for someone to ask. 'Oh, I could have wept when the flying boats finished,' said Bob Harwood, a retired BOAC pilot who'd flown them on the Africa route until the end in 1950. 'No other period in my service career was so enjoyable,' said Air Commodore Ted Williams, a BOAC first officer on its Sunderland flying boats from 1944 to 1947: 'to everyone who was connected with the flying boats it seemed romantic *at the time* – it wasn't something that just gained a patina afterwards.' 'The *smell* of the Empire boats . . .' reflected Peter Colmore, Imperial Airways' traffic officer at Kisumu in the early years of the Empire Air Mail service: 'Gasoline and aluminium – I can still smell it . . .' I received cigarette cards depicting the Empire boats, copies of the *Through Africa by the Empire Flying Boat* booklet, magnificent black-and–white photographs of Empire boats and Sunderlands alighting on the Nile silhouetted against the setting sun – all carefully preserved through nearly sixty years. Several correspondents had sat down and written me ten-, fifteen-page travelogues of the flying-boat voyages they'd made to Lake Naivasha or Victoria Falls – every last detail, from the goat curry served up at Malakal to the night-time roaring of the lions in Khartoum zoo that had disturbed their sleep at the Grand Hotel next door – clearly recollected as though they'd just got back yesterday.

And there was a further surprise. At least half the replies were from women. Wasn't aviation, with its Battle of Britain and Dambusters mythology, its *Right Stuff* and *Top Gun* pilots, its plane-spotting possibilities, its boffinry, its sheer *metal*-ness, stereotypically a male, even a boy's, preserve? But women, dozens of them, quite as many as men, cherished their flying-boat memories enough to trouble to write – as I'm sure they wouldn't if I'd advertised for memories of the Comet or even the Spitfire. The men who replied tended to place their reminiscences by historical co-ordinates: like George Blake, who remembered for me the BOAC Sunderland that brought him back from his war service in India with the Yorkshire and Lancashires, sideslipping down into Augusta harbour in Sicily between two lines of battleships from the captured Italian fleet.

But women retained, and articulated, images of simple and moving beauty. 'I was only a child when I went on a flying boat and so I only have a brief memory,' apologized Gillian Ollerenshaw, ringing from Cheshire: she had flown out to Egypt to visit her father, stationed there with the RAF. 'All I can remember,' she said, 'is the sun shining through the droplets of water blown up off the sea by the propellers.' In briskly recalling her wartime flight from West Africa back to Britain in the Boeing flying boat *Berwick*, Dorothy Babb could still demonstrate for me the peeling curve of its bow wave. 'No, not like that,' she mused, experimenting: 'like that' – and, ballerina-graceful, her arms swanned out like wood shavings curling away from the plane-blade.

Perhaps it is more than beauty. *Civil* aviation: today the word has lost its moral force, denotes a mere bureaucratic department. But by 1938, when the Empire boats had all entered service on the airmail routes, aviation was fast assuming a far less benign reputation. In August 1937 the *Times* war correspondent, G. L. Steer, had published a terrible account of the German bombing of Guernica during the Spanish Civil War, still one of the most graphic pieces of war-reporting. Aerial bombardment had shown it could obliterate an entire city. Over the next two years, as the arms race intensified and aircraft production was progressively turned over to the military, fears of similar bombing from the air spread to Britain. Aeroplanes had come to mean bombers.

The psychological shift in reality is impossible to overstate. The sky had become unsafe. Formerly the innocent blue province of skylarks and Wordsworth's clouds, now it held the potential to rain destruction and death, from which there was no escape, and aeroplanes were the agents. Bombers, as Albert Speer said after the Second World War, made every single street in every city the front line. In Virginia Woolf's *Mrs Dalloway*, published back in 1925, a plane had 'turned and raced and swooped . . . like a skater' over London, sky-writing an advertising slogan, and her Londoners stopped to look up and idly decipher the brand – 'the strange high singing of some aeroplane overhead,' writes Woolf of her protagonist, 'was what she loved.' But by 1939 planes were intruding into her last novel, *Between the Acts*, as an ominous bomber squadron, and it was fear of imminent bombing raids that at least contributed to Virginia Woolf's suicide that year. Where in 1933 Stephen Spender was celebrating the burring moth-like air-liner, in 1938 his poetry envisions 'the aerial vultures [that] fly/Over the deserts which were cities.' Louis MacNeice, William Plomer, Herbert Read, Jacob Bronowski, George Barker, Geoffrey Grigson: between 1938 and 1939, writes Valentine Cunningham in his survey of *British Writers of the Thirties*, 'Poems stirred by bombing-plane horrors simply poured out.'

But if, in the space of a few years, aeroplanes in general were transformed into malign instruments of apocalypse, flying boats never became un-civilized. During the war, their military duties were either defensive, escorting convoys, patrolling the coastline – or, when they were offensive (the Short Sunderland was so heavily armed with machine guns that the Germans nicknamed it 'the Flying Porcupine'), they were spiriting in Resistance fighters to Norwegian fjords, or directing their attacks not against innocent civilians but against enemy U-boats or fighters – old-style warfare, between professional soldiers, and far out at sea. Even then, the German navy's other nickname for these slow, tubby craft bumbling above the water on their endless patrols was *müde Biene* – 'tired bee'. But overwhelmingly flying boats flew, always have flown, civilians, on civil, peaceful errands, in a state of grace. They never lost their civility, and allowed their passengers to recapture theirs. I wonder if it's true to say that the women who contacted me loved flying boats *because* they hated aeroplanes.

At eighty-four, Rosemary Potter was still an active volunteer guide for the National Trust at Knole, near where she lived at Tunbridge Wells. A tall, elegant lady with a matter-of-fact directness, she dismissed her last airline flight, in a 747 to South Africa, as 'like a cinema taking off'. A refugee from Malaya separated from her husband after the Japanese invasion that had led to his incarceration in a prison camp, she had spent the war in Durban, a volunteer for the Women's Royal Voluntary Service dishing up large meals to young British soldiers on their way by troop-ship to the Far East. Early in the mornings, she told me, the Empire boats' engines bursting into life at the Congella base would remind her it was time to get up – 'It was sort of, "Hello, here we are again,"' she said. When she watched them circling in over the city for touchdown she used to say to herself, 'One day I'm going on that.' And though when she eventually did it was news of her mother's terminal illness back in England that qualified her for a 'compassionate placement' home, even such sad circumstances hadn't darkened her memory of the Empire boats. Why? I wondered. What was it about them? Mrs Potter thought. 'They were sort of friendly people,' she pondered; 'like gentle giants.'

Nearly sixty years on, it was with such affectionate and charming images in mind that I travelled to Africa for the first time. There were no flying boats in Africa any more, of course – at least, not flying scheduled passenger-services. And, except for sky-high seven-league-boot hops like our non-stop Kenya Airways flight KQ101, you couldn't retrace the whole magnificent trans-Africa route that Moorehead had flown. Great tracts of territory the Empire boats had serenely navigated were now barred to the casual traveller. Apart from Khartoum, which you could fly in and out of for a strictly controlled day or two, the whole of the vast Sudan was a dangerous war zone. The famous stop at Wadi Halfa on the northern border with Egypt, moreover, no longer existed at all. The entire town now lay under the waters of Lake Nasser since the building of the Aswan High Dam. Northern Uganda, prey to the unpredictable activities of the Lord's Resistance Army, was likewise out of bounds. And sadly, that meant that some of the flying boats' most recondite backwaters were now inaccessible: Malakal, with its Dinka tribesmen, which had been the highlight of Alan Moorehead's flight; the south Sudan city of Juba where Ian Henderson had built dykes and roads and set out from on camel expeditions into the bush; the remote Ugandan village of Laropi. But in any case, doggedly to try and shadow every one of the Empire boats' footsteps seemed a mere stunt, a factitious endurance test only begging the obvious and entirely reasonable objection, 'But you're not doing it in a flying boat . . .'

But, seeing how these romantic seaplanes seemed to have made their Africa service legendary *even while they were flying it*, how their ports of call had become so talismanic, I wanted to take Moorehead's way of looking, and the intense wave of nostalgia and affection that had rolled in from all over Britain – indeed, Britons all around the world – when I had simply uttered the words 'African flying boats', and test it all on Africa.

I have in front of me Imperial Airways' timetable for the Empire Air Mail service to South Africa, current from April 1939. Flying boats leave Southampton twice a week, on Wednesdays and Saturdays, to fly the full 7,201 miles to Durban. (They never completed the trail Cobham had blazed to Cape Town in his Singapore: a condition of the South African government's approval for the route was that its own carrier, South African Airways, retained the lucrative sectors into Cape Town.) The Wednesday departure, leaving Southampton Water at 5.30 in the morning, reaches Durban at 4.35 on Sunday afternoon: five days' flying. With a range, in the first years, of just 800 miles, the C-Class had to make plenty of stops, and, given the need to disembark all the passengers safely on to land away from the hazards of pumping in aviation fuel from a bobbing tender, this meant pleasant returns to earth several times a day for morning coffee, lunch and afternoon tea.

The first day's flying, therefore, was punctuated by touchdowns on Lake Marignane, for Marseille, in mid-morning, on Lake Bracciano outside Rome at lunchtime, and in Bríndisi harbour before the flying boat landed in Phaleron Bay for the night-stop at Athens. Thursday, the second day of the trip, took passengers and mail from Greece across the Mediterranean and up the Nile as far as Wadi Halfa, just over the Egyptian border. Sometimes they'd come down to refuel at Mirabella in Crete as well; and then it was on to Alexandria – a night-stop on the return service – where the seaplanes would anchor

B·O·A·C

TAKE OFF 06.00 L.T.

Station......LUXOR...... Service No...103/241

Money may be exchanged at......THE HOTEL

Exchange rate ....£1 = P.T. 97.5

Local time is .....2..... hours ahead/~~behind~~ G.M.T.

The stop here is for .....1..... ~~DAYS~~ NIGHT

You will be accommodated in room......64

at the......LUXOR HOTEL

Meal arrangements for the next 24 hours......

BREAKFAST......IN FLIGHT

LUNCH......IN FLIGHT

TEA......AT KAMPALA

DINNER......AT KAMPALA

You will be called at......04.40 L.T.

Your baggage should be outside your room at......05.10 L.T.

~~LEAVE HOTEL~~ ......05.30 L.T.

The next nightstop will be......KAMPALA

During this flight, stops will be made at......

KHARTOUM

B.O.A.C. STAFF

WILL BE PLEASED TO GIVE YOU FURTHER INFORMATION OR ASSISTANCE DURING YOUR STAY

Telephone ......5......

in the East Harbour next to the Royal Navy's Mediterranean fleet, and a further intermediate stop at Cairo, alighting on the Nile at Rod-el-Farag.

The third day saw the earliest start of all: a take-off at 4.45 a.m., for there were nearly 1,700 miles to fly all the way up the White Nile to its source, to reach Friday's night-stop at the Kisumu Hotel on Lake Victoria. The first stop, Khartoum, was reached by breakfast-time with a touchdown at Gordon's Tree. Next came Malakal, the isolated outpost with a swampingly hot climate where at least one Imperial Airways traffic manager is said to have degener-ated, unsurprisingly, into a hopeless drunk. Then the flying boat began to overfly the Sudd, the dense matting of papyrus that rendered the Upper Nile almost unnavigable, and Juba in southern Sudan was reached by early afternoon. If the weather was fine there would be a detour to view the Murchison Falls at the headwaters of the Nile, and then the first touchdown on Lake Victoria, at Port Bell in Uganda, for Kampala and Entebbe.

On Saturday it was east to the coast at Mombasa, before the seaplane commenced a long series of hops from bay to harbour all the way down to South Africa – the route that Cobham had pioneered: Dar-es-Salaam and Lindi in the then Tanganyika; and a night-stop at the Imperial Airways resthouse at Lumbo beside Mozambique harbour; then further south on the fifth and final day, stopping at Beira and Lourenço Marques, now Maputo and the capital of Portuguese East Africa as it then was, now the modern state of Mozambique – before journey's end at Imperial Airways' base at Congella in Durban harbour.

One additional station does not appear on the timetable. About a quarter of an hour before touchdown at Kisumu in Kenya, the weariness, even perhaps encroaching tedium, of a long day's flying would be momentarily enlivened as the passengers sensed the flying boat waggling its wings, or the nose dipping to duck under some invisible barrier. They had just crossed the Equator. Soon they would be presented with illuminated certificates, decorated by the artist Edward Bawden and personally signed by the captain, to testify to their exalted achievement in becoming:

one of the progressive band of travellers who cross the line by air. Over the waters of Lake Victoria, the Lingge Archipelago, the Empire flying boats pass in a moment from hemisphere to hemisphere, beyond the zone whose dwellers recognize no alteration in the length of night and day.

Air travel has almost entirely renounced such jollity. To print on the cover of your in-flight mag, as does the low-cost carrier easyJet, 'This is the only free thing you're going to get from us, so take it while you can,' is only to prove the rule. Now there are so many passengers aboard, and a culture of absolute safety is paramount, and business travellers can always switch their lucrative Club Class patronage to your competitor, established airlines are required to be entirely po-faced.

But sixty years ago it was still a bit of a jaunt. Air travel was a wondrous novelty; it was also something of a party piece. Even at the level of first-class luxury aboard an Imperial Airways Empire boat there was an air of the charabanc. The crossing-the-line certificate signed off with a quotation from Stephen Spender – already confirmed, as we have seen, as a futuristic poet of the air:

> Born with the sun they travelled a short
> Way towards the sun,
> And left the vivid air signed with their honour.

I hadn't realized the jocosity behind the inclusion of these sonorous lines until I traced the reference – to a poem entitled (with a lot less irony by the poet than it assumes in the context of a flowery airline gimmick) 'The Truly Great', in which Spender celebrates those individuals in history who 'from the womb, remembered the soul's history/Through corridors of light', and 'Who wore at their hearts the fire's centre'. And who were about to relax over a G&T at a rather nice hotel in Kisumu on the way to their up-country estates in Kenya.

I was going to pick up the route in the middle, as soon as it left the now-inaccessible Upper Nile. Though I was flying in to Nairobi my first flying-boat port of call would be Mombasa on the Indian Ocean – from where I would double back westwards to visit Kisumu on Lake Victoria and Port Bell in Uganda. But also I wanted to see all manner of the flying boats' haunts – rivers as well as lakes and coastal havens, and also I wanted to follow the history of their years in Africa, to the places that only hosted them on special occasions, or at the very end, even as the shadows were darkening over the era of the seaplane. So I would drop in at Lake Naivasha in Kenya's Great Rift Valley, a regular stop for Nairobi after the war when the longer-range Short Solents took over the service, and a once-weekly 'request stop' in the days of the Empire boats, 'Circumstances permitting and inducement offered', as the timetable stated – which usually meant when the wealthy landowner Sir John Ramsden and his wife, who had extensive estates around Nairobi, were aboard. And then after Naivasha I would stay inland and head south, as the Solents had, to Cape Maclear on Lake Malawi, and to the then Northern Rhodesia, now Zimbabwe, where they'd alighted on the Zambezi just above Victoria Falls. What side of Africa would I see if I let the heritage of the flying boats determine where I went? Would there be anything left for the seaplane archaeologist to discover – or had they skimmed from lake to river to harbour as lightly over thirteen years as a flock of migrating flamingos, and left as little trace as they had in the English Lake District? I knew how much people in Kent, and Wiltshire, and Norfolk, and Glamorgan, remembered of the African flying boats – but what of people in Africa?

But first I had some calls to make in Nairobi. It took a few days, indeed, for the gloom that descended on me on arrival to lift – a common affliction, I found, of those who make Kenya's capital their introduction to Africa. '*Not* Africa?' I find scribbled crossly in my notebook from the first days – but of course it was I who'd arrived from the imaginative non-regions of Africa. 'Ny-robbery' was what Ted, a Californian I met later in Malawi, called it: just the shameless rapacity of its taxi drivers could ruin your mood – and budget – for the whole day. Nairobi was not historic, far less antique. Depressingly it seemed both modern and worn, vigorously self-renewing but somehow also entropic. It had got rid of all its old buildings, but nothing looked new. Flying boats had never come here: no water. Stockholm, Seattle, Sydney: cities built around water always have a calm beauty, but even Nairobi's river was a trash-strewn ditch. This city was all in too much of a rush to notice itself, and I wasn't looking for rush but rather the lingering long view. Eventually I came to appreciate in Nairobi a gritty energy where initially I'd seen only the dust, soot, mud and tension – but coming with all those limpid intimations I'd read in Alan Moorehead was a handicap.

There was no aviation museum in Kenya – scarcely one in the whole of the African continent outside South Africa. I'd tried to sell a feature idea to a newspaper's travel editor about the fleet of vintage airliners South African Airways ran on first-class excursions up to Namibia and Mozambique – a Junkers trimotor, a DC-3 and a DC-4: 'But that's what Africa's like, isn't it?' she objected, puzzled and bored by the idea. 'When you fly in Africa, half the time it's some beaten-up old plane . . .' I suppose she had a point. But there was a railway museum in Nairobi. This was the kind of past I was looking for in Africa, so I started off there.

It was tucked away at one end of the main railway station – across the boundary fence I could see the faded chocolate-coloured carriages of the night train I was going to catch that night to Mombasa. A girl stationed at a table by the entrance put aside her Jackie Collins paperback to hand-write me out an admission ticket – slow, neat loops on her letters as though it was a school exercise. The collection of steam engines stood outside in grassy sidings, the rails mostly brown threads scoring a bumpy lawn. They were huge, saurian hulks, designs as improbable as sea monsters – odd pushmepullyou shapes designed by Beyer-Garratt with tenders front and back, the biggest weighing some 250 tons, painted mustard-yellow with proud names like *Masai of Kenya*. It was a sultry, ticking morning; a long-eared tabby cat was dozing in the shade beneath *Mount Shengena*'s wheels, and a quizzical heron hunted snakes in the long grass. A small party of schoolchildren was just leaving; that left me as the only visitor.

Britain, of course, is so crazy about steam engines that the scrap merchant in Wales who bought the hundreds withdrawn by British Rail in 1967 at the end of steam had to close his yard twenty years later: every last one had been purchased by preservationists. These days, whether in Sussex, North Yorkshire or the Severn Valley, we're used to seeing locomotives sixty, seventy years old completely rebuilt at a cost of hundreds of thousands of pounds, brass and paintwork so bright they could have been new yesterday. But this place had an air of simple abandonment. Kenya's behemoths were in poor shape: rusting, immobile, unrestored and just where they'd been left when they'd been shunted in however many years earlier. No question of any of these hauling a nostalgic steam cruise up the Great Rift Valley. My guide, a young man called Anderson, gangling and gawky in jacket and trousers, took me aside after our brief tour and told me confidentially that if there was anything I wanted off one of these engines – a nameplate, perhaps, or a brass number? – he'd be pleased to obtain it for me. English people, he said, were very interested in buying things like that.

'Most of our visitors are from Britain,' said Maurice, the museum's marketing manager – indeed, not only had the Brits organized the building of Kenya's railways back in the last century: they were still supplying the museum's quirkiest exhibits. A Mr John Wall had lent his collection of tickets, which in turn had prompted a letter from Edward W. Jones of Wrexham offering an English translation of Britain's longest station name, Llanfairpwllgwyngyllgogerychwyrndrobwllllandysiliogogogoch. Copies of *Bluebell Railway News* and the magazine of the Mid-Hants Line were scattered on a table. Here was the work of the prototypical railway enthusiast – groups of them probably came out from Britain on expensive group-holidays to tour places like this. But the young people staffing this museum weren't enthusiasts, far less volunteers – neither Anderson nor the girl selling tickets displayed the slightest interest in its contents. This was a – probably badly paid – job.

It hadn't struck me before I came to Nairobi's railway museum: how nostalgia is a luxury, materially a luxury – how much disposable time and income it requires. You only had time for the past when the present was taking care of itself. Outside my hotel on Moi Avenue one day I saw a Stagecoach driver and conductor actually trying to push their bus after it had broken down. It seemed wonderful enough that Kenya's rusting Beyer–Garratt locos hadn't been melted down into kettles long ago. All that money Edward Hulton had poured into his Sunderland; Vic Hodgkinson still changing fluorescent lighting-tubes inside Southampton's *Beachcomber* at the age of eighty. Why on earth should there be a flying boat in Africa in 1998 – what *use* could it be?

The Muthaiga Club, however, was different: the one place in Nairobi that was utterly different. I'd maximized the culture shock by catching a *matatu* there – one of Nairobi's honking, speeding, metallic-painted, crammed minibuses, this one thumping out Madonna's 'Like a Virgin' at top volume. Jump out at the roundabout by the police station, walk up the Muthaiga Road – and in through the gates of an almost eerily tranquil and picturesque oasis. Smart young women with clipped accents strode out jingling keys to climb in new four-wheel-drive Landcruisers and Shoguns. Shady, empty lawns stretched away under the trees beyond the car park, and a golf course beyond them. Mrs Travers was already waiting for me in the entrance hall, a large manila envelope under her arm. In the lounge deferential white-suited attendants lingered among deep chintzy armchairs. The week's copies of *The Times* were laid out in a neat overlapping spread. The dignified and immaculate lady of eighty-four who had taken me inside had first come here almost fifty years earlier, and it was the flying boat, both literally and in a much wider sense, that had brought her to Kenya. She waved her hand at the pink-washed exterior of the Club. 'This looks exactly the same now,' said Mrs Travers, 'as it did when I first arrived.'

In 1949 Joan Travers, then a war widow, was living on the Isle of Wight, and at Cowes, on its northern coastline, was the works of

Saunders–Roe, even this late after the war persevering with the development of the giant Princess. It was through Saunders–Roe that she met the man she married that year. 'Do you know I had no idea I was marrying anybody famous?' remarked Mrs Travers drily, showing me a wedding photograph from the envelope full of cuttings and pictures we'd spread out on one of the green-baize-covered tables. '*No* idea. And I came out of the church and there were all these photographers!' The groom was a tall man in dark uniform and peaked cap, with deep kindly eyes and a long, firm chin. The press, like Saunders–Roe, had been especially interested in his acquaintance because Dudley Travers was one of Britain's most famous and illustrious flying-boat captains.

'These are rather yellowed, aren't they?' pondered Mrs Travers in surprise as I sifted the slivers of newsprint, all pertaining to one man – they made a plump bundle. 'I forget how old I am,' she sighed. 'That's my trouble.'

I picked out one cutting from the *Aeroplane* of March 1950. 'Three million miles!' I marvelled – Captain Travers had clocked up all this distance without a single accident.

'Well, it's the hours,' Mrs Travers corrected me. 'The miles mean nothing, because most of the time they were only doing 80 miles an hour. It's the 20,000 hours . . .' In 1965, by which time, of course, he had retired from commercial aviation, but was still flying in Kenya as a volunteer for the African flying-doctor service, another article was noting how Captain Travers 'has been flying continuously since 1917'. 'He was a born flier,' said his widow.

Indeed, Dudley Travers was a legend even before he joined Imperial Airways. Enlisted in the cavalry in 1917 during the Great War, he had been given just two and a half hours' instruction before making his first solo flight with the Royal Flying Corps. After only ten hours' flying experience he entered air combat, and brought down a German plane. He went on to shoot down eleven more before the end of the war – in one engagement he and two other pilots attacked a formation of twelve enemy aircraft and brought down five. He was awarded both the Distinguished Flying Cross and the Croix de Guerre.

Between the wars he'd joined Imperial Airways. 'If you want to see what the pilots used to wear in open cockpits . . .' said Mrs Travers, proffering another cutting captioned 'Dudley Travers shaking hands with Carnera, the boxer' – whom he'd just flown to the UK for a fight at the Royal Albert Hall. Travers was done up in leather flying suit, flying helmet and thick fur collar – this was back in 1933 – but to me what was most interesting was how his own celebrity had been thought equal to that of one of the world's most famous heavyweights, to the extent of their being photographed together. Could you imagine Evander Holyfield being snapped alongside the American Airlines captain who flew him to Vegas? 'It was such a friendly, intimate profession in those days,' said Mrs Travers. 'Everybody knew everybody.'

When the Empire Air Mail Scheme had begun Dudley Travers had gone on to flying boats, and attained further distinction. He'd made the first night-landing at Durban – a safe touchdown on water by flare path no easy feat. 'As the *Ceres* flew over the Bluff,' the local South African reporter had written, 'the brightly lit saloons shone clearly against the cloud-covered sky.' Travers had retrieved a potentially disastrous situation at Laropi on the Upper Nile when an Empire boat's wing float had broken off on touchdown – the captain managing to stabilize the craft and prevent it capsizing. In 1940 he'd been given the command of *Golden Hind*, one of three 'G-Class' extra-big Empire-style flying boats that ran the dangerous wartime route from Foynes in Ireland down the west coast of Africa. Regularly, I heard, he'd forsake the comfortable hotel room provided at Empire-route night-stops to sleep aboard the flying boat.

But it wasn't just the nature of these pioneering civil airmen's exploits – Wilcockson, Travers, Bennett – it was the manner of them! Here was a rather funny article, said Mrs Travers: it came from a *Titbits* series on 'The Master Pilots' – 'There are only FIVE in All the World,' it shouted (who held British Master Pilot Certificates in recognition of their experience and accomplishments). Number Two was Captain Dudley Travers:

He has twinkly blue eyes and an inexhaustible fund of funny stories . . . He is tremendously popular with passengers. He has one peculiarity. Often I have stood half in and half out of the plane he is to fly; one look at the sky has told us all that it is going to be a dirty trip, and matters are not improved when Travers himself comes out of the Pilots' room with a *beaming* smile, humming to himself. This is an unmistakable sign that the trip is going to be not merely dirty, but exceedingly dirty. He has a passion for dirty weather, and a record second to none for bringing his plane in dead on schedule when other machines on the same route have had to turn back.

The anecdote recalls another Dudley Travers story – hallowed in Imperial Airways mythology – which I'd heard from too many sources for it to be apocryphal, and seemed to confirm the *Titbits* picture of a maverick nonchalance – perhaps forged in those First World War dogfights – and the aquiline hauteur of the exalted Empire-boat captains. Dudley Travers' passion was mint bull's-eyes – to the extent that it was the crew's job to ensure that a bag of them was always at his side on the flight-deck. One routine morning-departure, all passengers aboard, Travers taxied out into the bay, took off and circled to gain height – and then, once cruising and able to take stock, noticed. 'Where's my bull's-eyes?' (For all his imposing physique he apparently had a rather weak, piping voice.) No bull's-eyes. They'd forgotten Dudley Travers' bull's-eyes. So the captain turned the plane round, flew back to the harbour and touched down again so they could go and get him some.

'It was rather like being captain of the *Queen Elizabeth* that went across the Atlantic,' said Mrs Travers. 'These people were in the *flying* service.' 'Oh, Dudley Travers used to line his crew up,' Stan Prince told me – he'd worked at Imperial Airways' Durban base – 'and have them' (he clicked his heels together) 'salute him aboard the aircraft.' A 1942 memo Mrs Travers showed me from the B O A C press officer, enclosing a jocose news cutting referring to Travers as an 'air dog', hoped that the captain would not take offence at such a term. 'The term "sea dog",' I read, 'is not without honour in our long island story, and that our Service should take rank with the Merchant Navy is, I think you will agree, only right and proper.'

Mrs Travers and her new husband had flown out to Africa for their honeymoon – by flying boat, of course, stopping off along the way in Sicily and Egypt. 'It was a *gorgeous* way to travel,' she declared – Mrs Travers' way of drawing on the cigarette in her holder before answering each of my questions could not have made her pronouncements more emphatic. From the manner in which she described the Muthaiga Club she had encountered fifty years ago (her husband having been invited to join in 1936) as 'the snobbiest club in the whole world' I rather felt she would have told its ruling committee so, too. 'You sat back in, well, like armchairs,' she continued – 'it was like being on a flying yacht. You had the same crew all the way, so it was a big house-party. And Africa was just *full* of game, then. Herds of giraffe, herds of zebra . . . *hundreds*.' They'd touched down on Lake Naivasha (where they'd subsequently settled once her husband had retired from flying to become B O A C's East Africa manager): 'We'd board these great big buses and drive up the escarpment to Nairobi,' said Mrs Travers, 'and we'd have to stop to let the zebras cross the road. I didn't realize how wonderful it was until later, looking back.' Dudley Travers had died in 1970: Mrs Travers said she was much too fond of Africa ever to have considered leaving.

It was getting towards the late-afternoon rush hour, but Mrs Travers offered to run me back into town to my hotel. Soon her Fiat Uno was joining the frenetic near-gridlock of *matatus*, trucks and taxis jockeying for an exit on one of Nairobi's huge sloping roundabouts. 'Oh, somebody's clonked somebody,' she observed, steering us around a Peugeot estate and a van, with *matatus* bearing down on us. By the time we reached Tom Mboya Street in the centre, the traffic ahead was almost at a standstill, and Mrs Travers said she'd turn right and drop me there. As we swung across Tom Mboya the side-street we were headed for revealed itself as one-way, with two lanes of impatient traffic about to surge out in our direction as the lights were going green. Mrs Travers ignored my flustered suggestions of alternative setting-down places, completed a serene U-turn in the face of all this oncoming traffic and halted her little Fiat on the corner to let me out. A sanguine wave was the last I saw of her, and now the clamour of modern Nairobi was all around me.

Canopus

9

Naivasha

'I am *very* disappointed,' exclaimed the French guy. 'Have you seen the compartments? They are *small* and *dusty* – and the toilet is a hole in the floor! Already my blood pressure is up!'

'He was expecting something more like the Eurostar,' said his Kenyan friend wryly. 'I said to him, "Welcome to Kenya!"'

The Eurostar, however, doesn't pull out of Waterloo to the strains of Dolly Parton, whose silvery voice was quavering from Nairobi station's loudspeakers to a syrupy pedal-steel accompaniment. This was how Kenya Railways announced the imminent 7 o'clock departure. Black kites drifted on the air above the platform canopy; in the morning when I'd bought my ticket the empty concourse had seemed cavernous and dowdy – a station without trains is like a theatre fallen dark. But now, as night fell, it was coming alive with a bustle of passengers, parcels and packs. If the furiously smoking Frenchman was downcast, I found my mood upbeat. Dolly's piping country-and-western struck exactly the right note – somewhere between the jaunty and the wistful – to send off a night train.

I was headed, like the Empire flying boats, for the coast, and Mombasa. They'd boomed all the way up the Nile to Lake Victoria, and then from Kisumu or Naivasha continued east to the Indian Ocean, before harbour-hopping down the littoral as far as Durban. A Kenya Airways 737 could have shuttled me there in an hour, but what was the point of that? Here was Kenya's last great railway journey, the once-daily departure each way immutable as sundown, slowly descending from the central uplands to tropical sea-level, your ticket including a sleeper berth, three-course dinner and cooked breakfast. The Frenchman had a point: it was hardly Imperial Airways luxury, even my first class. The carriages were a faded brown, the leatherette seats torn, my toe went straight through the bedsheet, and from underneath the floors came a creaking and knocking as though you were at sea in an aged barque. But now that the flying boats no longer transnavigated Kenya, this seemed the most leisurely and civilized alternative. At 7 p.m. precisely, we began to roll.

Railways are, as Paul Theroux says, 'irresistible bazaars': you seek trains, you find passengers. On the way to the coast I shared my compartment with a Kenya Railways signals technician who'd been on training courses in York and Derby, and sighed, 'So many trains . . .' at the memory; on the way back it was Gitu from Nairobi, and his friend Dilip, visiting from Dubai, who turned out to have relatives running a jeweller's in Luton. They'd taken refuge on the train back after enduring 'eight hours of wild driving' on the bus to Mombasa. El Niño had wrecked the main road: 'You may not go to Mombasa,' said Gitu, shaking his head. 'You might go straight to God!' And when the steward came along the corridor banging a little xylophone *ding-doing-doing-ding* I found a dining car with a delightful sense of civic occasion – the staff uniformed in white linen, a wine waiter. All it lacked was for the train conductor to rap his ticket punch on the tablecloth for quiet and say a Latin grace. There, over onion soup, braised beef and three veg I chatted to a Nairobi University business lecturer and an American couple on vacation from teaching English in Djibouti, and as we jounced up and down and tried to spoon small squares of steam pudding and custard into our mouths rather than our ears, the American guy murmured, 'Like eating a meal on horseback . . .'

Not one of them had heard of flying boats. That isn't quite true:

the American guy thought hard and eventually said politely, 'The Spruce Goose – that's a flying boat?' which is correct, though rather like saying that a Delorean is a motor car. Everyone I met on the Mombasa train asked what I was doing in Africa, so I told them, but every time I met with blank incomprehension. The idea appeared too remote even to spark interest. No one knew what I was talking about.

It was dark by the time we'd left Nairobi, and we were nearly at the coast before the sun had risen and the land fallen away, curving around an escarpment among lush palm trees, tall cactus and red flowers. Green hills rolled to the south; suddenly there was blue water in the distance. From the station I walked in the early morning through the old town to the ancient Fort Jesus high above the shore, and stood at the ramparts to look out on the aquamarine Indian Ocean, white breakers curling on the reefs. After the grey gritty hubbub of Nairobi and the endless pitching and jerking and wallowing of the train across the sooty plain – I'd hardly slept – it was the most beautiful sight so far in Africa, and also the first flying-boat landscape, for there was the mouth of Kilindini Creek to the south, above which the C-Class would have circled in on the approach from Dar-es-Salaam.

'F/boat wd have been *just right,*' I'd already written in my notebook during the train journey: 'train too slow and jet plane too fast.' We'd travelled at night! Who knew how many giraffe, elephant or eland had stopped to turn their heads to the passing train? We'd taken twelve hours to miss all the scenery! Imagine, on the other hand, travelling in daylight hours only, retaining all the congenial civility of that dining car, flying low enough to watch all the land you were traversing float past in relaxing slow-motion, and even Kisumu (a further twelve-hour train ride west of Nairobi) to Mombasa a morning's ride – if we check the 1939 Empire Air Mail timetable – of just three hours . . .

But imagine was all I could do, for already, even at this first flying-boat port of call, a queer feeling of dislocation was setting in. In a café I got chatting to a young Englishman, John from Bristol, just a few days into a year's round-the-world travel, and together we spent the afternoon wandering along Mombasa's pretty coast road, past empty golf links, a giant baobab forest, bright yellow and pink flamboyant bushes, and plenty of families and courting couples out for a Sunday constitutional. John had done an apprenticeship as an aero engine fitter with Rolls-Royce in Bristol, but he had no idea what a flying boat was either. Like me, he was headed for Victoria Falls – but to do a bungee jump. For him it was the future – all that solitary travel ahead – that bore in on him and provoked a solemn phlegmatism, surely only intensified by Nairobi having been his first place of landfall. As we rode back and forth across Kilindini Creek on the Likoni ferry in the hot sunshine it was the present, the teeming present – these crowds streaming down the hill to board as though down Wembley Way – that suddenly seemed the only reality to me here in Africa. I'd found nothing in Mombasa of what I was looking for – not that I'd quite got clear in my mind what I sought. Even a single archive postcard in a shop, perhaps, just one photograph at the fort alongside those of custom houses and port tramways, or a port area not entirely hoarded away inside impregnable compounds – or merely a tiny spark of recognition from a mere human being. But though Mombasa still had a fort that had survived from the sixteenth century, and the same railway line ridden by travellers a century earlier, I couldn't find anything to take me back sixty years to the era of Imperial Airways' classic flying boats.

It was an immediate lesson for the rest of my travels in Africa, and indeed for any quest to find the lost village of 'Corsairville'. Sometimes people take their history with them: it is not vested in wherever they are visiting. It is in their lives that a place becomes fleetingly talismanic, not in its bricks and mortar. Places are the punctuation in the sentence, not the main verb.

Sometimes, indeed – what appeared to have happened at 'Corsairville' – the flying boat itself was the landmark, memorializing a small piece of nowhere. In 1945, Peter Hicks was working for the Kenya and Uganda Railways and Harbours department, the engineer responsible for all the jetties serving Uganda's trade along the Nile between Lake Albert and the Sudan border. The north, its tribes on either side of the river innocently naked, the banks noted 'sunbath stations' for innumerable crocodiles, was then the most backward, least developed part of Uganda, 'and for that reason,' one British colonial administrator told me, 'one of the most attractive.' One day, Mr Hicks wrote to me from West Beach, South Australia, while supervising the construction of a jetty at the tiny trading post of Laropi – little more than a few godowns and *dukas* – 'I was suddenly surprised to see a large BOAC flying boat coming down low from the north, and landing gracefully, throwing greenish spray from its bow wave on the river.' Not only Mr Hicks but also his Asian artisans and African labourers downed tools to watch a capacious launch set out towards the flying boat and convey its well-dressed passengers to the bank. (On one occasion the wife of the British District Commissioner at this out-of-the-way spot is said to have joined the re-embarking passengers and eloped with the pilot.) After a short interval for refuelling, the flying boat restarted its engines and:

in a majestic accelerating sweep along the river it rose from the water and thundered away southward, slowly gaining altitude until it was a speck in the distance.

I am writing to you [explained Mr Hicks] because it is still a clear and vivid memory of an event over 50 years ago. It left me at the time with a sense of the isolation of this place 'invaded' by what was then the latest technological advance in travel communication. I suppose these days anything of the sort would be commonplace to the locals – not that modern-day jet aircraft would require, or condescend, to stop down there. It was a sight such as I had never before seen or have since then.

'Or condescend . . .': that sense that a flying boat is only ever just visiting: a bird of passage. The point, indeed – what I had to learn from my fruitless wanderings around Mombasa – was that there would be no trace. Some history is sedimentary, slowly accretive – an ancient fort built and rebuilt upon the dust of its own destruction and decay – and sometimes epiphany makes history.

Nevertheless, as I continued stopping off along the old Empire route, I started to wonder if I'd gone slightly mad. Wherever I asked, or whenever the subject of flying boats came up, I drew an utter blank, and after a while – the solipsism of the solitary traveller – I began to feel like Pinter's caretaker muttering about how he must get to Sidcup. It was to remain the predominant response throughout my travels in Africa: 'When you say "flying boat" I haven't a clue what you're talking about,' declared a friendly woman called Julie several weeks later in Malawi – and she was a travel agent booking me some air tickets. I might as well have been searching for the Yeti or the land of the Jumblies. 'Anyway,' expostulated Uncle Holly in H. Rider Haggard's lurid romance *She*, which I'd bought for an undemanding read, 'I believe that the whole thing is the most unmitigated rubbish.' So much for the esoteric revelations codified in the Sherd of Amenartas bequeathed to his nephew Leo:

I know that there are curious things and forces in nature which we rarely meet with, and, when we do meet them, cannot understand. But until I see it with my own eyes, which I am not likely to, I never will believe . . . that there is or was a white sorceress living in the heart of an African swamp. It is bosh, my boy, all bosh!

I couldn't get to Laropi myself – the slumbrous backwater of northern Uganda that the flying boat had condescended to visit in 1945 was now the power base of a capriciously violent guerrilla organization, the Lord's Resistance Army – but I had doubled back west across Kenya to visit the capital of Uganda.

Apart from a handful of backpackers in my small resthouse by the market, there seemed to be no tourists at all in Kampala – I saw perhaps half a dozen white faces the whole time I was there, and they were mostly businessmen punching calculators over a beer in the Nile Grill restaurant where I ate an evening curry. There was no curiosity towards the white visitor: the occasional bantering 'Hey, *mzungu!*' from a bunch of youths, but none of the boisterous harassment of Nairobi. After the rackety entropy of Kenya, Kampala exuded the assiduity and businesslike assertiveness of a community tangibly and capably putting itself back on its feet: new white Toyota cars, Texaco gas stations, freshly black-tarmacked roads, and the smartest-dressed citizens anywhere, immaculate in pressed blouses, shirts and bright skirts: a large town bidding to become a metropolis. But the demeanour of its people was strangely chastened, a hammered, haunted reserve, an exceeding politeness as though welcoming you to a hushed church.

I walked out of town one sweltering afternoon, past the tatty marabou storks hunched in the park like abandoned umbrellas, through the villages of Bugolobi, Kitantale and Luzira to Port Bell. Along the way I found – at last, some kind of sign to prove I wasn't imagining the entire subject of my search – Sunderland Avenue and Solent Road. They were mere dirt tracks leading up to industrial units and a Colgate toothpaste factory. After several miles, at the road end I came upon a sleepy, lazy scene: railway boxcars being clanked slowly to and fro, a poor shanty-settlement by the roadside, clothes spread on the grass to dry, and a single cargo-ship in dock beyond the port gates. The odd white cattle egret flapped up out of the swamp at the lakeshore; beyond, Lake Victoria was hardly visible, a sluggish haze, soupy and inert. At the British Airways archive in west London they'd had the large brass bell that had been rung to signal the imminent departure of each flying boat from here. This was where *Corsair* had taken off that morning in March 1939, northbound for a next stop at Juba she would never reach. Port Bell.

There was a bar a hundred yards before the port gates, the New England Port View Inn. 'You are most welcome, sir,' said the teenage waiter when I ordered a Coke, his neat white shirt and black trousers the uniform of a smart hotel – that characteristically ecclesiastical courtesy at the same time oddly hesitant. African dance music – trebly, ringing guitars – skittered out of a radio inside.

As I sat on the patio with my cold Coke it came to me suddenly and with a pang of loneliness: this exploration I was embarked on, everything a flying-boat quest was leading me to look for, was all about Britain, British things, only about Britishness. Such an obvious realization, but I'd had to come to Uganda in Central Africa to have it. Kenya was still Anglophile to the extent that there were steam-train museums for British railway enthusiasts, little oases like the Muthaiga Club more English than Sunningdale, where you found an elderly lady who came from the Isle of Wight and showed you photos of her late husband flying planes at Croydon, and a sunshine coast of western package-hotels. There was nothing British about Uganda any longer: nothing I could presume, ethnocentrically, to be there for me.

I had never met such delicate courtesy as I was accorded by everyone I met in Uganda: the bespectacled proprietor of the Mukwana Guest-house, Joseph the student who walked with me down to the tranquil, deserted botanical gardens at Entebbe to ask me to sponsor his boy-scout troop to go on a 'Camporee', the moped rider who for 500 shillings gave me a ride back up the hill for the *matatu* back into Kampala – somehow it seemed both an unostentatious hospitality towards the uncommon guest and a democratic generosity towards allcomers. It made me see my own subject in another different light. Imperial Airways' flying boats held a halcyon place in British affection as a lost world of grace and civility and fine sensibility, these qualities presumed as further aspects of a uniquely British design feat, or in some way our property, like the game of cricket. Such nostalgia could so easily become self-congratulation – as though we had invented grace and civility to export across the world along with the airmail. Uganda taught me that, at the very least, the British didn't have a monopoly on grace and civility.

It was the first thing I'd noticed as the Akamba coach had climbed up the Great Rift Valley on the way to Kampala, and it was just as obvious grinding back to Kisumu and Naivasha. Mrs Travers had spoken of the airline bus that met their flying boat having to halt before herds of zebra in the road, the bush teeming with game wherever you looked. But I saw almost nothing. Apart from a couple of bemused zebra at the roadside near Eldoret, and a few egrets in the fields, I travelled across Kenyan and Ugandan landscapes empty of wildlife. The reason seemed just as obvious. Every square inch of earth was under cultivation. Patches of maize, small fields of vegetables, a few oxen, goats and chickens, parcelled around clutches of huts – not a scrap of wild land left, and the wildlife had had to retreat. At Kisumu, a decrepit place with an unappealing air of lethargy and entropy, where two grey hangars at the port were the only memorial to the flying boats, I walked out of town until I reached Hippo Point on Lake Victoria – as at Port Bell this vast inland sea was oddly inaccessible. It was billed in my guidebook as a quiet promontory from which good views of the lake's hippopotami could be had at dusk – but the framework of a large pavilion had already been erected there so that some kind of snack bar could soon destroy the spot's tranquillity. I had not expected wilderness to be so elusive in Africa, nor the press of people to be so ubiquitous.

There was a bigger shock when I got to Naivasha. The lake was some miles south of the town, which meant catching a *matatu* along the lake road from the main square. Naivasha itself was not an alluring place: dusty, poor and rather belligerent, with an evident drug problem, and the *matatu* stand was bedlam – the endless, crazed blaring of claxons, and the first really physical atmosphere I'd encountered since I'd been in Africa. There were quite enough passengers to go round if each *matatu* had simply waited its turn and driven off when it was full, but here the trade was in the control of young, stoned touts who kept your minivan waiting while they competed to fill each one to bursting point. I seemed to have picked the van with the craziest tout of all, slapping about in pulverized flip-flops, eyes rolling in his head, teeth blackened, who got into a desperate fight with another over the carriage of a PA speaker. It was an hour before, crunched right down on its springs with a solid entwined load of doubled-up old women and yowling infants, our Toyota juddered away.

We hadn't gone more than a mile or so when I was amazed and mortified to see a red double-deck Routemaster bus pass us, with just a handful of passengers aboard. How come I'd managed to catch something that made the Central Line look deserted, when there were London buses apparently going to Lake Naivasha? But on these old Routemasters' destination blinds it read HOMEGROWN, and a bit further down the lake road we passed the entrance to the Homegrown Flower Nurseries. They were works buses. The gates became a procession: Sher Agencies, Noordam Growers, Sulmac Growers – part of Brooke Bond. Beyond them I could spy acres of glinting glasshouses. The wait for the *matatu* to leave had taken us into late afternoon, and huge queues were waiting at one compound for their works transport; suddenly ahead of us, streaming down the road like fleeing refugees, was an endless mass of people. Alternating with the works gates were barrack-like estates of huts and shanty towns. Naivasha was no longer the empty, limpid landscape Joan Travers had arrived in with her new husband in 1949. It had been industrialized. That resonant line in Alan Moorehead's memoir of his flying-boat journey, of 'seeing Africa as Livingstone saw it': not here – I wasn't even seeing it as Moorehead saw it.

I knew what all this was: I just hadn't been prepared for the extent. This was where a large percentage of the western world's increasing predilection for giving one another flowers was satisfied. Fresh flowers – cut and air-freighted to be in Interflora bouquets in Europe the next day – had become a major industry in Kenya in recent years, and the British and Dutch combines that had set up here and annexed the northern lakeshore for its ready water had attracted a big labour migration. Cut flowers were the speedy air-traffic round here nowadays.

I stayed on the shore of Lake Naivasha at Fisherman's Camp, a tranquil clearing under the trees – but even here the blare of *matatu* horns rushed by at night along the road above, and cheers and chants came up from a football tournament next door beside another shanty town. It was a disappointment, certainly, that, however far I went, it seemed, the flying boats' old Africa route couldn't take me to the kind of isolated backwaters I'd been anticipating: the modern, busy world had got there first. I'd brought my Lake District way of seeing with me, and, here at least, it wasn't working in Africa. But that night, I realized, the melancholy that had come over me suggested something, too, about the intense nostalgia for the African flying boats I'd encountered in Britain. It was the dream of an innocent Africa: unspoilt and empty, and left to the animals. The vast herd of elephants, a landmark from the air at Bor in the Sudan; a continent that would suddenly yield a white rhino for the flying boat to swoop even lower and follow: gone now. It seemed a lot longer than fifty years ago. Just as I'd found no trace of the flying boats at Mombasa or Port Bell, so you remembered a strange extinct beast like a Short Empire or a Solent and it symbolized how completely the Africa you knew had gone, too.

The next morning I crossed the road and walked up the hill, until I came out on a terrace underneath some enormous bulbous *euphorbia candelabra* trees. A little white dog was snoozing on the lawn. From open French doors at the end of the house came the plonking of a manual typewriter. A rubicund man with white hair looked up over his half-glasses.

'Would you be Mervyn Carnelley?'

Mervyn had replied to one of my appeals for memories. He was the person who'd founded Fisherman's Camp, which had become the most popular place to stay at Naivasha for campers, hostellers and overland trucks. Sixty years earlier, however, in 1938, Imperial Airways had been offering special fares to enable children at boarding school in England to catch the flying boat back to Africa rather than the Union Castle steamer. Still in his teens, he'd caught the Empire boat *Cassiopeia* from Southampton to come home from Radley for the summer holiday. It was only mid-morning, but soon I was among a gathering of in-laws and friends on the terrace and cold beers were being opened. Mervyn had rooted around in his study and come out with a pile of documents: a long typed article entitled 'A Flight to the Equator' which he'd written back in England about his flying-boat journey and sent to his parents, a photographic album, and a full-colour fold-out Imperial Airways brochure containing exploded cut-aways of an Empire boat, which he'd preserved in pristine condition these sixty years.

'That was *civilized* travel,' he pronounced, 'not cattle trucks – never heard of *customs* in those days!' It had been the first time he'd ever flown. *Cassiopeia* had roared past *Maia* and *Mercury*, the piggy-back 'composite' that Wilcockson and Bennett had flown, as she'd taxied up Southampton Water – Mervyn was still proud of the memory. 'Spray all over the bloody place' as they took off. He remembered discovering, from his elevated vantage-point, that the flat roofs of Cairo were home to all the household menagerie, and watching as 'every living thing – sheep, goats and chickens – rushed into their respective hutches when the plane roared by overhead.' They'd descended to see a herd of elephants roaming through the trees just before they went over the Murchison Falls, and then the pilot had performed 'not quite loop-the-loop, but a sort of courtesy bump' as they went over the Equator. Mervyn unfolded the Imperial Airways brochure and found a black-and-white photograph of two sunny-humoured passengers in an Empire boat's dining cabin: 'Look – flowers!' There was even a vase of flowers on the table between them. 'And even when we circled the elephants the flowers didn't fall over – probably glued to the table!'

From their terrace we looked out on a vast view over Lake Naivasha, hazy in the morning sun. There was Mervyn's wife, Fay (who, like him, had grown up at Naivasha), their friend Chris and his wife and young daughter, another English couple who'd been staying for the weekend, and Akbar Hussein, a neighbour, who ran a camera store in Nairobi, and had done the sepia-effect enlargements of Mervyn's photos of *Cassiopeia* that were mounted in his album. 'It makes them look even more antique than they are,' said Mervyn. He'd just finished painting a truly superb illustrated map of Lake Naivasha (earlier maps of his, equally fastidious, were framed on the walls of the *banda* he and Fay kindly put me up in during my stay), and now the discussion turned to how to publish and market it.

'You should put a flying boat on it!' declared Akbar. 'Things to do with *nostalgia* like that!'

Mervyn regarded his crowded artwork. 'I think the fish eagle might have to come out,' he pondered.

Conversation was languid and slightly lofty: there was a kind of confidence in leisure, and in not having to take anything too seriously, as any more than a diversion. I had the sense of this gathering being more than literally above things. Mervyn turned to me and in his droll way murmured, 'Here you have a perfect picture of colonialism.'

There was a similar picture at the Lake Naivasha Country Club – the luxury hotel where the flying-boat passengers had put up overnight after the war. But despite the uniformly well-groomed white clientele taking tea on the immaculate lawn in the late afternoon sun, every photograph framed inside commemorated the visit of an African politician: when Robert Mugabe stayed here; when President Yoweri Museveni of Uganda hosted a conference . . . This had become the hotel's history. Not a single memento of the flying-boat days: 'Not any more,' said the guy behind the bar: 'there used to be some photos, but I don't know where they went.' I felt rather shameful even asking. To trade on the past in that way would have been to trade on a colonial feel. You could still check in here and experience the same luxury as you would have just climbing out of an Empire boat or a Solent, but that era was pre-year-zero. It was an African hotel now.

I couldn't connect the two worlds: in order to get from Fisherman's Camp to the hotel I'd had to catch *matatus* – an unbelievably crammed Peugeot personnel carrier there in which I crouched, fixed in the wide unswerving stare of small children, with a tousled chicken on my lap, and a Toyota back booming with UB40's *Labour of Love*, so full when it pulled up I had to ride the first few stops hanging on the outside. I walked down the drive of the Country Club pulling on a sweatshirt against a nip in the air as dusk fell; I clambered out through the rear window of the sweltering *matatu* half an hour later wringing wet and exhausted. Back at Fisherman's Camp that evening the British Open golf was on the television, live by satellite, the comfortable chestnut burr of Peter Alliss.

19. An Empire boat moored on Lake Victoria at Port Bell in Uganda, *Corsair*'s last stop on 14 March 1939 before her unscheduled arrival in the Belgian Congo

20. *Corsair* moored at Kisumu, Kenya – the last night-stop before her forced landing at Faradje

21. 'Thee put it in there: thee can pick it up again': Captain 'John' Alcock, the pilot of *Corsair,* on both her arrival on the Dungu and the first attempt to fly her out

22. The destination that *Corsair* never reached: the 'terminal building' for the Empire boats at Juba in the Sudan, 1939. Ian Henderson, who flew out from England on *Corsair* in 1938 to take up his position with the Public Works Department, is on the left

23. A young Hugh Gordon in Burma in 1936, having delivered a seaplane for Shorts to the Irrawaddy Flotilla Company

24. 'Why so desolate a spot should have been dignified with a name . . .': where *Corsair* had ended up in the north-eastern corner of the Belgian Congo

25. A native village near Faradje

26. Stuck in the mud: the sight that greeted the Shorts engineers when they arrived at Faradje to salvage *Corsair*

27. 'The hardest thing was digging it out of the mud . . .'

28. A team of native workers
carrying a log of ironwood
to construct a slipway for
beaching *Corsair*

29. Peter Newnham normalizing
rivets to repair the gash in
Corsair's hull

30. A hundred Africans are needed to haul the repaired flying boat back into the river

31. The second accident: *Corsair* marooned on the far bank of the Dungu after Alcock hits another rock on his ill-fated rescue attempt

32. 'Alcock Rock'

33. The second salvage team starts all over again: 'And suddenly . . . we could see it beginning to come up!'

34. Floating *Corsair*'s engines up the river for repair at Lacovitch's workshops

35. Running up the engines

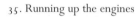

36. 'Ready to go'

37. Captain Jack Kelly-Rogers

38. Building the dam

39. Building the dam

40. The Imperial Airways salvage team at their 'mess': left to right, Radio Operator Wytcherley, the team's *askari* (standing), wearing a suit made from *Corsair*'s seat upholstery, Roy Sisson, Love, Ernie Arroll (standing), Alf Cowling

41. 'The plane that built a village': *Corsair* three years after her successful salvage from the Congo, at Gwalior in India in 1943

Somehow if you tried to follow the trail of the African flying boats by the human heritage, you either ended up with nothing, drawing a blank, or with uneasily bland images of luxury and exclusivity. But, as at Mombasa, if you got as close as possible to their own haunts – tracked their habitat as though they were rare creatures right to the water's edge – Africa revealed its beauty. For many years Mervyn Carnelley had led birding safaris in the area (his minibus still sat under a car port in his garden, all local approaches to acquire it for a *matatu* sternly rejected on the entirely reasonable grounds that it would be a wreck in months), and from my first morning at Fisherman's Camp I saw why. I had never come across anywhere that teemed with bird life like Lake Naivasha. Usually you had to go and look for birds. Here they were everywhere around you. Walking down from Mervyn's *banda* in the morning, the corrugated greenhouses below like upturned egg-boxes, I could watch flocks of slow-wheeling pelicans, floating on the air like aircraft in formation, white wings suddenly snow-white as they caught the sun, white as flying boats. I sat for a whole afternoon under the trees fringing the lakeshore, the glittering water beyond, and just let everything fly into view: Hadada ibises, pied kingfishers, shrikes, lovebirds, spoonbills, shrieking fish eagles, weavers, wood-peckers, dazzling starlings, darters and, above all, the tiny blink of the captivating malachite kingfisher with its glowing crimson beak. I could never predict when I'd see it next, and then it would flash across my vision again, so fast that only afterwards did my brain catch up and register its royal- and electric-blue plumage. It was like the sun striking glass, an ember pulsing in a fire: a release of pure energy. 'What a thrill to see again . . . Naivasha Lake, with its countless waterfowl and grunting hippo,' Mervyn had written to his parents sixty years earlier. The flying boats had touched down amidst that kind of wildness then, and you could still find it now.

Later that afternoon, my last at Lake Naivasha, Mervyn drove

me and his scooty little Jack Russell down to the post office on the
new South Lake Road where he could collect his mail. Between the
wars his father, who'd eventually retired as the chief magistrate in
Nairobi, had bought 6,000 acres around Lake Naivasha for just
£700; Mervyn had ranched cattle on it. Over the years, however,
the family had sold off most of the land, until now Fisherman's
Camp was just 50 acres. The expansion of all the flower-growers
during the previous decade, and the construction of this new road
five years ago ('Yugoslavs put it in,' Mervyn told me), had brought
a ribbon development of shops within a few minutes of his house.
As we were driving down the hill in his little Peugeot I asked him
if he minded all this encroachment.

'Good lord, no. It used to take an hour from Nairobi to Naivasha,
and then an hour from Naivasha to here. It was just a dirt track, grass
down the middle. Have you been in one of these shops?' he inquired
as we pulled up outside a little general store. 'Puts Harrods to shame.'

Here they'd just acquired a new Sharp photocopier, which meant
Mervyn was able to have the account of his trip on *Cassiopeia* and
his Imperial Airways brochure photocopied for me. The store was
lined with a vast array of provisions, from bottles of Ribena to toilet
rolls, and as the proprietor set about copying the beautiful thirties
brochure, and the yellowed original of 'A Flight to the Equator',
Mervyn commentated enthusiastically in Swahili to him on the
images of the Empire boat: the passenger compartments, the mail
bags, the flower vase on the table – how he'd flown on one of these
when he was just eighteen, and how they used to land on the lake
here. The man listened politely. Mervyn was pointing out the
propellers to him. Variable pitch airscrews! (He appeared to have
found the Swahili translation.) The shopkeeper went back to the
copier to try and fit the cut-away picture of *Canopus* on two sheets
of A4. Mervyn turned to me and said, 'That's not bad for 1938,
is it?'

10

Wartime

When *Cassiopeia* had touched down at Bríndisi, Mervyn remembered, there'd been 'a lot of evidence of Italian aggression – military flying boats and things'. Her sister craft *Corsair* had paid her unscheduled visit to the Belgian Congo the following spring, and she was still there in autumn 1939 when war finally broke out in Europe. The Empire Air Mail Scheme was soon abandoned – even though the C-Class boats had only started carrying all-up mail through to Australia a year earlier. The postal revolution for which Britain had turned its long-haul air services entirely over to flying boats was remarkably short-lived – and airmail has been surcharged ever since. Southampton, vulnerable to German bombing raids, was abandoned by Imperial Airways for a base at Poole, where the flying boats left from the large harbour, and the airline established its terminal in the premises of the Poole Pottery.

But the Empire boats – still almost new planes – flew on. Ironically, a fleet of aircraft hallowed for a world of leisure and luxury spent more than half their operational life at war. Two aircraft, *Cabot* and *Caribou*, were taken over by the RAF, first for radar patrols of the sea north of Scotland, and then were both destroyed flying special missions into Norway. From 1939, too, once war seemed only a question of when, not if, people's memories of the African flying boats are of a different order. Before the war, Ian Henderson and Mervyn Carnelley are spectators, celebrating with innocent wonder an absorbing new phenomenon. From 1939, passengers tell you about their lives. Often the flying boat becomes the messenger of, or the transport towards, a personal world never to be the same again.

For women, travelling alone to visit partners posted overseas, the flying boat marks an especially final step into the unknown. 'For Heaven's sake don't marry the man if you don't want to,' were Veronica Berry's sister's parting words on the platform as she prepared to board the train to Southampton. The man, William Berry, was working for the Colonial Medical Service in the then Nyasaland: now he'd sent the money to cover the £100 cost of a return sea-passage to Africa. When he'd cabled one day to suggest flying, Veronica had rung Imperial Airways straight away and blown £120 for a single ticket on the flying boat. The Empire boat was not cheap! 'Oh, then it isn't so much more?' her father had said when confronted with the change of plan. Mrs Berry was living in Brentwood when I went to see her, a quietly spoken, scholarly woman, who remembered the conversation with guilt and wonder at her youthful recklessness: she hadn't dared to admit that she had no return ticket. She was twenty-four, William was thirty; although they'd been corresponding for three years, they still hardly knew each other. It was April 1939.

The invasion of Albania, placing Italy on a war footing a couple of weeks before she was due to depart, added further suspense to the flight, but on the eighteenth she set off, as she remembered later, 'for a stay of unknown length in an unknown country to meet an almost unknown man!' At Southampton the Empire boat *Corinna* 'was swaying in a depressing manner by the quay'. Once aboard, she found a cabin crew – all men – amazed that a young woman should be flying half-way across the world all by herself.

There were just two of them for Africa: her and a roly-poly man called Richard S. Jukes, 'like two peas in a pod', and, after an uneventful Channel crossing, *Corinna* soon tested their powers of mutual support:

After that we ran into clouds [Veronica wrote home from Rome]. I don't know whether you realize the significance of that remark. It means that *Corinna* became possessed of a devil – she bounced, she lurched, she twisted her tail, she caught an upward current and your inside was pressed to the chair, she fell into a precipice and your chest jumped into your throat and remained there. Jukes and I stopped talking, my knitting sagged in my nerveless hands and presently Jukes left his seat in a hasty and decided manner . . . When we eventually skimmed down to Marseilles I wished I hadn't come.

At Marseille Mr Jukes, 'hideously bright', said they would probably get used to it; 'Nelson didn't,' snapped Veronica, and they returned to *Corinna*, 'who looked smug and smelt of petrol'.

Over Corsica the captain climbed to 15,000 feet and Mr Jukes looked after the young woman 'like a father', piling rugs and coat on her and putting her feet in a muff – 'It was desperately cold up there!' Mrs Berry exclaimed. The bumpy ride continued all the way through Africa whenever the flying boat dropped below 10,000 feet, and without Richard S. Jukes to giggle with, Veronica wrote back from Africa, she'd have been quite miserable. 'It's a tremendous strain going on and on,' ran her final letter, 'being relentlessly woken any time from 3.00 to 4.15 a.m. and flying and flying and flying and flying.'

But there was no animus towards *Corinna*, then or now. Far from it: the crossing-the-line certificate Mrs Berry had received when the flying boat had hopped the Equator was still framed on the wall, and those letters back to England had spoken of *Corinna* like a capricious friend. 'It seemed like home,' said Mrs Berry. 'We became very fond of *Corinna*.' *Flying and flying and flying* . . . Once William had met her in Blantyre off the landplane from Beira all thought of a prudent three-month courtship went by the board. Within two days they were engaged; three weeks later they were married. They'd remained in Africa for the rest of her husband's working life. She was widowed forty-four years later.

Almost a year after Mrs Berry's voyage, in May 1940, Patricia Arber's husband was given 'local leave' from the Sudan, and wrote suggesting she join him in Alexandria. 'Would I!' she wrote to me from Oxfordshire. (She also told me she'd once been up on a pleasure flight at an early airshow with Sir Alan Cobham.) 'So I parked our new baby with a nanny and my mother, and set off from Poole Harbour. This was an agonizing parting, but was to be only for a few weeks.' *Canopus* flew her across Europe, and while they were crossing the Mediterranean a couple of days later from Athens to Crete, the captain confirmed over the public address that Germany had suddenly over-run Holland and was half-way through Belgium.

We all then realized that we were completely cut off from England for the duration – a traumatic situation. My husband had, of course, never seen his daughter, and I didn't see her again till I returned in 1944 on the first convoy through the Med.

When Italy entered the war in June 1940, and France fell at the end of the month, the Empire route from England across mainland Europe and the Mediterranean was cut altogether. But keeping lines of communication open was more important than ever – no longer to corner the airmail market: rather to fly diplomatic mail, civil servants and military staff around. The Empire boats were regrouped at Durban, and soon the famous 'Horseshoe Route' had been inaugurated – flying from South Africa the length of the continent up to Cairo, and then all the way round to Australia.

Getting from Britain to Africa, meanwhile – let alone on to the subcontinent or the Antipodes – was much more of an expedition. The airline had converted half a dozen military Sunderland flying boats – taken the gun turrets out, and put in canvas paratroop-type seats. 'They were bare-as-bones,' one of their flight engineers, Ralph

Lawes, remembered for me. 'They rattled, they were draughty, the heating was very primitive so you either baked or froze.' A Sunderland like this would rumble off from Poole Harbour westwards to Foynes on the west coast of Ireland. There it'd wait until dark, before taking off again and setting course for 10° south, 'and after flapping along for six, seven hours you'd see the lights of Lisbon. One of us would go back into the cabin and dish out the lunch-boxes,' said Mr Lawes, 'because that's all you got – a stale sandwich and an apple – and if it was cold you'd give them a blanket.' Lie low all the next day in Lisbon, and then at nightfall again fly on, down the west coast of Africa to Bathurst in the Gambia, Freetown in Sierra Leone, to end up at Lagos in Nigeria. There you'd pick up an Empire boat that flew across the French and Belgian Congos – Libreville, Leopoldville, Coquilhatville and Stanleyville – to connect you with the Horseshoe Route at Khartoum. Tank spares used to be flown east by this route; many of the ferry pilots delivering RAF fighter planes across Africa for the Middle East campaign then used to catch this Empire boat on its way back. When the Empire boat's pilot turned out to be one of Imperial Airways' pre-war '*crème de la crème*', as Mr Lawes put it, the crew of the utilitarian Sunderland would watch him walk out on the jetty with his briefcase, clad in white kid-gloves. 'We used to call it their "bullshit bag",' said Mr Lawes. 'We used to think they were a bit toffee-nosed.' At Lisbon in neutral Portugal, and again when the Empire boats were touching down at Lourenço Marques and Mozambique Island in Portuguese East Africa, British military personnel had to do some hurried changing into civvies.

There was also a more luxurious passage available to Africa than the utilitarian Sunderlands. Short of large flying boats in the early years of the war, in 1941 BOAC had purchased from Pan-Am three of its fleet of huge Boeing 'Clippers', to enable it to restart a transatlantic flying-boat service. (The acquisition wasn't covered by the Lend-Lease agreement that enabled the US to supply munitions on a 'buy now – pay later' basis: the British government had to pay cash, and it seems that Pan-Am's canny president, Juan Trippe, saw it coming. A quarter of a million pounds was a prodigious price to extract – especially since Pan-Am had already foreseen the end of the flying boat and was not unhappy to be offloading several Clippers anyway.) BOAC christened its new craft *Berwick*, *Bristol* and *Bangor*, and set the three fabulous seaplanes to work flying from Poole down the west coast of Africa as far as Lagos, before setting off westwards across the Atlantic for Belem in Brazil and up to Baltimore.

Inside, the Boeings were perhaps even more opulent than the Empire boats – the fuselage lined with a beige damask imprinted with the Pan-Am logo. There were bunks in the rear cabin for overnight sleep, and even a sumptuous honeymoon suite that was later to be used by Churchill on his transatlantic air crossings to meet with Roosevelt.

During the war Dorothy Babb was a young woman working for the Ministry of Economic Warfare – a branch of the Special Operations Executive – in Nigeria. Due some home leave, she and her friend Margaret were scheduled to go by sea – 'but round about Accra it was absolutely *black* with boats that had gone down'. Fortunately they happened to know John Brancker, the son of the government's former Director of Civil Aviation, Sir Sefton Brancker, and himself a senior BOAC manager. 'I think I can get you a sort of hitchhike by plane . . .' they were told. And so Dorothy and Margaret found themselves departing from Lagos in the luxurious Churchill suite aboard the Boeing flying boat *Berwick*.

Sharing a drink with John Brancker before departure, Mrs Babb remembered, one of their party asked for a whisky. 'No, I don't want that kind,' the barman was told when he brought the standard issue, 'I want Haig.'

'Oh,' observed a sardonic John Brancker, 'you don't want *landplane* whisky.'

During the stop-over in Lisbon Dorothy and Margaret bought

some stockings and, under way again in the middle of the night, they washed them through in the honeymoon suite's hand-basins and hung them up to dry. *Berwick*'s captain, Tony Lorraine, was an urbane man with a prototypical upper-class stutter and a house in Knightsbridge: Mrs Babb was delighted to recall his coming aft to behold the Prime Minister's suite festooned with cheap nylons, and exclaiming, 'What on earth are you girls doing, using my aeroplane as a laundry?'

A fire aboard another transatlantic Boeing flight threatening to fill the rear sleeper cabin with smoke, Victor Pitcher, the navigator, was sent aft to fetch an extinguisher. One of the passengers turned out to be the young Yehudi Menuhin, lying on his bunk practising violin frets on a finger-board. So rapt was he in his practice that the navigator's fire warning fell on deaf ears. So then – 'I don't know what came over me,' Victor told me – 'I went up to Yehudi Menuhin and said, "*Nero fiddled while Rome burned!*"'

Since the spring of 1940, however, the diminishing C-Class fleet had at least been swelled by one prodigal flying boat. A postcard sent from Maritsburg in South Africa in 1942, from Tessa to her uncle,

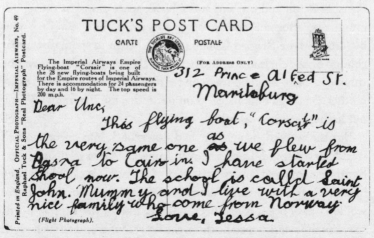

shows on the reverse a photograph of the flying boat taking off from what looks like the Medway. Like Mervyn Carnelley, Tessa Smith had taken the flying boat to school: her father was working for an oil company in Iran, and as the war intensified thought it better for her to go to South Africa for her education. She was nine years old. The memory Mrs Smith retained of the flying-boat journey nearly sixty years later when I went to visit her in Colchester has the isolated brilliances and shadows of a still-young child's: oranges heaped by the roadside in Tiberias, a colourful canopy of bougainvillaea over the terrace at the meal stop in Lourenço Marques, huge herds of wildebeest near Kisumu and, from the before-dawn start at Khartoum, darkness in the hotel. 'It's an odd memory I have of Khartoum – just darkness.'

This was *Corsair*. At the British Airways archive, Fred Huntley had pulled out a large map-drawer to reveal the red-lined charts on which the Empire flying boats' movements had been mapped in those days, place against date. In March 1939 the red-ink line representing *Corsair* had come to a sudden halt: Mr Huntley leafed on through the charts, running his finger down the other Empire boats' lines, on and on, and still a blank space amongst them. But eventually, after the epic struggle to escape from almost a year becalmed in the Belgian Congo, red ink began to spool down that column on the chart again, and here was *Corsair* now (despite engine trouble in Cairo that laid them up for three days and enabled Tessa's mother to take her on a local tram out to see the Pyramids), seeing out her war service unscathed.

But the rescued flying boat had flown back into an unadorned world far removed from pre-war Imperial Airways luxury. Mrs Smith remembered 'a very basic sort of aircraft – it can't have been bare fuselage, but I can't remember anything pleasurable.' There wouldn't have been: it had been refitted, like all the Empire boats, to wartime austerity specification, the flower vases and all such plush fittings removed to fit as many seats in as possible. The present of a board-game called *Aircraft* 'which must have been thought appropriate', pondered Mrs Smith, was no distraction from a week of incessant noise and unpleasant turbulence that left the young girl 'practically comatose' from airsickness by the time they touched down in Durban. At least one person, had she known of her privilege, would not have been hugely grateful for Imperial Airways' engineers' efforts to salvage her flying boat from the Congo.

The world *Corsair* re-entered after her long absence had changed around her in another large respect. This was no longer an Imperial Airways flying boat. By April 1940 Imperial Airways was no more. In its place was the British Overseas Airways Corporation: BOAC. The transformation was the single, in retrospect somewhat gratuit-ous, achievement of Imperial Airways' last chairman.

The appointment of Sir John Reith, the imperious founder and first Director-General of the BBC, had in itself been a strange and perverse one. He had absolutely no experience of civil aviation, and he didn't want the job – felt it, after the monument he had built to himself at Broadcasting House, a considerable underestimation of his calibre. In his own eyes he was War Cabinet material. But the BBC had outgrown him and wanted rid, and it was more a question for the government of what else to do with the dour Scotsman if they didn't give him Imperial Airways.

Taking up his post in the summer of 1939, Reith was appalled by Imperial Airways' tatty headquarters, by its rudimentary organiz-ation, and by how little this semi-private company in receipt of major government subsidy appeared to conduct itself as a publicly accountable institution. 'The dividend motive,' he wrote later, 'was, in my view, incompatible with the public service motive.' (Fifty years later another Conservative government was to conclude that only restoring the dividend motive, by privatizing British Airways, could solve the problem of excessive subsidy and enhance the public service motive.) One suspects, too, that the kind of jocose company spirit behind the Empire boats' larky crossing-the-line certificates, or Captain Wilcockson's wooden medal for crashing *Syrinx*, also accorded Reith himself less deference than his Olympian ego had entitled itself to at Broadcasting House. Excessively tall, he was soon dubbed 'Wuthering Heights'; Imperial Airways trainee Hilary Watson claimed to me that Reith's first act on moving into his office at Victoria was to have the ceiling lowered, to enhance yet further his towering stature. And what would the puritanical, teetotal Reith have made of the news that Captain Caspareuthus, one of Imperial Airways' senior flying-boat captains, heedless of his passengers puttering by in the launch, regularly stripped naked and dived off his flying boat for a swim while it was being refuelled? Or that the nocturnal carousing of some Empire boat crews was such that you couldn't go near the flight-deck in the morning for the alcohol fumes, and one pilot once cheerily inquired of the ground crew, 'Did you see my pissed-cat take-off?'?

A highly critical, and in many ways unfair, report recommended the merging of Imperial Airways and the much smaller British Airways into one wholly publicly owned corporation. Despite a wave of protest inside the company Imperial Airways' popular and capable managing director George Woods-Humphrey was edged out. But on 3 January 1940 Reith had been summoned to see Neville Chamberlain, and the following day was offered – not quite Secretary of War, his own valuation of his destiny – but, tolerably, the Ministry of Information. Even before *Corsair* had flown off the River Dungu Sir John Reith had already moved on.

As the war progressed, more of the Empire boats were lost. *Cassiopeia*, which had taken Mervyn Carnelley home for his summer holidays in Africa, and at the end of 1941 had been ferrying a cargo of ammunition to Singapore, was wrecked trying to take off from

Sumatra on the way back, with four passengers drowning. *Corinna*, which had given Veronica Berry such a devil of a ride over France, was destroyed in a Japanese air-raid on Broome in Australia in the spring of 1942. *Circe*, which had conveyed her and Richard S. Jukes on from Kisumu, went missing around the same time near Java with twenty people on board, probably shot down by Japanese fighters.

Out of the forty-two Empire boats built, *Corsair* was one of a mere sixteen to survive the war. Two-thirds of the fleet were lost. A service life of ten years had originally been projected for the Empire boats, which was nearly up anyway – but some of them had already clocked up more than 2 million miles. *Corsair*, despite almost a year's inaction on the Dungu, had flown 13,262 hours. The Horseshoe Route the Empire boats had flown since the fall of the Mediterranean, arcing round from Australia and India to South Africa via Cairo, finally closed in 1947. With the end of the war plenty of military Sunderland flying boats were available to BOAC: converted to carry passengers, they had a longer range than the battle-worn C-Class.

The decision was taken, unsentimentally, to scrap the lot. Originally, according to John Pudney, BOAC's plan was to break them up wherever they ended their last service, perhaps at Congella in Durban, or at Kisumu. But (so claims the author of *The Seven Skies*) such was the outcry from former passengers, in Africa in particular – a flood of indignant and horrified letters – that the airline was persuaded to fly them all home to its Hythe base to be cut up. British Airways' archivist seemed unaware of any bulging folder of correspondence from Disgusted of Naivasha, but even if the anecdote is apocryphal, the sentiments we can identify with now. It seems inconceivable, today, that such a famous, genuinely historic class of aircraft – a social institution, no less – could be done away with, every last one. It would be like scrapping every single Concorde. When, a few years ago, the RAF retired its spectacular Vulcan

V-bombers, a *dozen* were preserved by museums and collectors.

But after the war nostalgia was a dispensable luxury. People wanted to look forward, not back. And the world was awash with redundant aeroplanes. Vast aircraft-manufacturing industries needed to be kept at work, at least enough to help prevent mass unemployment, building new planes for peacetime. Warplanes could not be scrapped quickly enough. BOAC did, in fact, make an effort to see one of the Empire boats saved for posterity. *Cathay* was offered to the Science Museum. Sorry, replied the Science Museum, which had seen a third of its exhibition space put out of action by enemy bombing: no room. So *Cathay* went under the torch, too. (Pan-Am did away with all its magnificent Boeing Clippers as well: another extinct breed.) Just over seven years after her spell in the Belgian Congo, on 20 January 1947, *Corsair* was broken up at Hythe.

Camilla

I I

Cape Maclear

'Cape Maclear,' Vic Hodgkinson had read out from his captain's log-book as he recalled for me the times he'd flown BOAC's flying boats down through Africa. He looked up, blank. 'I don't remember going there . . .'

Not only did flying-boat services through Africa not end with the demise of the C-Class, but a kind of Indian summer ensued for the seaplane. As late as 1949 British flying boats were alighting on African waters they had never visited before. A whole new stratum of society travelled out to the continent on them for new reasons, and remembered the experience in new ways. Most remarkably, perhaps, a fleet of brand-new flying boats, the biggest and most powerful ever, was introduced by BOAC to fly them there, even as the days of this irredeemable elemental hybrid were rapidly numbered.

I couldn't get to Malakal or Laropi – the back-of-beyond haunts of the Empire boats that had given Alan Moorehead his sense of seeing Africa as Livingstone had seen it – but I could follow the flying boat's wake to two post-war stops where David Livingstone had been less than a hundred years before. That was the wonderful thing about the plane-that-could-land-on-water: you could give it bigger fuel tanks, stronger engines, a greater range so that it could soar over half the places where it had previously had to refuel – but it could still just drop down on any remote stretch of blue it fancied.

To the modern spectator the introduction of the Short Solents on

147

BOAC's 'Springbok' service from Southampton to Johannesburg in
1949 seems more than a little indulgent. By now it was the only
major airline in the world still running flying boats. In 1947 BOAC
had lost more than £8 million. 'It is a moving thought,' mused the
Daily Telegraph, 'that we should have been in pocket if all the
passengers travelling by air had been paid £50 not to go.' A year
later the 'load factor' (the percentage of seats BOAC had to sell to
make a profit) still stood at a frankly absurd 115 per cent. The bill
for maintaining its flying-boat facilities was over a million a year.
When Sir Miles Thomas became the new BOAC chairman in
1949 he was horrified by 'the cloying sense of lushness, that money
did not matter'. You could not have defined the charisma of flying-
boat travel better. Meanwhile, airliners like the American Lockheed
Constellation were setting new standards of speed and comfort for
flying long routes like the Atlantic – even BOAC was buying them.
The Comet, to be the world's first jet airliner, was in advanced
development. Landplanes, both British and South African, already
offered a quicker passage from the Cape to London. Half a dozen
of the new seaplane fleet were actually converted from military
planes when the RAF cancelled the last part of its order. A few
months after Shorts completed BOAC's final Solent flying boat,
its historic seaplane works at Rochester on the Medway closed for
good.

At a glance a Short Solent looks pretty much identical to the
Sunderlands and Sandringhams it replaced – slightly larger; just as
bull-nosed and bulbous. But it had a range of up to 3,000 miles –
think of the early pond-hopping C-Class having to drop down to
earth three times a day for fuel! – could cruise at up to 280 miles an
hour, and carry almost forty passengers. The Solents cut the flying
time to South Africa nearly in half: all the way to Sicily on the first
day, Khartoum on the second, Cape Maclear or Victoria Falls on
the third, and you were in Johannesburg in time for lunch on the

fourth. BOAC built a completely new flying-boat terminal for their entry into service in April 1948 – the ruins of which I had seen at Southampton with Vic Hodgkinson. The occasion was deemed sufficiently auspicious for the Minister of Civil Aviation to perform the official opening, though he used the occasion to wonder aloud how much longer travellers would continue to prefer the leisurely passage of the seaplane.

Taking the flying boat to Africa was no longer an expeditious decision – the fastest way there – as it had been before the war with the advent of the Empire Air Mail Scheme. Now it was a stately luxury – even with these powerful new Solents – for those with time on their hands. Perhaps consequently, where the First Class of the Empire boats was marked by understated affluence – a gold-rimmed card welcoming each passenger by name – the Solent service stressed the unashamedly sybaritic. There was a semicircular bar at the rear of the passenger saloon: the rush to congregate around it as soon as the craft was airborne not infrequently led to an urgent call from the flight-deck for everyone to take their seats again – because the weight concentration at the back was threatening to stall the plane. You could browse in the Solent's own on-board library. There was a Gentlemen's Dressing Room, and a Ladies' Powder Room, containing a couch scattered with glossy magazines and a free and plentiful supply of Elizabeth Arden Blue Grass perfume. 'Every female on the aircraft had applied it liberally to their persons,' Gwendolen Hughes wrote to me from Norwich of her flight home from Uganda in 1950: 'for the next few years I simply couldn't stand the scent!' On the face of it, there also seems a leisurely caprice about a big silver flying boat dropping in once a week to a remote peninsula on the southern tip of Lake Malawi.

Livingstone discovered Cape Maclear for the western world in 1861 – naming it after his friend the Astronomer-Royal in Cape Town

– but his attention was focused elsewhere. He was more interested in circumambulating vast Lake Nyasa by its western shore to reach its northern tip. He never managed that, and the southern peninsula was relegated to an intermediate stop on an expedition counted a frustrating failure. The good doctor's transitory visit seems, in retrospect, to have set the keynote for a place fated always to point the way to elsewhere, that has never succeeded in detaining visitors long enough for them to put down roots, and build a community.

Though Livingstone's evangelizing aspirations had been almost utterly defeated by Africa – in all his time as a missionary he appears to have managed to convert just one person – his lonely death in 1873 at least proved a good career move. Within two years Lieutenant Young, a veteran of the doctor's 1862 expedition and leader of the first search party for him, had gone back to Cape Maclear, to found and build the Free Church of Scotland's mission of Livingstonia, named in honour of the dead explorer. But though this time the missionaries had much more success bringing their native charges to God, and the Free Church was to become established in Nyasaland for the long term, it was not to be at Cape Maclear. The lakeshore proved to be rife with malaria, within six years five of the missionaries were dead of fever, and the mission had been abandoned.

Between the wars Sir Alan Cobham's Singapore flying boat had actually visited Lake Nyasa during his 20,000-mile proving flight for a flying-boat service the length of Africa. In February 1928 he'd touched down just 30 miles round the lakeshore at Fort Johnston, as the town of Mangochi was then called. In Zomba, Nyasaland's administrative capital, he spent a week attempting to interest the governor in subsidizing an air service, as Uganda and Kenya had already agreed to do. But Nyasaland was to miss out on what would eventually be the arrival of the Empire boats. 'In the study of administrative history one can identify "hinge-points",' writes Malawi's historian Colin Baker: 'points at which the graph of progress had the opportunity, to a greater or lesser extent, to change direction. One such hinge-point occurred in Nyasaland in 1928.'

It's easy to dismiss questions of transport and communications as a rather anorakish preoccupation with timetables and machines, but Baker is not guilty of overstatement. It's a big historical point. Communities only thrive if you can get to them. If their citizens feel isolated from where the action is, they'll move elsewhere for good. One only has to compare a town like Windermere in the Lake District – entirely a creation of the railway that could bring in thousands of trippers from the northern conurbations – with a stillborn cul-de-sac like Canvey Island, where the Victorian speculator who planned a seaside resort to rival Southend failed to lure the railway in. The rapid prosperity and growth that followed the French town of Lille's successful lobbying campaign to be on the route of the Channel Tunnel rail line is recent corroboration. 'If you invite them, they will come,' runs the line from *Field of Dreams*. How does a tinpot dictator assuage the nightmare of international indifference? He builds a Pharaonic new airport.

But the Governor of Nyasaland in 1928, at the time of Cobham's visit, was a cautious accountant by training, and already worried about balancing the governmental budget. The matter was closed: no money or sufficient encouragement would be forthcoming to finance a dream of flying boats touching down on Lake Nyasa. Cobham flew on south, and eventually, ten years later, when the Empire Air Mail Scheme commenced, the C-Class went down the coast. Little landlocked Nyasaland, a slender streak of a country with a fabulous flying-boat lake, had let any chance of a direct air service all the way to Britain pass it by. When Veronica Berry had caught *Corinna* from Southampton in 1939 on her way out to meet her future husband in Blantyre she'd had to leave the flying boat at Beira on the coast and catch a landplane.

*

But twenty years later, with the advent of the Solents, Nyasaland had another chance. The story of what happened is worth telling in some detail, not only as an illustration of the wide and sprawling net that history sometimes spreads to catch a small fish, but also as an ironic prologue to what I came to find at present-day Cape Maclear. The advent of BOAC's new 'Springbok' service, forsaking the coast to head due south from Lake Naivasha for Victoria Falls, offered a new occasion to lobby for Nyasaland to be connected into an international air route. This time the new governor took a view as enlightened as his inter-war predecessor's had been short-sighted. Sir Geoffrey Colby, who took up his post in August 1948, didn't actually like flying – but using the flying boats while on diplomatic service in Nigeria during the war seems to have convinced him that Nyasaland must now pull out all the stops to ensure the international seaplanes from Britain came to call.

Several felicitous, if appropriately recondite, coincidences helped Colby's cause. In June 1949 Sir Miles Thomas became the new chairman of BOAC. In his former post as head of the Colonial Development Corporation he'd actually visited Nyasaland and stayed with the governor to deal with development matters. Then there was the disastrous failure of the Groundnut Scheme. After the war the British government had poured money into Kenya and Tanganyika to grow peanuts on a large scale – they had already proved a valuable cash crop in the West African colonies. But the project was bedevilled by unserviceable machinery – the only bulldozers available were converted from rusted Sherman tanks the US military had previously dumped into the sea after the Pacific campaign. Crop yields were paltry because the light topsoil disappeared in the first breath of wind after all the tree cover was removed; and incompetent organization resulted in spectacular wasting of money. 'I can remember porcelain toilets, rows and rows, as far as you could see,' Jack Beagle told me – he'd got in touch to tell me about the Solent flying boat that had brought him home from Lake Naivasha in 1950, after a year on the scheme overhauling diesel rollers in Kenya. 'But there wasn't any water out there – all our toilets were holes in the ground. Somebody'd ordered thousands – as far as I know they're still there.' (The only use found for his diesel rollers – rows and rows of them, too – was to roll out a tennis court.) So by the middle of 1949 the Colonial Development Corporation found itself needing to airlift out of Tanganyika in a hurry a hundred tons of the scheme's redundant agricultural machinery before it all rusted to scrap. The solution led to the first flying boat to touch down on Lake Nyasa since Cobham's.

For six weeks that summer, BOAC's freight-carrying Sunderland *Helmsdale* touched down at Nkhata Bay on the western lakeshore with consignments of harrows, disc ploughs, tractor wheels and brick-making machines for Nyasaland. (The conditions the flying-boat crews on 'Operation Ploughshare' seem to have endured hark back not a little to the salvage of *Corsair* in the Congo: one captain described the life as 'do-it-yourself bushwhacking', with clouds of ants obscuring his view through *Helmsdale*'s windscreen, and a dug-out canoe for paddling out to the seaplane.) When the work was over, however, the resourceful governor stepped in, to extend the flying boat's charter by twenty-four hours – so that before it returned to Southampton it could make a trial landing at Cape Maclear.

Far sight also conveniently coincided with folly. A new luxury hotel had just been built at Cape Maclear, on the site of the old Livingstonia Mission – a malign precedent, it must have seemed, when the first building supervisor took ill and died of malaria. The Cape Maclear Hotel was a huge Xanadu of a place, complete with golf course, billiard room, swimming pool, even an airstrip for light planes – and opened with a firework display. The only problem was: no road access. Unless you had your own light plane, or fancied chugging round the coast from Monkey Bay in a motor launch called *Odd Spot*, or you came in the dry season when the rudimentary road through the hills was still passable, you couldn't get there. But the hotel company had got its plans right in one respect – unsurprisingly, since its head was a former squadron leader. This lavish pile could have been designed for the kind of opulent comfort passengers disembarking from a luxury flying boat would be expecting for the night.

There was precious little else there, however, and the shopping list of facilities the Nyasaland administration would have to provide in order to host the big silver Solents is a good index of why BOAC was soon to decide that running flying boats was just too expensive:

> customs and immigration officer;
> coxswain;
> radio beacon;
> passenger landing jetty;
> fire crash launch;
> passenger launch and tender;
> two small thatched huts with rails and cradle for launch repairs;
> additional mooring buoy;
> storage facilities for 1,000 gallons aviation fuel;
> equipment for air-wave signals and meteorological observation.

Colby's persistence paid off. Eventually the BOAC chairman agreed to divert one flying boat a week each way to call in at the lake. The governor's reported satisfaction at 'a minor triumph' sounds very like muted mandarin-speak for 'How the hell did we pull that off?' So, from November 1949, the Solents started calling regularly at Cape Maclear. But in the same October issue that heralded the event – on the same page! – the *Nyasaland Times* reported that a De Havilland Comet had just flown all the way from London to

North Africa and back again in a lightning eight and a half hours. Once again, just at the moment when it seemed as if the wider world had finally discovered Cape Maclear, the wider world was already looking away. Nyasaland was twenty years too late. It had just acquired what soon nobody else would want.

In April 1950 Patrick Spencer flew from Southampton out to Cape Maclear to take up a post with the Nyasaland Department of Agriculture – 'The officer will take part in stimulating production of crops generally and cotton in particular by African peasants on Native Trust Land,' reads the brief of his duties from the Crown Agents. Still a young man, and weary after four years' seven-day-a-week work tending dairy herds in Ayrshire, he was going out to Africa for 'an element of adventure', he told me – and a very attractive salary for those days of £600 a year. 'And there was this dream – every man's dream – that you were going to be given a block of land. We knew it wouldn't be like that, but . . .

'I'd not flown before – I'll be honest with you,' he told me when I went to see him in Cambridge. 'I remember where I sat' – Mr Spencer still had the exceedingly elegant brochure he'd been given aboard the Solent nearly fifty years ago, which folded out into a full-colour exploded illustration of the flying boat depicting every seat, every bag of mail. Like Mervyn Carnelley's Empire boat brochure it was fabulously intricate – as though those who commissioned and drew it knew that all the passengers would in future years want to recall their flight in every last detail.

It's a paradox of the post-war flying boats: as the whole concept of a slow seaplane-voyage out to Africa comes to seem more of an extravagance and a luxury, so the leisured classes and pillars of the establishment who formerly constituted the majority of the passenger list give way to a classless post-war meritocracy – people like Mr Spencer. No longer the aristocracy, the wealthy landowners and farmers, or just the highest echelons of the diplomatic service and the military: it was the eager demobbed middle classes with tickets out paid for them and jobs to do. The one-off flying-boat journey – most still got the single chance in a lifetime – continues to mark momentous opportunity, a genuine turning-point in one's life, the bow waves peeling away like one's past existence. But now the Solents are taking out nurses, colonial policemen, agriculture workers, publisher's representatives. No wonder there was such a run on the Blue Grass in the Ladies' Powder Room: as with easyJet's in-flight mag, take it while you can . . .

And history has moved on past the flying boat far enough by now to highlight another curious irony. These Solents were almost-brand-new aircraft – only eighteen months old by the time Patrick Spencer went out to Africa. By comparison with the old C-Class, which Ian Henderson had admired in 1939 for its flaming exhausts and speedboat celerity, they had a stupendous range and top speed, and unrivalled standards of spaciousness and comfort. But to hear all the reminiscences of the post-war flying boats you would think the conveyance was battered old *Corsair* that had just heaved herself out of the Congo mud. 'It was almost like a submarine,' said Mr Spencer – 'you wondered when you were ever going to come up!' 'I can remember it being slow and *lazy*,' Jack Beagle recalled: 'this lumbering thing – it couldn't go very high. At Lake Naivasha we just got off the water at the end – it seemed we just cleared the tops of the trees. If one of us had coughed we'd have been in trouble.' Mr Spencer was struck by how the creeping, unpressurized Solent didn't like the hot air-pockets they met flying down through Africa during the afternoons: 'It's a bit disconcerting when the airscrews don't seem to grip any air. It all goes a bit quiet . . . and then they hit some air again and start to bite again and the old plane would start to shudder . . .' He eventually flew back from Africa on a pressurized Constellation, and remembered a cruising height of

20,000 feet as much more comfortable. 'The old plane . . .': the Solents' passengers could already see the writing on the wall, even if BOAC couldn't quite yet.

But yet again, as with so many people's lives, the flying boat, and in this case Cape Maclear, had consecrated a moment of personal history for Mr Spencer that had never left him – I imagine that when he noticed my tiny advertisement in the newspaper it was the image that came immediately to his mind's eye and compelled him to get in touch. 'There was a little jetty,' he recalled, 'and a doctor met us – and that was it. You were really out in the sticks. And my *lifelong* memory is seeing that plane taking off. The heart sank a bit – they just dropped us boys off, and they didn't want to know any more. But there was this beautiful trail of spray – it was rather like that comet at the moment.' At the time I went to see Mr Spencer in Cambridge, Comet Hale-Bopp – coming round once in a lifetime – had been flared in the night sky.

Mr Spencer had gone on from that lonely landfall on Lake Nyasa to the Shire river plain to the south. Initially living under canvas, he'd ridden around by bicycle to 'preach the gospel to the villagers' on more efficient ways of harvesting cotton. He and his colleagues had sunk wells – 'the money was used for Africa,' he said, 'that's what I liked about the Cotton Marketing Board'; they'd relied on hurricane lamps after dark, and a primitive 'saucepan radio' would sometimes get him the cricket commentary from London. It was nine years after that first arrival in the Solent before he went home from Nyasaland for good. And it was that plangent image of the young man fresh out of dairy farming in Ayrshire, watching the flying boat leave him behind on a remote jetty, that stayed with me, as it had with Mr Spencer himself, and drew me out to Cape Maclear. Swish hotel or not, it was, Mr Spencer had been quite clear, 'really out in the sticks'.

*

It took me all day to get there – twelve hours' grinding overland travelling. For many years a quaintly semi-closed country under the benign dictatorship of Hastings Banda, Malawi even today seemed squeezed into almost-invisibility by its far bigger neighbours, like Tanzania and Mozambique. When I came eventually to fly out from Lilongwe airport, a British Airways Jumbo was standing on an otherwise entirely empty taxi apron, wing lights winking red as the setting sun burnt the last light to gold: it seemed a bewilderingly vast phenomenon to be marooned amidst these empty miles of biscuit-brown bush. I'd flown down from Nairobi – only four hours in a 737 to the capital, even with a stopover in Lusaka, and on the map Cape Maclear appeared to be a mere 80 miles or so east of the capital, at least as the crow would fly.

The Stagecoach bus that pulled into the grimy city bus station at 7.30 in the morning bound for Monkey Bay, the nearest town to Cape Maclear, was encouragingly blazoned SPEEDLINK. There seemed to be some discrepancy among the various Stagecoach officials as to how many hours it would be to Monkey Bay, but I'd teamed up with a New Zealand couple and a Californian college teacher called Ted Foster, and by the time we boarded, the maximum estimate we'd elicited was a reasonably encouraging five and a half hours. Four hours, labouring south to skirt Malawi's central highlands, took us not even half-way – no nearer our destination than when we had pulled out of Lilongwe. It was already dusk when, after nine and a half hours, and about two thousand pick-ups and set-downs to maintain the load at a constant crush of thirty standing, and a mêlée at every stop to buy giant cabbages – even once a squawking chicken – through the open windows, we staggered out in the dusty centre of Monkey Bay.

A Peugeot pick-up was waiting to take us the last 12 miles to Cape Maclear. Not until it was horrendously overloaded – fifteen of us piled in the back on top of rucksacks, plastic bags full of shopping and a consignment of wide straw hats soon regrettably misshapen by the crush – and the light had quite gone did we creak away. Then, a couple of hundred yards along the road we jerked to a stop again, so that half a dozen hundredweight sacks of maize could be hefted aboard literally on top of us. Soon we were bouncing and swaying on a dirt track through the darkness, the acacia trees rushing by in silhouette, the track plunging to cross small ravines and swerving around bluffs. ('Elderly and unadventurous persons,' the BOAC station manager at Cape Maclear had memoed the airline's booking staff in London and South Africa in 1949, 'should be advised not to use this route.')

About half-way there the young African behind me, perched straight as a sentinel on the tailgate, removed his shirt and wound it slowly and ceremoniously into a turban about his head. When we halted so that the driver could hop out and pee at the roadside a man on the left side of the truck pointed at a flickering fire-light among the trees, and dissolved into hysterical laughter. Animated conversation in Chichewa broke out around us. It was late, it had been a very long day, longer than we had ever anticipated already and we still weren't there, and I was too tired to follow all the broken English of the guy in the turban as he began to explain to me. But I know he was talking about witchcraft, and whatever gathering was taking place out there in the bush had something to do with 'the lizard that looks like a tiger but is not a tiger'. This was how we got to Cape Maclear. Not for the first time in my travels seeking out the haunts of extinct seaplanes, I found myself wondering, 'Has anyone thought of inventing a *flying boat* to get here?'

In the morning we found a clutch of backpacker's lodges, a campsite, and a sprawling fishing village where the villagers were hollowing out baobab trunks for canoes and drying tiny silver fish on long tables in the sun. Cape Maclear was now a young traveller's hang-out, a place to scuba-dive, sunbathe and just chill out – a

Goa for Africa, with an air of purposelessness and languor. Most time-warped of all was The Gap, a resthouse and bar run by Australians: music surged out of a ghetto-blaster there all day – and there can hardly be a more disagreeable confirmation that somehow you have been beamed back to the early seventies than hearing the Electric Light Orchestra as you munch your eggs and bacon at breakfast. This place was definitely out on a limb. Zomba, the administrative centre of the British Protectorate of Nyasaland (it had become Malawi on independence in 1966), was 150 miles' drive to the south. Blantyre, which had then been the state capital, was 50 miles further still – another entire day on a Stagecoach bus even today. Apart from the haphazard pick-up shuttle to Monkey Bay, the only way in or out of Cape Maclear was a weekly ferry boat taking several days to creep up the west coast of the lake to Nkhata Bay. How on earth had huge, luxurious British flying boats ever come to touch down just out there between Thumbi Island and Dombwe Island and disgorge their First Class passengers for the night?

It was a thoroughly pretty spot – a vast blue lake fringed with hazy mountains, a long curving beach of pale sand, and at Otter Point, the western extremity of the bay, a silent rocky cove where orange and azure fish flicked below the surface of the glassy water, and fish eagles pealed aloft. But there was an odd, unsettled ambience about Cape Maclear: my Lonely Planet guide to Malawi hailed it as the kind of place where you found yourself losing track of time so comprehensively that you overstayed your visa, but I and the travel companions I'd arrived with found ourselves more than impatient to leave after a couple of days, and I realized later that things had always been like that.

For it was not a peaceful, relaxing spot: the local young men hassled you with a desperate persistence: buy our carved ebony tables; how about this necklace, that nice bracelet?; let us cook you a barbecue of catfish and cabbage on the beach, come out in our small boat across to Thumbi Island. Everywhere you turned there would suddenly be a guy fallen in at your heels hoping you hadn't noticed, murmuring 'Hello, my friend . . .', dogging your steps in the pretence of a healthy taking-the-air stroll – and soon the bag of carved elephants or chess pieces would be produced, until eventually you were on the brink of raging, 'Yes, I will buy one of your ebony letter-knives – *if I can personally disembowel you with it!*' It was a level of harassment – an almost autistic refusal to take no for an answer – far beyond any previous experience. There was no other work or money here, of course: just this client economy around the increasingly irritable community of surfers and backpackers – who after a couple of days of this suffocating attention couldn't get out fast enough. Still, such haplessness I hadn't encountered anywhere else in Africa. In Kenya the hawkers who swarmed around the bus whenever it stopped had worked out what their customers wanted, and it was almost an open-air supermarket that waved and clamoured at the window. Here these young men sat all day making far more ebony tables and chairs than they'd ever sell, but you couldn't find anyone with the right change to sell you a banana. (I exempt the guy at Otter Point, for his ingenuity in trying to ingratiate himself with Ted and me by announcing his name as Shakespeare.) There was a depressing sense that everyone here knew the visitors had all the answers, but didn't know how to ask the right questions to elicit them. It was as though Cape Maclear was still waiting for the big idea to float out of the sky and skid magically to a halt on the blue water.

At first I couldn't find any trace of the majestic Solents. The old hotel, said my Lonely Planet, was up at the west end of the bay, in the National Park, but the only substantial building was an ugly and dilapidated pile now housing a bare café where, five minutes after opening, the proprietor had no change whatsoever and was glumly unable to sell me a Coke. But there were two older men chatting on the verandah. Did they know if this was formerly the Cape Maclear Hotel where the flying-boat passengers stayed? For once I did not receive the blank look accorded to a hunter of the Yeti or the unicorn. No, said one of them, a short man in his sixties wearing a brocade waistcoat and flip-flops, but he would show me . . .

His name was Donald Khumate, and he was a retired primary-school teacher, who'd lived and worked at Cape Maclear all his life. Nowadays, to supplement his small government pension and support his extended family, he worked part-time for a non-governmental organization promoting Malawi's national heritage, and it was for one of its meetings that he was waiting at the National Park headquarters today. But now he had time to show me everything I wanted to see, and his final regretful words were to warn me off the so-called guides who pestered for money, and confide his disappointment that these days so many in the village would ask for it.

It turned out the guidebook had got it wrong. This had been a hotel, but not until the sixties – Mr Khumate remembered the man who had run it throwing coins into the sea for him and his young friends to chase after. The grand Cape Maclear Hotel had been back along the bay – the jetty had been (Mr Khumate pointed to where the beach protruded in a small spit) just there. But there was nothing left of it now – nothing. He took me back along the dirt road past a fenced-off agriculture research station and a tangled thicket of willowy trees. Here was where Livingstonia, the ill-fated mission, had been. Quite gone. We found the missionaries' graves up a steep track at the foot of the escarpment encircling the bay: a line of grey weathered wood crosses stuck into the bank, each tall as a man – a scrubby spot devoid of any melancholy atmosphere. To the immediate east was the old hotel golf course, said Mr Khumate. It had been long swallowed up again by the bush. The expanse of flat scrub we crossed on our way back down was the remains of the airstrip. And across the track Mr Khumate stopped to behold a sprawling jumble of rubble and foundations. This was the opulent Cape Maclear Hotel. 'It used to be really big – five storeys!' He peered down into a deep brick-lined pit in the bottom of which, for some reason, blackened pots and pans were smouldering. The generator house, said Mr Khumate – there had once been a big turbine in here. This sooty hole held his attention – to him it was obviously the vanished hotel's most fascinating aspect of all. 'They could put a plug in a point,' said Mr Khumate, 'and have power twenty-four hours a day!'

To me, though, what seemed fantastical was the scale of dereliction, and the brevity of this era of luxury. When Patrick Spencer had come ashore here from the flying boat in April 1950, the service had been calling at Cape Maclear for just five months – and by Christmas the Solents would have gone for good. After all that complex lobbying, that long shopping list of launches and beacons and customs houses and weather stations, Cape Maclear lost its flying boats after precisely a year. The very last Short Solent touched down in the channel between Thumbi Island and Dombwe Island on 30 October on its way to Johannesburg. Without the lifeline of its regular twice-weekly supply of guests, the improbably remote hotel closed down the following year. In the almost fifty years since, nothing comparable had materialized to replace it. At Stephens' resthouse in the backpackers' quarter – the equivalent of £3 a night – we were given a candle for our rooms once night had fallen (though no matches to light it with). Nothing but cold water to wash in. You could have egg on toast for breakfast: they cooked it squatting on the ground in the yard at the back, on a wood fire. One night the four of us who'd come in on the bus together yielded to entreaties and let young Victor and his two friends cook us a beach barbecue: we could eat little more than half the catfish and rice they prepared, and when we set our plates down the three boys fell on the leftovers with quiet intensity.

Mr Khumate had been a child when the flying boat used to call. He answered my questions about it carefully, politely – no, it used to land on that side of the island, and taxi down this way, and take off over on the other side; no, although it was so big there wasn't that much noise when it took off. But his answers had the detachment I'd come to find from African people. It was not their flying boat: it had decided to show up for a while and then, like the banana company in *One Hundred Years of Solitude*, it had gone away again. They had been spectators. Did he know of anyone here at Cape Maclear, I asked him, who'd actually worked with the Solents – maybe as a boatman? Mr Khumate thought. There was an old man who now worked as a watchman for one of the surf shacks, he said: he used to work in the hotel's kitchens . . .

But in the way Mr Khumate spoke about the flying boat there was a kind of magic realism. Pointing out to the west of Thumbi Island to show me where it used to take off up the lake, he called it 'the floating flying machine', which seemed both wonderfully literal and utterly fabulous. 'It used to carry *a hundred and fifty passengers!*' he informed me solemnly. 'Someone could make a *lot of money* if they brought the floating aeroplane back.'

Perhaps because the era of Cape Maclear's flying boats seemed so short and improbable you wondered if you'd dreamt the whole thing, there was, remarkably – the first time I'd come across any such thing in Africa – a memorial to them. Mr Khumate took me into the National Park's visitor centre, where there was a rather good exhibition tracing Cape Maclear's history from the earliest days of human settlement. At the far end a whole panel was devoted to the Solents. There was a black-and-white photograph of a Solent taxiing out past Thumbi Island, and another of the Cape Maclear Hotel, a villa-like construction with a long arched colonnade that looked as though it ought to be in Tuscany. And, in a big glass case, suspended above a painted backdrop of lake and hills, was a white Airfix model of a Short Sunderland, commemorating what must have been a magically unique achievement by a flying boat in getting airborne with its entire beaching chassis attached! A panel of explication confirmed that 'the fate of the flying boats was already foreshadowed when the Cape Maclear service was introduced,' and that, 'with the departure of the Solents, the hotel was doomed . . . Thus ended,' it concluded, 'an era of colonial luxury at Cape Maclear.' Mr Khumate wanted me to see the aquarium next door to the visitor centre – but we found only a succession of empty tanks filled with murky brown water. It seemed there wasn't any money for its upkeep.

That afternoon Ted Foster and I climbed from Otter Point up the northern slope of Mount Nkhunguni, the highest peak on the peninsula. Dozens of baboons crashed away into the woods as we toiled up the steep path, or swayed among the trees ripping leaves off the boughs. Rose-pink humming-birds fled with a tiny fizz; hornbills hooted. We halted on a col woven with giant ancient baobabs, from where there was a huge view north out over the lake. On this overcast day it was smoky with haze, its northern shore, so much more alluring for Livingstone than here, invisible far beyond the horizon, and the little ribbon of settlement below. You needed the great height of this vantage-point to confirm the conclusion each step on my flying-boat itinerary had been nudging me towards. Water – its lakes, its rivers, the littoral of the Indian Ocean – is what is most beautiful about Africa. No wonder people remembered their flying-boat journeys with such wonder and affection: the craft sought out the best bits of the continent the whole way, all the way down.

Ted, a pragmatic historian of science, was used by now to humouring my recondite obsession – he'd even got into the spirit as we reached the summit by suddenly recalling that seaplanes used to fly from Long Beach, California, out to Avalon on Santa Catalina Island. So he laughed, but did not demur, when I pronounced the one thing missing from the view. You have to walk up a mountain to find enlightenment, and while Erich von Däniken looks at the Nazca Lines in Peru and concludes they can only have been put there by spacemen to land their chariots of the gods, a view like that from Nkhunguni – our altitude that of a Solent pilot on final approach – could suggest only one thing. What other possible reason could they – whoever they were – have had, aeons ago, to crack the earth apart and inundate this immense lake, unless they were waiting for something? They had built this giant watery runway *for only one reason* . . .

Unfortunately we could not leave Cape Maclear by flying boat, nor, owing to the high winds and waves the next morning, by boat to Senga Bay, a fishing village and holiday resort on the western shore. But Ted and I got there anyway by a high-speed pick-up round the lakeshore road to the town of Salima – two and a half hours an exhilarating advance on the 'chicken bus' that had brought us – and Senga Bay turned out to offer an odd coda to the Cape Maclear story. Ted spent the afternoon in the market negotiating complex deals with local craftsmen that concluded with him in possession of an astounding quantity of wood-carving; I stretched a pizza, a Coke and Rider Haggard's *She* out to take advantage of a whole afternoon on the sunlit lakeside terrace of the Livingstonia Beach Hotel, one of Malawi's very finest. (When I beheld in the mirror of the Gents the wind-ravelled urchin that had arrived off the back of the pick-up I was amazed they'd let us in.) This was *it*: turquoise water ahead frilling the pale sand; flamboyant bushes on every side, and guests padding off to the pool – for a few hours I was defiant in my own enjoyment of that colonial luxury. Waiting in the hushed lobby for Ted to change a traveller's cheque (a battered and barely functioning pick-up that he'd hired to collect us was parked right outside), I studied the period photograph blown up on the wall. I recognized that long arched colonnade. 'Ted – here's a picture of the old Cape Maclear Hotel.' I realized as soon as I'd said it that I was wrong. It was an old picture of this hotel.

Back in England, in an article about Cape Maclear I'd been sent in response to one of my appeals for information, I discovered the cause of my confusion. When the very last Short Solent had taken off from Lake Nyasa and the luxury hotel had gone belly-up, its owners hadn't simply closed it and demolished it. They'd dismantled it piece by piece, transported it round the lake by the route we'd just come, and re-erected it here at Senga Bay. No wonder it was called the Livingstonia: the site of the old Scottish mission, that jumble of vegetation and rubble, was where it had started out. But the mission had left Cape Maclear, and so had the hotel, and so had the flying boats, and so, after a couple of days, had we.

Castor

I2

Victoria Falls

Mathematicians and physicists have their own formulaic definitions of infinity, but there are better. The number of people who saw the Beatles at the Cavern Club, for example, or the number of South Wales working-men's club managers who gave Tom Jones his first break. And there is the number of passengers on BOAC's very last flying-boat service to leave Africa.

'I flew home on, if not the *very* last, then one of the last . . .'; 'I was present at the *last* departure from Victoria Falls . . .'; '– the last flying boat.' Many letters I received began with such words. The final departure was not flown by Howard Hughes's Spruce Goose, but nothing less than such a behemoth could have accommodated a passenger list so immense. How, so ponderously freighted, did it get off the water at the elevated altitude of Lake Naivasha? Imagine the Elizabeth Arden Blue Grass perfume having to be trundled aboard by the *drum* . . . And how had the pilot avoided a catastrophic tail-down stall when the huge congregation unclicked their seat-belts and surged aft to the bar for a wake?

In fact, it was the Solent flying boat *Somerset* that taxied out from Berth 50 in Southampton for the very last service to Johannesburg, on 3 November 1950. A commemorative photograph shows the ground staff waving their caps in valediction as they watch her slide away into Southampton Water. She returned eleven days later, on the 14th, trailing a 20-foot long pennant through the air, and that was that.

The last flying boat. 'My daughter Rachel Dufton, then aged ten, offers her recollections of our 1950 flight from Port Bell to Southampton,' Arthur Williams wrote to me from Cockermouth in Cumbria, 'on what it seems was that aircraft's last flight.' Rachel remembered a steward walking down the cabin during the long taxi up Southampton Water telling them they'd be seeing Queen Mary in a few minutes, and 'expecting to see a grand lady smothered in jewels' – but also 'being told that the Solent was "going home to be broken up" and being rather worried that it might not last the way'.

The last flying boat. There is no self-aggrandizement involved, no boastful ego, in claiming to have been there at the end – as there is for all those who knew the Beatles or Tom Jones when they were nothing (and without which patronage would doubtless have stayed that way). The pathos of the image is in its haplessness: by then it was too late to save. The insistence of all those who were there, even if their final flight left six months earlier than November 1950, has to be a kind of gratitude, at the privilege of being able to say goodbye.

The last flying boat. The huge sense of loss – that even I, who was still ten years from being born, feel when I dwell on the phrase – is nothing to do with, or is much more than, aeroplanes. It is the end of a transforming magic: of a wondercraft that could fly you across the horizon of your own life; in which travel became a consecration of your personal fate. It took you not on a mere journey, but to your destiny. I wish I had not missed the last flying boat – that there were still the chance to travel *that* far: to *be* travelled with so much *art*. As Eileen Murray, now ninety, sighed to me when I visited her in Bournemouth – her late husband Bill had been an Imperial Airways Empire boat captain – 'Now we'll all just have to go to the moon . . .'

Right up to the end, the African flying boat was offering memorable adventure. Sometimes it was just small things: Olive Burkitt remembered the captain coming to the rescue after a bumpy passage north of Luxor had made one of her daughters sick over the smart dress she was attired in for their arrival in Uganda. (This was seven months before the flying boats finished.) Don't worry, said the captain, taking it away: they'd wash it and hang it from the flagstaff to dry – and returned shortly with a clean, dry garment having done just that. 'I laugh now,' Mrs Burkitt wrote to me, 'when I think of my daughter's cotton dress flying from the mast of that flying boat as we flew across Africa.' And of all the written reminiscences I received, two of the longest described flights made during the flying boat's final two years. A good definition of travel-writing is a journey worth writing about, and the accounts A. E. Lorriman of Gloucestershire and Roy Marriott of Somerset sent me of their journeys each ran to eleven pages. I'd asked for recollections, and these were theirs, fifty years on, in every detail. A book about a flying-boat service needs its own passenger list – a shotgun congregation, all aboard together, and as many as possible: here are two more, two of the last.

'It was mid-June 1949,' began Mr Lorriman, 'when I was told by the Crown Agents that I had been accepted for work as a Postmaster with the East African Posts and Telecommunications Administration.' Then working at the head post office at Rugby in Warwickshire, in a few weeks he'd received instructions to leave for Nairobi on the Sunday flying boat. It was already Friday – and the need to get a Kenyan visa in London meant he had just a couple of hours to prepare and pack! 'As soon as I had sufficiently recovered from the shock,' recalled Mr Lorriman, 'I cycled to work at Rugby, where I was immediately asked by my overseer, in an extremely strident voice, why I had come to the office instead of being on my way to Long Itchington sub-post office, where I had been scheduled to check the office account.' Mr Lorriman explained why he 'felt unable to go to Long Itchington'.

Equipped with a new Antler suitcase and a camera, the proceeds of a hurried office whip-round in Rugby, Mr Lorriman set off for Kenya. The eventful and portentous nature of his trip manifested itself even before he reached the flying boat *Sussex*, when the BOAC coach carrying them to their Saturday nightstop at the Lyndhurst Hotel had to detour across farmland and scrub to bypass a Dorset village where a wood-burning lorry had overturned and set several thatched cottages ablaze. 'I thought later,' reflected Mr Lorriman, 'that this was my very first experience of "going into the bush".'

To someone whose only previous flight had been in the bomb-bay of a Liberator bomber, being 'air-trooped' from India to the UK in non-stop legs of ten hours, the Solent itself seemed the height of luxury – deliciously confirmed when the stewards' reluctance to open the bar was overruled by some prompt and high-handed insistence from the Duke of Manchester, who was flying back to his Kenyan estate with his wife. But over Uganda the *RMA Sussex* hit a dreadful thunderstorm, 'with ferocious rain hammering on our flying boat'. The aircraft was tossed about at all angles, on one severe drop a lady passenger was suddenly somersaulted over the table in front of her, and the plane descended to such low altitude – since they couldn't fly above the storm, said the captain, they had to duck under it – that the passengers could easily make out the elephant and giraffe below. 'We really felt,' wrote Mr Lorriman, 'that we were very close to Africa now.' Eventually the ghastly turbulence communicated itself to his insides, and to be nearer the toilets Mr Lorriman took a precautionary stagger to the men's room. 'On entering, I found one of the crew finishing off his shave with a cut-throat razor. When I suggested that holding a lethal piece of steel so close to his throat in a pitching aircraft seemed a highly dangerous thing to do, he carried on scraping the shaving soap from his face, and told me that conditions were "normal" for this part of East Africa.'

In later life, 'after Africa', Mr Lorriman was to find his British Telecom engineers complaining vehemently if sent on training courses at less than the full six weeks' notice – even when the destination was 'usually well within 100 miles of the Gloucester telephone area' – and frankly incredulous, too, whenever he countered with a tale of 4,000 miles by flying boat at one day's notice to a job which would, in his words, change his whole life. 'So I stopped telling the story,' he concluded – 'until now.'

Mr Marriott's flight was differently auspicious. For twelve years, he told me, the intervention of the war had separated him from his parents: in 1950, a few months before the service ended, the flying boat finally took him from southern Africa home to England to see them again. What he sent me was the account he'd written to them later of his 'great adventure'. It began at Victoria Falls, the airline bus cresting the brow of the hill to drop down to the forest clearing on the Zambezi, 'and there, a little upstream, with the morning sunlight gleaming on the hull, lay the *City of Cardiff*. I must confess,' wrote Mr Marriott – and who cannot share it? – 'I had a great thrill on seeing her for the first time.' Every account of a flying-boat journey seems to notice something new: though Mr Marriott is hardly the first to have felt, as his Solent forged ahead through the water, that he was on a ship rather than a plane, once the flying boat had risen off the river and circled the Falls, he looked out of the window at the wing: 'One had the sensation again of perhaps being at sea, for all the time the tip was rising and falling against the horizon of the sky.' It is that mysterious indeterminacy that transfixes us: a Saint-Exupéry moment. You're in the hands of something you can't quite understand and thereby limit – when your reason and your senses give you conflicting reports, to leave a lacuna that lets in the imagination. It reminds me of the golden-winged mare that gallops across the sky with young Kay Harker on its back in John Masefield's fantasy *The Midnight Folk*, 'the hooves

. . . treading the air much as a swimmer will tread water'. In a flying boat you were being – all these words it rescues from numbness – *transported*.

Mr Marriott's return journey from Southampton to Victoria Falls, following the Nile all the way south, touched down at Luxor for a nightstop, with time to spare for an afternoon's sightseeing around the ruins of the temple of Karnak. His narration needs no ironies pointed: here's what happened:

Our mode of transport was in the form of very ancient gharries through the streets of the town. Our guide, who seemed to appear from out of the blue, hardly stopped talking all the time. He was, however, interesting, if a little long-winded in all his stories. It was getting dark by the time we finished.

Just before it was really dark, the flying boat on the service from Nairobi to England came roaring up the river on take-off. It made a brave sight with its lights shining against the setting sun, the last rays of which were still in the sky. I thought that here I was watching one of the marvels of the modern world from a site which had stood for so many thousands of years.

Fifty years on, there seemed a chance that if I travelled to Victoria Falls I would find a flying boat. 'The lush tropical vegetation on the Southern Rhodesian shore and the sun shining on the calm water . . . a glorious sight as we slowly moved upstream': a seaplane anywhere in Africa was rare enough, but here apparently I could count on replicating Mr Marriott's ascent from the Zambezi, at least in a floatplane, and nowhere else on the continent held even the faintest promise of a flight in a Second World War vintage Catalina.

As usual with reports of mythical beasts, the evidence was tantalizing, vague and contradictory. A small photograph had appeared one month in *Flypast* magazine: a bright red- and yellow-painted Catalina, one of two apparently under conversion in British

Columbia from a Canadian fire-bomber to carry passengers, for a Malaysian hotel group planning pleasure flights off the Zambezi. That could only mean Victoria Falls. Correct, said the Africa Travel Centre in London: but though there *had* been two out there, one had already crashed. Never heard of such a thing, said the tourism representative at the Zimbabwe Embassy, her bewilderment seeming to extend to the very concept of a boat that flew. Several there, confirmed Jürgen, a Reuters manager I got chatting to at Lilongwe airport while our flight to Harare was delayed for several hours, who also told me a tale of how, some years ago, Reuters had scooped all its rival news organizations with the first pictures of the Italian cruise-liner *Achille Lauro* going down in the Indian Ocean, by chartering a Catalina flying boat at ruinous cost from some buccaneering aviator in Mombasa. So from Harare I flew on to Bulawayo, and then took the night train to Victoria Falls. A second place in Africa on which David Livingstone had conferred a name on the map, and Alan Moorehead's flying boat, beguiling him with a sense of Africa as the explorer himself would have seen it, had called here, too. Sure enough, when I walked down into the small town, a big billboard on the side wall of the first travel agents blazoned: KAYAKING, BUNGEE-JUMPING, SAFARIS, SEAPLANE!

Half an hour later I had an inkling of how Livingstone must have felt on arriving back at Ujiji after three years' exploration of Lakes Nyasa and Tanganyika to find all his medical supplies, food stocks and letters from home had been pilfered. In that first travel agents my confident presumption that their large sign might actually bespeak what it read prompted not just surprise but irritation. I suppose I was a little persistent. *Of course there was no seaplane.* The disillusion was confirmed in every agency along the street. No Catalinas had arrived here recently. The floatplane running pleasure flights had crashed over a year ago. Would I like to go on a safari?

No flying boat.

So I did the next best thing. I went on a boat, and took a flight – and the combination took me nearer Mr Marriott and Mr Lorriman's adventures than I anticipated.

Once you'd beheld the sheet of pouring roar that was the force itself – an hour's excursion – there wasn't actually a great deal to do at Victoria Falls, especially if you weren't into strenuous, and expensive, outdoor activities like white-water rafting. So everyone, it seemed, went on a booze cruise. 'Sunset cruise' was the official terminology: pile aboard a riverboat in mid-afternoon and pass a few hours puttering up and down the Zambezi until sundown, drinking your way through all the free liquor aboard – not bad for eight quid a head. I certainly had the time.

I was lucky, too. I'd expected some kind of Mississippi sternwheeler – and indeed we passed some big pleasure craft plough-ing up the middle of the river like floating saloon bars. But just eight of us climbed aboard what was little more than a small verandah mounted on a couple of pontoons. Perhaps it was a good thing for our flimsy vessel that there were no longer Short Solents touching down on the river: when Norman Ramsay and his wife had kept a sailing dinghy at the Zambezi Boat Club above the Falls, his letter recalled for me, and sailed upstream every Sunday for a relaxed picnic on one of the islands, they'd get no peace at all from the flying boats:

My understanding of the rules to avoid collisions at sea was that airborne aircraft gave way to surface craft, and that when in contact with the water they became steam-driven vessels which gave way to sail.

The persons operating the flying-boat service did not seem to know this, and we were continually buzzed, badgered and pestered as we sailed through.

We, however, faced no threat from low-flying steamships. We nosed in so close to the banks that we could almost touch the overhanging foliage. Darters, slender black seabirds like flying thorns, perched

on tiny tufty islands at eye-level. We were as close to the Zambezi
as Mr Marriott had been in the small launch taking him out to the
City of Cardiff.

When we talk about wilderness we always think of land. Desert;
tundra; moorland; ice shelf. But land is actually the surface of the
earth most vulnerable to man: nothing that cannot be built on,
deforested, ploughed up or quarried, remade as humanscape. All
the way west across Kenya to Uganda that day on the Akamba bus
I hadn't seen a single stretch of uncultivated land, and no more than
a solitary handful of zebra. Nairobi gave you no sense of history
deeper than a few years. But though we can pollute the seas, dam
and divert the rivers, we can never do away with them. The oceans
yield coelacanths that have survived in the depths since prehistory.
A mighty river just flows on through the future, and back into the
earliest past. Water is wild.

An idle diversion of an afternoon, then: the equivalent of sitting
in the hotel bar – but afloat: and yet for the very first time in nearly
a month in Africa I had a sense of unchanged and unchanging
wilderness. This afternoon on the small boat it didn't matter that
conversation was polite and halting among us, or that, with the four
women from an overland party chatting together and the Austrian
couple taking photographs of each other, myself and Matt, the guide
and boatman, were left the odd ones out. All I wanted to do was
look and listen. Half a dozen giraffe teetered tremulous amongst
the trees on the Zambian shore. An elephant swished its trunk shyly.
Monkeys scooted and bounced after one another – 'They're playing!'
laughed Matt. And near sunset, on our way back to the landing
stage, I suddenly saw a grey mound motionless under the branches,
which rose in the water and yawned a chasmic, snaggle-toothed
mouth, and then the hippo had submerged again to wallow just feet
away from us, a shimmer like an oil-slick on the surface. Most of

the time there wasn't another cruise boat in sight: it was just us and the wildlife and the forest.

At the Falls themselves, the cliff from which you viewed them had been tidied and organized into footpaths, overlooks, signboards, railings, a visitor centre and toilet block – neatly enough done, but a modern tourist environment all the same. But the Zambezi, splintering into countless sinuous channels as though a giant bottle had broken and spilt across the landscape – this was Livingstone's Zambezi. A green-walled corridor of ageless motion, nothing about it could change. I understand now what Alan Moorehead meant. Until I'd been to Victoria Falls I'd suspected him of a journalist's sentimental conceit, but now I know he was right, and that only a flying boat's course down the interior of Africa could have let him see it.

Several miles upstream Matt shut off the outboard for a moment beside a weathered and stalky wooden jetty. This was the old flying-boat landing stage; behind it, now closed in by the thick dark trees, the former slipway. He filled in the other passengers with a brief history of the B O A C Solent's stop-offs here on the Africa services. I'm certain Matt also told us that Queen Victoria once arrived at the Falls by flying boat . . .

The next morning I caught a plane. This was July: the southern African winter. Many of the trees around Victoria Falls were brown and leafless; the railway station was hardly the riot of flamboyant floral colour the guidebook heralded – but the weather was a rich dry heat; no rain. That didn't prevent my flight over the Zimbabwean bush and the Zambezi turning out every bit as tumultuous as Mr Lorriman's storm-tossed passage in the Solent. A twenty-minute 'Flight of the Angels' circling the Falls in light planes or helicopters was a staple tourist attraction – the sky above the town whined and *chuckerchuckered* all day with them. It seemed a lame, commercialized mockery of my dreams of stately take-off in an antique Catalina. So, with the grim recklessness born of disappointment, I went the whole hog: a 'game flight', twice as long at forty minutes, to take in some African wildlife at low-level before you reached the Falls.

We didn't find any. That was the problem. It was all the same to me – I knew what a lion looked like. I'd seen my game, the previous evening on the booze cruise. A seven-thirty start, three of us and Charlie the taciturn young pilot in our Southern Cross Aviation Cessna 182 – for my forty quid I'd have been quite happy with a spot of aerial car-touring in our Ford Escort of the sky. The *leisureliness* of it all! – that was the halcyon refrain of every flying-boat wayfarer! But we'd been flying out over the Maindi region west of Victoria Falls for over ten minutes already, and seen nothing but gritty umber bush. I could feel the tension, even the beginnings of desperation, sat alongside me. There was honour at stake here – no less than had our pilot been a Battle of Britain ace scrambling his Spitfire at Tangmere. Charlie had promised us game, and game he had urgently to deliver.

Suddenly we peeled off and dived as though a Focke-Wulf was on our tail. The ground loomed up, we levelled out, and Charlie said, 'Buffalo.' It was a start. We climbed again, and then plunged at the Zambezi, from this height leaking an amazingly wide mess of broken brown channels across the bush. We gunned down the river, it seemed just inches above the rapids – scatter of grey backs: hippo. The waterway ravelled back at me at a speed that made my eyes want to retreat to the back of my head. Only the final scrape-and-thud of impact and the windows slopped with suds were missing: had we been on a Catalina we could not have got closer to a water-landing. But already Charlie was turning us inside out into a near-vertical climb, stick full back and pulling huge G, before flinging us away 270° as though by catapult over to where he thought he'd glimpsed a rhino.

Dodgy guts over the previous three days didn't help. We plummeted at elephants, then reached for the sky, and while my stomach was still on the ground we swung across the bush on sudden centrifugal parabolas. If it had been a rare Grumman Albatross lurking down there . . . but for a few animals . . . ! The two guys in the back – their names must have fallen out of my mind's pockets when we'd ascended to touch the hand of God – were hunched over their cameras in excitement; I was trying not to imagine the consequences of losing control below the waist in a small four-seater cabin at 3,000 feet. By the time we were over the Falls themselves I couldn't care less. *Yeah rainbow very nice yeah big aren't they can we go now?* I'd got my trip back in time to the golden age of African air-travel. Charlie was giving me a close look. 'Are you starting to feel a bit sick?'

'Launch promotion idea,' I see I'd scrawled in my notebook the previous evening. 'Get Plane Sailing Catalina to land on Thames.' I'd had a brainwave. Other books received Godspeed at small edgy gatherings in publishers' boardrooms where thirty people sipped white wine and picked at twiglets: *Corsairville* was going to be the first to forsake a party for a *flypast*.

There was just one airworthy flying boat left in Britain. I remember the first year it came to the Biggin Hill Air Fair. I had a Saturday job in those days at a local newsagents, and I thought I had privileged knowledge in announcing to one of the brothers who ran the shop that my dad and I were going to see the Catalina the following day. 'I was up there last night when it arrived,' said David softly. Owned by a syndicate called Plane Sailing, and based at Duxford airfield in East Anglia, this immaculate white-painted amphibian became a regular on the airshow circuit, and over the years my father and I had often seen it – just two engines, that skinny, shallow hull, a skiff where an Empire boat was a liner: there was a milling breeziness to a Catalina's flypast. Some years later, living in Cambridge by then and birdwatching one afternoon near Duxford at the tranquil Fowlmere nature reserve, I looked up from moorhen and grebe on the lagoon to see the slim white Catalina sailing and circling overhead.

Apart from a couple of touchdowns each year on a lake in Sussex to retain its seaplane licence, however, this seaplane now never went near water. But it would for my book. Trailing a large sky-pennant like the last Solent returning from Africa, it would hove in sight above the mirror-glass towers of London's Docklands, rolling slightly on the air as though already riding the water. Canary Wharf workers in their lunch-hour would glance up at the unfamiliar rumble from its Pratt and Whitney radials rolling around the stainless-steel-clad canyons. Declining gracefully on to the Thames somewhere near Rotherhithe, it would taxi up the river to Tower Bridge (forty years ago one of BOAC's new Solents had also done this), where the press, tipped off a deliciously short time in advance, would scramble aboard from small boats, and the author of this *coup de théâtre* would make all the front pages as though he were Howard Hughes and had just landed the Spruce Goose. Now I just had to get back to London and write the book.

A few years ago a Catalina had regularly visited Victoria Falls. It was not an aircraft that had ever ventured into the interior of Africa during the trans-war heyday of the flying boat – exclusively designed as a military reconnaissance plane, it had come no closer than a few RAF seaplane stations on the west and east coasts. Over 3,000 had been built by the end of the last war; by the mid-1980s just forty were left flying. But in 1987 a Frenchman who ran adventurous safaris in Africa decided to try and re-create the longest aerial safari of all: the African flying-boat route. The best he could come up with as a substitute for a fleet of four-engined Empire boats was a solitary Catalina purchased in Reno, Nevada, that had previously

42. Short Sunderland at the Gambia, West Africa

43. Two Sunderlands of RAF Coastal Command on their take-off run

44. Boeing flying boat *Berwick* touches down on the lagoon at Lagos in Nigeria after a wartime flight across the South Atlantic. One crew member is already stationed in the nose to make her fast to the moorings

45. The BOAC ground crew work on *Bristol* at the wartime BOAC flying-boat base in Baltimore

46. A Qantas crew unloading their Catalina in Karachi on the Australia route

47. Churchill at the controls of *Berwick* during a flight from the USA to Bermuda in January 1942

48. The actress Yvonne Arnaud emerging from the Ladies' Powder Room of a Short Solent

49. Brochure for the post-war BOAC flying boat service to South Africa

50. A Short Solent on the 'Springbok' service loading at Lake Naivasha

51. 'The Solent was like a millpond': the Saunders Roe Princess is launched in the middle of the night at Cowes on 21–22 August 1952

52. A Saunders–Roe advertisement from February 1952 for a flying boat utopia that was never to be

53. 'The flying beer bottle': Pan-Am Air Bridge's Mallard at Watson's Island, Miami

54. John Wagner lets his seaplane turn itself round on the tide at Fort Jefferson in the Dry Tortugas off Key West

55. PenAir's Goose waits while Fred Ball fishes for salmon in Miam Lake on Kodiak Island, Alaska

56. Nick Brigman checks all aboard the Goose at Hidden Basin on Kodiak

57. The sudden end to BOAC's flying-boat service to Africa. *Somerset*, the last Solent to depart for Johannesburg, taxis out into Southampton Water on 3 November 1950

58. *Islander*, the last airworthy Short Sunderland left in the world, with Captain Ken Emmott at the controls, bids goodbye to Windermere in the Lake District in the summer of 1990

ferried fishermen around British Columbia. The southern Sudan was now a war zone requiring sensitive avoidance. The pariah status of apartheid South Africa meant he could go no further south than Victoria Falls; and the cost of the whole enterprise required a fare of no less than $13,750 – for travelling conditions (at least aboard the flying boat) some way short of Imperial Airways luxury. An early proving flight from Cairo as far as Mozambique was immortalized by the BBC in a classic television documentary, *The Last African Flying-Boat* (though the British flying-boat veterans I met tended to harrumph, 'Did you hear the state those engines were in!' and 'They didn't even empty the bilges!'). But for four years Pierre Jaunet and his tiny team sustained their elderly craft, sufficient bookings, and his bank balance, in the best seat-of-the-pants flying-boat tradition, to ply a perversely heroic migration up and down Africa.

Mike Honmon remembered Pierre Jaunet's Catalina fetching up on the Zambezi. The one difficulty the old flying boats had had, he told me when I met him in the garden of the Pink Baobab café, 'and the Catalina, too, when it came, is that the jetty is 3,150 feet above sea level'. A Catalina, in particular, was essentially designed for sea level – to carry a handful of crew on immense endurance sorties just a few hundred feet above the waves. Two engines were not much to unstick a fifty-year-old amphibian laden with sixteen passengers and all their luggage from a glassy Zambezi, especially where the air was thinned by the altitude. 'Many times Pierre used to have trouble on this river. I used to see him try and take off, be unable to – and then he'd have to unload all his clients, bus them to the airport, fly over there and pick them up.'

Mike Honmon was the guy who'd started up the floatplane service at Victoria Falls – though he'd sold the company on before the plane had crashed, killing five people. A youthful, stringy man with a bright, open manner, he now owned several shops along the town's main drag, which sounded a lot less fun but was no doubt compensatingly easier. He'd flown sixteen twenty-minute flights a day off the river in his Cessna seaplane – 'for most people twenty minutes is all they can take going round in circles without getting sick.' Still only a couple of hours after I'd taken frail paces away from the Cessna at Victoria Falls Airport, the other guys enthusing, 'You went *yellow*, Graham!', that helped restore my equilibrium.

'I thought: a floatplane – that'd be different!' said Mike. 'I just wanted to set it up as a challenge – and, man, it was a challenge. I had to teach everybody in Zimbabwe about floatplanes.' The precedent of the big BOAC Solents, and irregular Empire boats before them, visiting Victoria Falls had obviously faded from the country's memory. I told him how, since I'd been in Africa, any mention of flying boats had met with blank incomprehension. 'Exactly. I'd go into the Department of Civil Aviation, all these officials in suits, and it'd be, "OK, we've got a madman here." I had to find out about everything.' It took six years, from getting his Air Service Permit to doing the first flight.

In partnership with an American seaplane company that flew trips between New York's East River and Long Island, Mike set himself up as Seaplane Safaris Africa and took delivery of a five-seat Cessna floatplane. Its arrival in kit form on the bank of the Zambezi brought home to him what he described as 'the maintenance night-mare' of a seaplane. 'At the airport you have tools and cranes and things, but, down at the river – nothing!' Several flying-boat pilots had remembered for me how dropping a spanner while changing an engine was to see it disappear for ever beneath the water. 'If you could dig down in the mud,' said Stan Prince, who'd worked at Imperial Airways' Congella base in Durban, 'there'd be a fortune in aircraft tools.' Eventually, to put the Cessna together again Mike and his team had to hang the fuselage from a tree, and it took forty men to lift the reassembled Cessna off the tree and into the water. If there was ever a next time, he said, he'd make sure he bought an amphibian.

But once his operation was up and running he was carrying 1,500 tourists a month. He'd cut back the undergrowth from the old flying-boat slipway, and replaced the rotten planks and rusted pontoons so his passengers could board from the old jetty. He'd fly them up the Zambezi to touch down in places that submerged rocks put out of bounds to the pleasure boats, and everyone would get out on the wing with a few Cokes to watch the sun go down. On some October and November days, the river smooth as a mirror, to unstick the Cessna he'd have to lift one float off the water and plane along on the other before lifting that off, too. And though his passengers would always expect a big bump on touchdown, 'on clear, glassy days,' said Mike, 'I could land that thing and people wouldn't know – I'd hardly know!' The river's hippos were an extra hazard. 'Landing, you could see them, but taking off, at that speed, up he popped and you'd have to' – Mike did a shimmy with his hand – 'and go round him. Once or twice I came quite close to hitting one.' Flying the Cessna off the Zambezi, he said, was simply 'a nice environment. You don't have to go up to the control tower and fill in all these forms – you're just out there by yourself.'

The trouble was, inside his seaplane Mike Honmon was probably the only person on the Zambezi, even in Victoria Falls, who felt that. 'The noise! An incredible amount of noise!' For the performance needed to get his seaplane off the river he needed a propeller with longer blades and turning faster than on a landplane – on take-off the Cessna's would be spinning faster than the speed of sound, with a deafening high-pitched crackling. 'You could hear it from here,' said Mike – in the garden of the Pink Baobab we were a good 6 miles away from the old flying-boat jetty. 'You and I couldn't talk. And when you're taking off every twenty minutes – some of the boating enthusiasts used to get quite upset.' He didn't think anyone would ever restart a seaplane service at Victoria Falls. 'You've got to be very environmentally aware landing on the river here these days.'

In any case, he eventually gave it up because he got tired of flying round in circles – those endless circuits of the Falls, *wow-wow-wow* – and because, said Mike, who'd learned the hard way, it was tough flying seaplanes: negotiating the current, taxiing in the wind, pumping out the floats after every flight because the wind had blown water into all the watertight compartments, hippos . . . 'You have to try so hard, and go through so many channels, to bring everything together. I think that's why people love them . . .'

Though Zimbabwe's civil-aviation bureaucracy had forgotten about the flying boats, Victoria Falls itself had not quite. Mike Honmon suggested I take a look inside the Tourist Information Bureau up the street. In the corner by the window, slightly dusty and as though shunted to one side, was a Perspex case containing a large silver model of BOAC Solent *Salisbury*, exploded along its starboard profile to reveal an intricately modelled interior. Mounted on the sides of the display plinth were nine black-and-white photographs of the flying boats on the Zambezi, including one superb front-on shot of the crew on top of a Solent's wing repairing the leading edges. A framed, illuminated citation in finely calligraphed antique script ('Presented by Councillor J. G. Blunt') celebrated the short era – just two years – of the service landing at Victoria Falls. The walls of the bureau were covered in racks of colourful leaflets for youth hostels, bungee-jumping, jet-boat hire, safaris. There was an odd cumbersome redundancy to this meticulous, monotone monument – could no one quite bring themselves to get rid of it? Paying for a handful of postcards with lions on, I asked one of the young guys manning the desk if they produced any of those superb flying-boat photos as postcards. A queer look of bafflement: 'No, there are no postcards of the jet-boats.'

And then there was the Victoria Falls Hotel, its idyllic gardens looking out over the falls, where I found a large and rather beautiful mural in the arched front porch paying further homage: BOAC

flying boat G-AHIN tracing its route down a vast map of the
African continent, with special prominence given to the point where
'the Solents landed and were serviced on a reach of the Zambezi
above the Victoria Falls, permitting an overnight at this hotel, the
stop being affectionately known as JUNGLE JUNCTION.' I had
never, in all the letters of reminiscence I'd received, or my conver-
sations with former flying-boat pilots like Vic Hodgkinson or Ken
Emmott, or any of the books of aviation history I'd read, heard of
this nickname for Victoria Falls. Why should it be? Here was neither
jungle nor junction.

But the Victoria Falls Hotel was a wondrously thorough exercise
in myth-making. Pre-war travel posters for shipping lines and airline
destinations lined the walls of the lobby. The lounges were cool
repositories of stuffed animals, busts of explorers and glossy mags
on coffee-tables. Sprinklers ceaselessly drenched the emerald lawns
(in my hotel a notice in the bathroom exhorted guests to help conserve
Zimbabwe's scarce water-resources). Out on the rear terrace, the
'I Presume' Bar, where I ordered a meal, snatches of conversation
drifted across from the next table – an urbane, immaculate woman
languidly recalling for her companion the time when she was wearing
that Versace necklace. Groups of middle-aged American tourists
hobbled down the steps, every last one kitted out in pristine, pressed
safari-wear: sandy shirts, bush hats, razor-creased shorts, thick socks,
desert boots – evidently for going no nearer the bush than the inside
of a tour-bus. Nosing along the corridors after lunch I passed a
young English family letting themselves into their new room to a
loud exclamation of 'Oh, there *is* a piano!' The penny suddenly
dropped: no wonder a ticket for the African flying boat had been
so expensive – they put up every evening at these fabulously posh
hotels! How large a proportion of the entire fare had gone just on
the overnights?

But the unease I felt padding around the Victoria Falls Hotel –

undeniably classy, no sickly ostentation – was more than that of the budget traveller half expecting to get thrown out and half indignant at such easy luxury. I'd just come from a conversation with a guy who'd been evoking for me the hassle and difficulty – viscerality, even – of running a seaplane operation here at Victoria Falls. We'd been talking about how Pierre Jaunet, despite herculean efforts, had never seemed to have enough money behind his African Catalina, and Mike Honmon had nodded his head in vigorous sympathy: 'I had an overdraft when I started up.' If I had to choose one word to sum up what the term *flying boat* evoked for me, it was *adventure*. The point wasn't the Grand Hotel in Khartoum – it was the lions roaring at night in the zoo next door. It wasn't the Winter Palace Hotel at Luxor – it was Mr Marriott watching the southbound flying boat thunder up the Nile in the last light of the day. It wasn't the Cape Maclear Hotel – it was Mr Spencer suddenly abandoned on a little jetty with a new life ahead of him.

But this place was inert. Perhaps all swish hotels are. Luxury is inert – it means: do nothing. We'll make sure you're not disturbed. *Jungle Junction*; *David Livingstone, I presume* – reduced to vacuous brand-names, heritage industry, history-with-the-history-taken-out. The same kind of indulgent comedy was evident in an endless series of period cartoons hung along the hotel's corridors, depicting 'The English Character'. In the drollest, captioned 'Adaptability to Foreign Conditions', a party of dinner-suited, monocled, pipe-smoking Englishmen sat at a card table in a jungle-clearing playing bridge, while a scarcely clad black native brought a tray of drinks. Yet it was an apathetic, hapless comedy – can't help it; lovably incorrigible. But how many times had all the people who'd contacted me with their flying-boat memories of Africa used the same words: . . . *changed my life* . . . ?

Here is what the interior designer who'd planned the recent refurbishment and remodelling of the Victoria Falls Hotel had had

to say about the brief – a cutting of Graham Viney's article from
HL magazine was framed in the porch:

> . . . we felt we had succeeded in recapturing something of the romance
> of the place. For many, this is now a half-remembered romance, whose
> scents are a muddle of dust and veld, of mown kikuyu, of Cobra polish
> and the watery smells of English cooking. Its night sounds are the shrieks
> of cicadas, the distant hoot of a goods train, the band's persistent foxtrot
> rhythms in the dining room and the constant, thunderous roar of 620,000
> kilolitres per minute pouring into the mighty chasm.
>
> For all the endemic smugness of its colonial domesticity, it is a romance
> conceived, visually at least, on a heroic scale . . .

The architectural expression of that heroic scale Viney goes on
to articulate in the hotel's 'imperially planned and newly restored
main axis' leading all the way through the building from the hall,
past the teak and trophies, through the courtyard and the lounge
with its palms and punkahs, all the way to the graceful prospect of
the bridge across the smoking Falls.

The whole is a splendidly atmospheric, and not uncritical, piece
of rhetoric – and yet, when I come to the end of it I think: so where
is the romance? What *happens*? It's a peculiarly common strain of
English nostalgia: all backdrop, noises off – picturesque, historically
utterly unspecific: a stage-set for no play. But in medieval literature
a romance was an adventure story – *Gawain and the Green Knight*,
or Malory's *Morte d'Arthur* – and the French word for a novel is still
roman. Romance is falling in love: something happening between
two people, casting both lives anew, making every moment count.
That's what I understand by romance, and what, by now, I'd come
to comprehend as the romance of the flying boats. It was the
difference between leisure and idleness – all the difference in the
world. There was never anything idle about flying boats, but when
people commemorated this most leisurely way to travel – during

one short, momentous historical epoch when the world remade itself – what they meant was, *I had time to realize what was happening to me.*

I caught an Air Zimbabwe HS146 back to Harare and had a spare day in the capital. In a city-centre stationers I picked up the new issue of *Aeroplane Monthly* magazine – and read a report of a Catalina flying boat preserved by the Confederate Air Force in Minnesota that had just been tipped over by a hurricane and wrecked. The following morning, waiting to fly out of Zimbabwe, I telephoned my parents in England from an airport payphone. 'You know that Catalina we see at airshows, Graham?' said my father. 'Well, it was doing a display at Southampton over the weekend, flying over the sea, and it got too close to the water and crashed in.' Its flight over Southampton Water had been to promote the city's plans for a huge seaplane festival to mark the millennium. Two passengers, including the Mayor of Southampton, a non-swimmer, had lost their lives, drowned. 'That was the only one, wasn't it?' said my father.

Cavalier

13

Corsairville

So what about Corsairville?

From the moment I first read the story of the flying boat that came down in the Belgian Congo, and flew away ten months later leaving its own little village by the shore of a new lake, I had wanted to go there. I'd wanted to find for myself this forgotten memorial to a forgotten episode. How had this hazard-created settlement grown into a community oblivious of the reason for its foundation? What did the people of the village beside the River Dungu do these days, now they were no longer salvaging a huge flying boat? Where could be further into the back of beyond?

Getting there wouldn't be easy. Indeed, while too many of the wildest places in the world have been brought within range of a charter flight, a package tour and a chain hotel, Corsairville was actually even less accessible than it had been sixty years ago. The Belgian Congo had become the independent Central African nation of Zaire, a vast and ramshackle domain which, under the dictatorship of President Mobutu, had seen much of its colonial-era infrastructure – its metalled roads, its provincial administration, its internal air-services – fall into disrepair and chaos. Not only was there no longer a direct Empire Air Mail service from Britain to Juba, a 150-mile drive away: but access from southern Sudan, the most convenient way in, which the Shorts engineers had taken to get to the River Dungu, was also closed out altogether by the civil war. Overland ingress from the east was further complicated by the guerrilla activities of the unpredictable Lord's Resistance Army in the north-west of Uganda, and by the tribal violence between Tutsis and Hutus on the Zaire–Rwanda border further south. 'That really *is* the heart of darkness,' exclaimed John Hatt, the author of *The Tropical Traveller* handbook, when I told him of my plans. 'It will cost you a great deal of money' (he meant in bribes); 'you *will* get malaria.' The last sounded almost like an order.

But there was a point of contact, for a flying boat's freak visit was not the only unusual thing to have happened here by the bank of the River Dungu. It was the only place in the world where the African elephant had been domesticated. The name of the National Park – one of the remotest and least visited of all – where the last of these tamed elephants survived was Garamba, and for the last ten years it had been run by a courageous couple called Kes and Fraser Smith.

The African elephant, larger and fiercer than its Indian counterpart, is not supposed to be amenable to training. But in the largely forgotten colony of the Belgian Congo the Belgians had, since the last century, been running a quite unique project. The idea of domesticating the African elephant had been King Leopold's, back in 1879 – with the aim of providing what was then effectively his private fiefdom with a team of animals to clear woodlands for planting, pull cultivation machinery, and carry around baggage and officials. His initial attempt to import four domesticated Indian elephants via the east coast of Africa failed, when all of them died of disease or grief. Instead, some five years later, the king sent some of his soldiers into the interior of the Congo and, though the brutal pursuit of young animals by teams of Africans with lassos would cause the deaths of many elephants and men alike, by the 1920s forty African elephants had been successfully trained. Twenty years later – by the time *Corsair* was on the Dungu – there were three times that number in the Congo.

The Garamba National Park had been founded in 1927, and the training school for the African elephants relocated there to a small settlement beside the Dungu. Seventy years later, there were just four trained animals left in the park – the only place in the world where, on the rare visit of a tourist, he or she could have a ride on the back of an African elephant. Nowadays Garamba's extreme inaccessibility had enhanced its value as a wildlife refuge: it was the only place where the northern subspecies of the white rhinoceros survived in the wild – just two dozen animals – and the principal task for Kes and Fraser Smith was to protect these pricelessly rare creatures from poachers. I sent them a letter: they, of all people, would have the best idea how to get to Corsairville.

Then, at the beginning of 1997, Corsairville, and Garamba, were put completely out of bounds. After decades of plundering his country's finances to reduce it to bankruptcy (a slow leaching that only consolidated Zaire's subjection to his rule), an ailing Mobutu was suddenly confronted by an unstoppable rebellion. The uprising started in the east, led by a roly-poly figure in a safari suit called Laurent Kabila. In the civil war that followed, the rebel army rolled south-west across Zaire in miraculously quick time. When the capital, Kinshasa, was certain to fall, Mobutu slunk out of the country, to die of cancer in exile soon after. Zaire received a new name: the Democratic Republic of Congo.

But in the mean time, even though I hadn't yet got there, my destination dematerialized. I realized one day that I no longer believed in Corsairville. At least, my expectations changed: I met retired district officers and colonial officials stationed in Central Africa at that time, I saw some of Africa for myself, and common sense crept up on me. Even at somewhere like Port Bell, where the British flying boats had touched down at least twice a week for some thirteen years, I'd found no trace and no memory of them. The little village by the lake to which the flying boat had given its name – it came to seem as credible as the vision of bygone Africa articulated by the architect who'd renovated the Victoria Falls Hotel. Africa didn't work like that, even if British nostalgia did. It had been a gradual disillusion, and this new negative was the result of recognizing other new positives.

For one thing it was such a *static* picture, this fairy-story village, frozen and ageless. Like those limpid echoes of the steam train's whistle and the band playing the endless foxtrot, or Orwell's sardonic vision of a past England of warm beer and spinsters cycling to church, it was only another backdrop, when in this case the story had already happened. It didn't ring true. Africa taught me that it is never stationary, never memorializes itself. Literally it cannot afford to. The choice is either the future, or decay: the past is no use. The more I dwelled on the myth, the more it seemed to have nothing to do with Africa at all: it seemed the kind of mirror England sometimes held up to itself – benevolent self-regard as a refuge from thought. The image of Corsairville told you about the person regarding it, not the object of their gaze. It was the languid pleasure of looking at something unchallengingly empty. This was supposed to be the appeal of the flying boat – a vague amalgam of luxury, grace, leisure and classiness.

It had nothing to do with Africa in another crucial respect. There was a serious and moving resonance to the legend as it had been passed down through the history books, and I realized now, when I thought of Rosemary Potter, say, recalling the 'gentle giants' circling in above Durban during the war, what it was: the corner-of-a-foreign-field-that-is-for-ever-England. The epitaph of that pastoral image – it needed reshaping only slightly to become the clutch of cottages around the millpond, even the village overlooking its cricket field – said, *I was far away and you brought me something of home.* As I'd journeyed through Africa – Port Bell, Kisumu, Mombasa,

Lake Naivasha – from one former flying-boat stop to the next, finding no relics, no mementoes, no flicker of recognition, the conclusion had become obvious and unavoidable: I was looking in the wrong place. Africa told me about Africa – the driver and conductor of the bus I caught in Harare one day, who communicated over its shattering engine-noise by whistling to each other – *Do you want me to stop here?* (piercing warble through the teeth); *Yes, please* (fluting thrush's lilt). Flying boats didn't matter to Africans. They'd never flown on them. It was an era that had finished and left them nothing. Africa sent me back to Britain for what I was seeking.

In any case, I'd discovered something different from the idle mirror-gaze. I'd heard – from pilots, cabin crew, ground staff and, above all, almost too numerous to mention, passengers on the flying boats – so many stories! They'd all been members of that club, and discovered that it conferred life membership. I could see why the British *wanted* a memorial to the great flying boats. They'd all gone, every last one – cut up with oxyacetylene torches. There was nothing left of them, and something ought to have been. For actually the truth of their history was not to do with idleness or languor, but the very opposite: excitement – thrill, even; now I'd flown on the Pan-Am Mallard I understood and shared that. It was about countless individual destinies, times when history itself had happened to people – when those lives were most intensely lived. That, it seemed to me, was at the root of my longing for a Corsairville to exist. In a way I had proved the existence of a small, forgotten community founded by a strange and extinct kind of boat-plane, a monument of gratitude for its civilizing beneficence. I'd actually found what I was looking for, and I'd found it not in the heart of Africa but in the heart of Kent, on the Dorset coast, in retirement flats in Hampshire and Somerset, and in Egham, in Cambridge, in Maidenhead.

*

RECORD OF

| Date. | Aircraft. | | Engines. | | Journey. | |
	Type.	Markings.	Type.	H.P.	From.	To.
						Brought forward
39. 14/3	C Boat	Corsair	4 R.R.	.	Risumu	P. Bell.
"	"	"	"		P. Bell.	Faradje.
						Carried forward

Still, something was out there. Flying boat *Corsair* had come down at a certain point on the earth's surface: the River Dungu, near a town called Faradje. You couldn't eradicate a set of coordinates. Months after I'd written to Kes and Fraser Smith – when I'd just given up on hearing back – I got a reply. The civil war had enforced their withdrawal from Garamba: finally, they wrote now, they were starting to make progress in getting back there to pick up the pieces. There was a phone number in Nairobi for them when they weren't in the Congo: as soon as I was installed in my hotel in the Kenyan capital I called it, and was amazed to hear a quiet, composed voice saying, 'This is Kes . . .'

They lived south-west of the city, in Langata, and I took a cab out to them that evening, a little grinding Nissan with Chris de Burgh's 'Lady in Red' playing on the radio and a driver who, as soon as I'd got in, asked if I wanted to buy his sister. We drove for miles, crashing over speed bumps, fields and trees disappearing into deep darkness. Eventually the way ahead got bumpy, and when it seemed we'd reached the end of the road the driver flatly refused to get out and check if this single gap in the trees might be a gateway.

FLIGHTS.

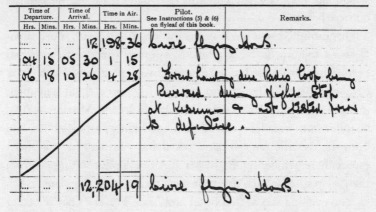

We nosed in to a clamour of barking dogs, and I swear a cowled figure approached the car, the face invisible, carrying a longbow. And then a slightly clipped voice was saying, 'You must be Graham,' and Kes and Fraser's English friend John Watkin took me inside their spacious, cosy house, an open fire burning in the living room.

There were five of us gathered for supper, including Gerard, an American naturalist, and Kes and Fraser's young son, Dungu, named after the river that formed the Garamba National Park's southern boundary, who swung a stubby handmade club and chattered excitedly to me about his new craze for golf; Chyulu, their daughter, was at a disco for the evening. While Kes was getting the meal Fraser, a hale, rosy-cheeked southern African, told me how he'd first come across the story of *Corsair*. A while back he'd gone to Canada for a wildlife conference, and during his stay taken several trips out into remoter territory by seaplane. Back at Garamba, he'd been talking to one of his African guards down by the banks of the Dungu. 'You know,' Fraser had remarked, 'I should get a floatplane' – he could fly in and land it right there on the river. 'That'd be a new thing for round here, wouldn't it!'

'Oh, no,' his guard had replied. 'We've had a really big one landing on here before . . .'

Fortuitously, just a few months earlier, they'd heard more about *Corsair*'s sojourn on the Dungu. Missionary friends of theirs had been visiting from the United States – two generations, Herb Cook Senior and Junior, father and son, who between them had spent many years in the Congo with the African Inland Mission at Aba, 50 miles from Faradje – and Herb Cook Senior, it turned out, had been there at the same time as the flying boat and her salvagers, especially remembering the Imperial Airways pilot setting off from the Aba resthouse each day to inspect progress on the plane.

'You couldn't stay at that hotel now,' said Fraser. 'They're taking the roof and bricks off it.' Just to drive from Aba to Faradje these days would be three-quarters of a day's expedition. Kes had rejoined us: they had some friends who ran an insurance company in Zaire, she said. In former times, they'd told her, you used to be able to order any make of car in Aba – there was actually a Chevrolet dealership there – have it sent up the river to Juba and driven across, and they'd insure it for you in Aba. 'Aba's now a wreck,' said Fraser.

He was hoping to fly out to Garamba in their light plane again the next week. It had been a slow and arduous process re-establishing their presence in the Congo – building relations with the new government, for whom wildlife and the environment were far from a high priority, and starting to reconstruct Garamba's infrastructure. The bright news, however, was that the park's white-rhinoceros population had survived the war better than anyone had expected. Fraser had recently done an aerial survey and counted twenty-five animals. At least four calves appeared to have been born. But all their vehicles had been stolen during the civil war; rebel soldiers had been billeted at the park headquarters for months after Kabila had come to power; their own house, the visitor huts, the park's records and sup-plies – all had been looted and wrecked. Everything they needed to enable them to work there for a few days at a time had to be flown in – there was no room on the little plane for passengers like me.

According to Fraser there was only one way I might get to Faradje: a little airline called T M K ran a twice-weekly commercial flight from Entebbe in Uganda to Bunia in the Democratic Republic of Congo, and then I'd need to charter a light plane from the Congo arm of M A F, the relief airline that flew aid workers and missionaries around, to take me as far as the Garamba airstrip at Nagero. But that would still leave me an uneasy distance away from Faradje, where the flying boat had come down. 'We'll give you all the help we can,' said Fraser – but the best suggestion he could come up with for the 6 miles from Nagero to Corsairville was a push-bike.

It was time for Kes to go and collect her daughter from the disco; my taxi – the driver had obviously decided that if he went away he'd never find his way back – was still waiting outside. There were two other people I might talk to, said Kes. Steve and Debbie Wolcott were American missionaries with the African Inland Mission who'd been running a guest-house in Nairobi since the civil war had forced them to leave Zaire – but in 1994 they'd been part of a team that had gone to work in Faradje. She looked up their number in her address book – try them while you're in town, she said.

The missionary arrived on a motorbike. Steve Wolcott strode into the lobby of the Hotel Ambassadeur, beard and black leather jacket, a man with a strong, stern voice. On the phone he'd sounded a little dour, grim even, but as soon as we'd sat down in the restaurant, had a couple of sodas and I'd shown him the photographs I'd brought of *Corsair* wallowing on the Dungu he let out a shout of laughter. 'Oh, man! I had no *idea* it was this big! I mean, it's not much of a river . . .' He couldn't take his eyes off the pictures: the Empire flying boat half-submerged in the mud; beached on the bank with a big rent in its hull; engines being floated upriver on a raft. The

thought of this huge thing, *there*, where he used to live: he didn't
have to tell me he was amazed. Every so often he would break off
what he was saying, gaze again, and just laugh. 'The impression *I*
got,' he said, 'was that it was something to do with the war. I'd
figured it was some twin-engine thing – but now I can see. It was
like a . . . civilian transport plane!'

Steve himself had grown up in the Belgian Congo, subsequently
Zaire and the Democratic Republic of Congo, and the team of
missionaries he'd been part of had first gone to Faradje in 1992 to
survey it for a possible mission. Historically the town had been a
district administrative centre for the Belgian government, and it was
still a 'main territories office' for the Congo, though the government
buildings hadn't been maintained or repaired since colonial times –
'the wood's all rotting,' said Steve, 'the termites are eating everything,
the bats are in.' These days, he reckoned, there must be between
eight and ten thousand people living in the area: Faradje had a big
market, shops, a girls' school, a maternity hospital founded by
Belgian nuns, and a big Catholic church. The strong Catholic
tradition in Faradje was the reason why the African Inland Mission,
a Protestant organization, had originally centred its activities around
Aba, to the north-east, but the accession of a new local chief, who
didn't share his father's antipathy to Protestantism, had opened the
way for AIM to try again, and they'd begun to construct a mission
there in 1994. They'd had to leave at the end of 1996 when war broke
out; Steve still hoped to go back.

This was how he'd first heard the story of the flying boat at
Faradje. 'One of our missionaries suggested that we put a hydro plant
on the river.' You'd struggle not to feel a western developed-world
smugness at such an idea, I thought – clean hydro-electric power
to bring light! refrigerators! computers! to the town. 'And when the
question of it came up with the people there they said, "Oh, this
river's been dammed before." A plane crashed there. But I kept

questioning: "Did a plane *really* crash here?" So they told me: the first time they tried to take off without damming the river. And then, they told me, they came back and dammed the river. I think that story – everybody in the area knows that story, or at least the older people do.

'I have seen where they dammed the river,' Steve added. 'From a distance, not up close. I was just taking this trail one day and these guys I was with said, "Oh, over there, that's where there used to be a dam."' Remnants were still visible of where it had been keyed into each bank. 'I didn't take much of a look . . .' He was hoping to go back to Faradje in the fall to visit his church friends there – driving in overland in his Toyota Landcruiser would take a minimum of three days: if I stayed in touch he'd be happy for me to join along. 'I'd *love* to come out with you and take a proper look,' said Steve – 'now I know what's really out there.'

But Steve Wolcott didn't get back to Faradje in the fall of 1998, and neither did I, and we still haven't. I flew on south from Kenya to Malawi and Zimbabwe, and then back to London, picked up a copy of that morning's *Guardian* at Heathrow and opened it on the Piccadilly line train jogging back into the city to read – the timing could not have been more exquisite – that the Congo was again at war.

This time it was much worse. Kabila's government had steadily squandered the credit it had come to power with, both with its neighbours and its own citizens, and now it faced rebellion from an alliance of all those it had offended, from its own soldiers, whose wages had continued to go unpaid, to factions remaining loyal to the memory of Mobutu. The crucial difference now was that even the Democratic Republic of Congo's gigantic territory could not contain the conflict. Neighbouring Uganda and Rwanda, their patience with Kabila used up after he had failed to suppress guerrilla movements attacking them from inside Congo, were aiding the rebels; Angola, Chad and even Zimbabwe, fearing that Kabila's fall would destabilize the entire region, were sending their own troops in to back him up. On both sides in the civil war all this outside intervention led to an extreme suspicion of outsiders. Several parties of foreign soldiers were taken hostage. Once again western embassies advised all their citizens to leave.

'Greetings from Nairobi!' read Steve Wolcott's e-mail in November 1998:

> As you know, the war in the Congo continues even as I write. It appears that this will be a long-drawn-out war with possibly no definitive winners. Although Eastern Congo, including Faradje, are securely in the hands of the 'rebels', we have been told that anyone entering Eastern Congo will be considered 'persona non grata'. Up until the present we have not been willing to risk being considered as such and have been advised by our church partners to not set foot in 'rebel'-held territory. We are honoring that.
>
> I cannot tell you when the situation may allow for us to make a trip to Faradje . . .

So that was that. Corsairville would have to be left to the imagination, just as it had been for all those historians. But what had amazed Steve — and those of us gathered for supper that night at Kes and Fraser's — were those pictures: the actual photographic record of *Corsair* having landed on the Dungu and, even more miraculously, managed to fly away again. 'It's enormous!' Gerard the naturalist had exclaimed. 'How did they ever get that off there?' How indeed? Seeing through the myth had told me that the story was the story. *There* was the romance — and one that led back to Britain just as the flying boat herself eventually had. Who had taken part? How on earth had they brought it off? What had actually happened?

14

'Thee Put It In There . . .'

Following the trail that led back sixty years to the true story of *Corsair* at Faradje took, on and off, seven years. The British Airways archive out at Hounslow turned up a file devoted to the flying boat – and the then-archivist, Ron Wilson, had a hunch that he'd once seen a photograph of the little village built by the new lake. Where, tantalizingly, never came back to him. Then one day in the spring of 1991 a spread of superb photographs of the episode appeared in an aeroplane magazine – the flying boat stuck in thick mud beside a big rock the shape of an avocado pit; engines being towed upriver on a raft of oil drums; three Africans in a boat running a hose from the hull to pump the water out.

They'd been taken by a member of the second salvage party. His name was Alf Cowling, and I found him in a big, gaunt house in Salisbury from which his current ill-health was forcing a move, a correct, slightly stern man with a shock of white hair. He had a whole album of magnificent pictures, though his recollections of Faradje, like that fastidiously preserved photo collection, were those of the engineer, not the whimsical adventurer. But another of his salvage colleagues was still alive, he told me – 'he's now *Sir* Roy,' said Mr Cowling – and *Who's Who* led me to Hertfordshire, and a superb raconteur.

From there came an address in Somerset, which put me in touch with the leader of the first salvage effort, and Somerset led to Wiltshire – and along the way other photographs turned up in the albums and collections of people who also unexpectedly turned out to have dropped into the Belgian Congo to lend a brief hand. There were even supposed to be in existence not one but two ciné films capturing the episode. The saga of *Corsair* hadn't quite receded beyond the pale of living history. But, just as amazingly, it seemed to be a story the protagonists hadn't been asked to tell before. I'll tell the tale in the order in which it all happened, and begin with the person I actually met last.

Peter Newnham was the first of the Shorts salvage team out there. In April 1939 he'd been repairing a Sunderland down at Calshott, when the order came to leave for Africa. 'I thought, "Here goes"' – and he caught an Empire boat out to the Sudan. Arriving at Juba in the afternoon several days later, he was taken to a guest-house. 'There was nobody about,' he remembered, 'so I opened a door, and I thought, there's a dog in the room. But it wasn't a dog – it was a lion cub. So I shut that door quickly.'

Nearly sixty years later Mr Newnham was living quietly on a housing estate outside Amesbury in Wiltshire – he'd moved there after the war when Shorts had been testing their new naval monoplane, the Sturgeon, at nearby Boscombe Down. Since the death of his wife it was just him and his cats; a devout Christian, despite a stroke a short while back he still regularly read the lesson at his local church. His cats plumped themselves on the back of the sofa, quizzical and proprietorial, and had to be scraped lovingly off the table as we talked.

He'd soon made friends with the mischievous lion club, which used to inch its way along narrow window-ledges 'with great big paws as big as my hand', said Mr Newnham. 'But he did like to get hold of your hat, and if you left it around he'd run off with it and chew it up.' Then a driver took him on to the border with the Belgian Congo, some 150 miles distant, where the Shorts team was to stay in the small frontier town of Aba's solitary hotel. Ian Henderson, who'd flown out from Southampton in 1938 on *Corsair* to return to his job with the Public Works at Juba, and read me his absorbed young man's letter about the voyage, stayed at the same Aba resthouse one day on his way over to view the salvage site. 'Very Belgian' was his verdict. 'Sanitary-wise, it stank.' From here it would be a further hour's drive to the flying boat *Corsair*. On the way to Aba they ran into a cloud of locusts so dense that the driver had to stop the car.

Faradje. In *Merchant Airmen* Dudley Barker had wondered rather magnificently why so desolate a spot should ever have been dignified with a name. (Not that it ever had been by his presence, either.) But this was where the flying boat lay. 'Anything that could irritate the skin and bite you was flying around there,' said Peter Newnham. 'It wasn't a very friendly environment.' *Corsair* had come down in the quietest corner of one of Africa's largest countries, administered by its Belgian masters with a combination of slumbrous neglect (for the British at Juba it was a handy source of cheap cross-border wine) and iron repression. 'We ran the Sudan on the basis of trying to do good and make it better,' Ian Henderson asserted to me: 'the Belgians ran the Congo as a colony.' They'd built roads – though the route from Aba to Faradje was for part of the way merely a pair of tyre tracks through the long grass – but little else. Mining companies had been granted concessions to exploit the Congo's valuable mineral wealth of gold and diamonds; education and health provision were left to the efforts of (mostly Catholic) missionaries. South-east of where the flying boat languished, along the border with Uganda, the Congo landscape became lush and mountainous, the volcanic Virunga range home to the rare and famous mountain gorillas. South-west, towards the interior, was dense rain forest. But this north-eastern frontier, abutting the Sudan, was flat waving scrub, and marsh where the River Dungu inundated the flood plain during the rainy season.

'Frames nos. 12–25 inclusive extensively damaged including keel plating, formes, stringers and floor supports for 24 feet,' read the report from Imperial Airways' Central Africa staff on the accident on the River Dungu. In plain language, Captain Alcock's misadventure had torn the bottom out. Either whole new sections for the hull of the flying boat would have to be transported, somehow, all the way out from Rochester in Kent, or, ran the telegram, 'Only alternative Shorts repair gang carry out complete repair.'

Shorts estimated that that would take about six weeks, but they'd sent the leader of their salvage team, Hugh Gordon, out for a brief survey. Having returned to England fleetingly to confirm that, yes, it could be done but, yes, it would be extremely difficult, he had his team assembled at Aba by 18 April 1939. 'It appears the conditions under which Mr Gordon and his men will be working will be very exacting' (Shorts' Works Manager, Mr Jackson, wrote to Imperial Airways), 'and for this reason Mr Gordon has been instructed that if he finds the men are not able to cope . . . he is to have no hesitation in giving the job up.' Already, between March and April, the estimated duration of the task had stretched to three months.

I found the pretty cottage where Hugh Gordon now lived all on its own along a winding leafy lane in Somerset. From here, dapper and sprightly at eighty-six, he still motored around England with his wife, regularly revisiting Cambridge, where they'd met during the war, Hugh managing the Shorts factory that repaired battle-damaged Stirling bombers, Irene a driver for the Ministry of Aircraft Production. After the war he'd followed Shorts' managing director to their great flying-boat rivals, Saunders–Roe, on the south coast, subsequently to design and build Wasp and Scout helicopters. Then he'd worked on Saunders–Roe's development of the hovercraft, before going back to helicopters and retiring as the Sales Director of Westlands here in Somerset.

Even before the first Empire boat was launched in 1937, Shorts were sending him across the world. In 1936 he'd been to Burma, to deliver a small Scion Senior seaplane to a former Imperial Airways captain who was setting up the Irrawaddy Flotilla Company. The five-week sea voyage on which he accompanied the crated-up craft was so stormy that at least once the ship had to hove to, and the crew feared that several hundred-ton steam locomotives lashed to the deck would topple over the side. When, finally, Hugh got to unpack the crates in Rangoon to reassemble the Scion, he told me, 'I thought: they've sent the wrong plane!' The order had been for ten cane seats in the passenger cabin – but these seats were red plush! Only slowly did it dawn: water had penetrated the packing cases during the stormy sea passage, oxidized the metal seat frames, and a luxuriant red fungus had grown over every seat . . . Until the seaplane was fully tested, Hugh stayed on to fly with Captain Phillips, whose habit of urinating into a Player's cigarette tin and emptying the contents out of the window gave the Irrawaddy's passengers an alarming sensation of streaking rain – though still less alarming than the alternative procedure (also tried) of leaving the sensitive controls of the Scion temporarily pilotless while he and Hugh blundered to change places so he could visit the toilet at the back.

In the two years following, Imperial Airways' new fleet of Empire flying boats kept Hugh very busy. March 1937 had found him on a French hillside at Ouroux, near Lyon, picking through the wreckage of *Capricornus*, the first Empire boat crash, not only for parts to salvage but to recover £10,000-worth of gold bullion that was being carried in great secrecy. He'd repaired wing-floats and a main spar at Marseille, collision damage with a submarine at Naples, and found the Imperial Airways traffic staff at heat-swamped Sharjah in the Persian Gulf, just an isolated desert fort in the days before oil production, eager for each evening flying boat to arrive because it was bringing ice for their gin and tonic.

'It so happened,' Hugh told me, 'that before the Congo accident I was offered another job at Shorts. It would have been a promotion. And I said no – I didn't want it. I found a lot of salvage work interesting, and I felt that I'd like to do a big job – I'd always mentioned Africa. Little did I ever *dream* it was coming along like that . . .' He was still only twenty-six.

'Well, there was nothing there, really,' he remembered of where he'd found *Corsair* marooned. The Belgian district commissioner lived somewhere not far away; he supposed there must have been a few native huts near by. '*Precious little.* It was very wild.' Gordon had five men commuting with him from Aba to Faradje in their two Ford station-wagons. Besides him and Peter Newnham there was a young cockney riveter called Blake who'd crawled out of an Empire boat wing-tip in Naples to introduce himself, then Hern and Robinson, and Howard Rayner – they'd already been out to places like the Persian Gulf together on other repair missions. 'It was a good core of people I could rely on,' said Hugh. 'We grew up together, as a matter of fact.' Imperial Airways' wireless operator Dangerfield, who'd been on *Corsair* when she came down, travelled over from Juba to operate the radio set in the cockpit and maintain contact with the outside world. No telephony, just Morse messages, and everything having to be routed through Juba, and a recalcitrant generator to keep going to power the flying boat's batteries.

'The hardest thing was digging it out of the mud,' said Peter Newnham. His photographs show it dried and crazed up to the top of the hull. Captain Alcock had got *Corsair* to the bank of the Dungu after hitting the rock, and there she had wallowed, half-submerged in the swamp, and stuck fast. Hugh laughed when he thought of 'John' Alcock. ' "What maddens me, Gordon," he used to say, "is that this is the first aircraft I've ever damaged . . ." Of course, he'd forgotten the one before that, and the one before that . . .' *Coriolanus*'s heavy landing at Marseille, which had pushed the wing-float up into the main spar – that had been Alcock. Gordon planned to construct a coffer dam between the craft and the river, inside which the water could be pumped out, but first he went to see the assistant district commissioner and got him to hire a gang of native men, each at about a penny a day. Hoisting sheets of corrugated iron piled with earth on to their heads to carry away, they helped to dig *Corsair* slowly out. 'When I say we reclaimed land,' said Hugh, 'we did, in a way.' All the water was pumped out of the barrage with small diaphragm pumps – by hand. 'It was a laborious job, it really was. Every morning more water had seeped in.'

Then they had to try and get the flying boat up on to the riverbank where they could work on it. To position hydraulic jacks underneath to lift it on to its beaching wheels, they had to bring in huge logs of ironwood – 'terribly heavy, it only just floats' – dig down further around the hull and, as Hugh put it, 'build up a kind of mineshaft – wood, fill in, wood, fill in – until we could lift the whole thing'. Then, with ironwood also laid down to the water's edge to form a slipway, perhaps a hundred Africans, as one of Peter Newnham's pictures shows, all laid hold of a rope tied to *Corsair*'s tail, and hauled her out of the Dungu.

But now other members of the cast emerge from the surrounding bush. The surviving engineers' memories reveal how the small team's vulnerability gradually drew in, or at least came to require, the assistance of the few other westerners dotted about this empty territory. 'There was a man by the name of Lacovitch,' remembered Hugh. 'He was a very clever chap. Out there they had to work out their own salvation, and he did all sorts of wonderful jobs. I liked Lacovitch.' An Italian engineer for the Belgian SHUN company, which managed the hotel at Aba and also ran lorries to the gold-mines south-east at Watsa, and exporting coffee to the Sudan, Lacovitch was in charge of their workshops and trading post. In addition he made the tombstones for the local community, and Hugh also remembered him cutting a lorry in two to install extra gearboxes. Lacovitch helped out the Shorts team with their water pumps and on metal-working jobs, and extended Hugh a regular invitation to take the nightly dose of quinine with him and his wife – washed down with the host's South African whisky.

'Meester Gordon,' said Lacovitch one day when Hugh went to visit him, 'you come into the magasin. I'd better tell you,' he confided inside his store, 'the natives here, now and then you have to give them a shampoo. But don't let anyone see you! It's against the law. If you get them alone and give them a shampoo they won't go out and tell the others – they're too ashamed. But watch your hand! – because their teeth stick out, some of them.' Hugh demonstrated Lacovitch's advice for me: not like this – back of the hand across the face – but like this: flat of the hand; otherwise you'd bark your knuckles ... Every morning Lacovitch had a line-up of all his people, called out their names and, if someone was misbehaving, his way of doing things was to have them in the back of the magasin and give them a shampoo. 'That was Lacovitch's expression,' said Hugh. 'A shampoo. Well, you asked me about salvaging, but there you are!'

The native Africans spoke no English, the salvage engineers no Bangala, and one day the task of marshalling the large gang to try and dig the flying boat out of the mud had suddenly seemed insuperably difficult to a non-Bangala-speaker. 'You know they don't understand,' said Hugh, 'but you still shout ...' Then he realized that they seemed to be doing what he wanted. Gordon looked up from the large hole in the ground he was down in to see a pair of rimless spectacles and a broad grin under a solar topee. 'We heard the flying boat was down here,' said the man, who spoke with an American accent, and had been unobtrusively instructing the Africans in Bangala. He introduced himself as the Reverend

Harry Stam, the senior missionary at the African Inland Mission the other side of Aba. Gordon climbed up the bank covered in mud, and shook hands.

'A very sincere man,' recalled Hugh – the Gordons and the Stams stayed in touch for many years after the war. Harry Stam and his wife had three sons, who Hugh remembered being put to bed on the verandah at night in 'rabbit hutches' to protect them from leopards and other marauding animals. The Bangala-speaking minister, friendly and outgoing, was a godsend down at the flying boat – Peter Newnham remembers his strong voice getting the African team singing together as they tried to pull *Corsair* free. But also – 'Oh my God,' recalled Hugh, 'he served us *food*.' Since their arrival in the Belgian Congo the team's diet had even extended to snake sandwiches. Harry Stam had the young salvage engineers to dinner, sat them down on the grassy bank at the end of his garden with his family and served them ice cream. It was also the first time Hugh Gordon had ever eaten corn on the cob.

I found one tiny and inconsequential historical reference to Stam, Rev. Harry, in the index of *The New York Times*. Four years earlier, in November 1935, the newspaper reported, 'The New Jersey authorities were unable to find a law covering the use of his Belgian Congo driver's licence.' I never met the man, but when I dwell on the detail I imagine the American missionary returning from Darkest Africa, amazed there should be any doubt over whether the damp-swollen documents that permitted him to drive dirt roads through the bush should also let him get behind the wheel of a Packard in downtown Newark! He'd come from a place where you had to work out your own salvation. Harry Stam's missionaries had stepped in where the Belgian government had failed, and ran local schools, also training African teachers to set up their own 'mud and wattle' schools in the bush. They travelled the bush in a truck painted with biblical quotations, and ran a hospital, too. 'Bear in mind, it's such a long time ago now, and I was young,' Hugh mused, 'but I met some *wonderful* people.' In the mission hospital a surgeon called Klein-schmidt operated under paraffin lamplight at an enamel table, on native Africans suffering from elephantiasis so severe that a man might have to wheel his swollen testicles there on a handcart. People would walk 200 miles from the north to reach Dr Kleinschmidt's hospital, the Revd Herb Cook Senior remembered – I'd caught up with him living in retirement in Kentucky: they'd cut notches into their walking sticks to keep count of how many days they'd walked. Christian evangelism had to contend with local pygmy tribes among which cannibalism still lingered. They wouldn't eat human flesh, Peter Newnham told me, but they'd boil it up and wear a small pot of the grease round their necks to dip their finger into and lick when they went hunting.

And there is one more figure in the landscape, who seems to have stepped straight out of a Joseph Conrad narrative. Hugh didn't think much about his first encounter with the handsome Belgian who showed up at the salvage site and asked if he'd write him a letter in English to send off for parts for his Triumph motorbike. But soon after, there was a commotion at the resthouse in Aba. Batten down the hatches!, Hugh was told: de Voss is back! The Belgian on the Triumph was an official with the health authority studying the tsetse fly out in the bush – Hugh and his team stopped their cars one day before a crowd of people and found the centre of attention was de Voss, seriously ill with fever. From these excursions, it appeared, he was prone to hit town and smash the place up. One image had never left Hugh: de Voss being carried through the bush on a litter, an African woman walking behind, naked except for a trilby hat, and carrying a tin kettle. Above all, de Voss and his mistress are responsible for introducing a note of magnificent, Byronic scandal to the graceful world of the Imperial Airways flying boat. As a mark of gratitude to M. Appermans, the district commissioner who had been first on the scene when *Corsair* had come down on the Dungu, Imperial Airways had arranged free flights to Europe for him and his wife. The couple were to break their journey from Faradje to Juba, where they'd pick up the northbound flying boat, at the Aba hotel. And when the proprietor's wife showed the dignitaries to their room, they opened the door to find de Voss's black mistress installed in bed there . . .

'At last we have the machine on firm ground,' Gordon was able to write to Shorts by 9 May. Cleaning out the inside of the punctured and flooded hull, in order that repairs could commence, was not a pleasant task. 'With the mud and stagnant water, not to mention dead toads etc. the stench was intolerable.' Already two of his men were sick – when he wrote this letter one had been in bed with fever for four days. Frequently they endured terrible thunderstorms, and Hugh Gordon had to fit earth wires all over the flying boat.

But now at least the engineers could get to work. 'The other repairs had just been wing-floats,' said Peter Newnham: here they were having to replace a whole section of the hull – 26 feet of it. Back at the Rochester factory they would have had the benefit of pneumatic-powered drills, and electric light to illuminate their work inside the aircraft. Out at Faradje the only electric tools they had broke down, and every single rivet hole had to be drilled by hand – one African also employed at just a penny a day merely to sit and blow away the swarf as Peter Newnham drilled. A great deal of the jointing compound Duralac went into making the rebuilt planing bottom absolutely watertight again. Howard Rayner struck up a relationship with one local man Hugh told me he'd recognize if he met him today in Yeovil high street – who, like several of the Africans, used to borrow his metal files and sit on top of the flying boat filing his teeth to a point. 'What about a round of golf this afternoon?' would come Rayner's disembodied voice from inside the hull; 'are you all right for eighteen holes?' and the man would grin and hand Rayner the hammer when he'd asked for the hacksaw.

On 22 May they had a visit from Major Herbert Brackley, Imperial Airways' Air Superintendent. 'Shorts' men are doing magnificent repair work,' he wrote in his diary, 'under trying conditions of heat, humidity, flies, mosquitoes and hornets. I've had my full share of bites from a small black beetle-shaped fly with a sting like a hornet. I've never met this type before and I don't want to again!' Brackley returned towards the end of June, with the repairs now nearing completion, already pondering how to get *Corsair* off the Dungu again.

At first sight [he wrote in his Memorandum], the reach does not give the impression that it is 100% safe for take-off because of overhanging grass, but a close examination of the banks along each side . . . for over 800 yards reveals the possibility of widening the river by cutting the elephant grass and the few trees and stumps which now form obstructions. I am satisfied [Brackley concluded] that the reach can be made safe for a take-off provided *Corsair* is handled by an experienced and skilful pilot and taken off as light as possible.

The following week, Captain John Alcock got a letter from the manager of the Empire Division detailing him to report to Hythe for some test flights in an Empire boat. The final proviso of Brackley's recommendations now throbs with irony, but no one seemed to notice then. Remarkably, perhaps, the same flying-boat captain originally responsible for *Corsair*'s plight had now been chosen to retrieve her. As a contemporary Imperial Airways trainee recalls it, the airline's insurance agent decided the issue. 'Thee put it in there,' was Captain Lamplugh's blunt, even retributive, verdict: 'thee can pick it up again.' Alcock's brief was to essay take-off runs from Southampton Water, simulating the likely loading weight, and ascertain the length of river he would need. 'As far as is humanly possible,' ran Alcock's instructions, 'the take-off of *Corsair* must be a practical certainty from every point of view.'

It is easy, at this historical distance, to malign Captain Alcock, of whom contemporary memories are warmly fond. Peter Colmore, then Imperial Airways' Traffic Officer at Kisumu, *Corsair*'s nightstop before her vagrant last leg, evokes a big, bluff north-country man with a florid face and ginger hair – 'great tombstone teeth, a fruity way of talking, always cheerful'. The genial Alcock would always do a circle over Lake Victoria, the most romantic announcement of arrival, before coming in to touch down. 'Very jovial and easy to get on with,' confirms Peter Newnham; 'always a crack.' There are no half-measures in aviation: risk-benefit analysis, playing the percentages, is not acceptable policy – and when the subject in question is an almost new flying boat desperately needed for service, which has just spent months under repair at extreme financial and human cost . . . But perhaps one can still feel a little sorry for Alcock, saddled with his implacable brief. How could anyone, unless comfortably cocooned behind a desk at Imperial Airways' Victoria HQ, envision circumstances under which getting an 80-foot-long seaplane, among the biggest aircraft of its time, off a minor African river scarcely wider than its wing-span, would be 'a practical certainty from every point of view'?

Out at Faradje, the repair of *Corsair* complete, the assistant district commissioner provided a large contingent of native prisoners to haul her down into the water for launching, who arrived shackled around their necks in a chain-gang, roughly treated by their guards. Meanwhile, 'I have no hesitation in saying,' Alcock was blithely reporting from Hythe on 3 July, that, provided all the trees and pampas grass along the take-off run were cleared away, and the height of the river rose to allow a draught of 4½ feet below the flying boat's datum line, 'the taking-off of RMA *Corsair* from Faradje offers few difficulties and should be carried out quite safely.'

But the imminent summer rains did not come. Instead of rising, the River Dungu was falling. 'I remember the assistant district commissioner coming down,' said Hugh Gordon, 'and saying, "Usually at this time of year it's not down there, it's up here."' Imperial Airways' Central Africa manager, Vernon Crudge, sent an unequivocal telex from Juba back to Hythe: 'It is not considered that a take-off should be attempted until there is a further rise in the river or until further steps are taken to achieve the same effect.' Nevertheless, Alcock and his first officer departed for Central Africa. At Faradje, he and the Shorts team waited. Still no rain.

'So, John Alcock decided he must have a go,' said Hugh. His team removed every superfluous component possible from *Corsair* until they'd brought the weight down to 13 tons – a lot of the internal fittings, like the porcelain hand-basins, he gave to Harry Stam's mission. Back at Aba the night before the planned take-off, Alcock told Gordon he was still worried about that rock he'd hit near the port bank five months earlier. Although it had been blasted by engineers from the Kilo Moto gold-mines at Watsa, its stump was still only 14 inches below the surface of the river. Hugh Gordon assured the pilot that, within the planned take-off course, the flying boat would be up on its step and planing by the time she reached it – and capable of clearing it without tearing her bottom out again. But Alcock, who had only collided with it accidentally while trying to avoid another near the starboard bank, understandably demanded further precautions. So the team staked out the rock with saplings driven into the river bed, and threaded a cord flagged with white streamers between them to mark the danger area. Gordon and another Shorts engineer would stand at intervals along the bank – 'I know this sounds crazy,' said Hugh – to signal frantically to Alcock if he drifted too near. Alcock worked out a take-off path that would leave 20 feet between the port float and the riverbank, and 20 feet between the starboard side of the craft and the rock. He checked that both wing-tips would stay well clear of the banks.

The night of 13 July 1939 it rained for three hours, and the river rose 6 inches. The take-off was set for early the next morning. By now the bank of the Dungu was busy with activity: an Imperial Airways maintenance team had come over from Kisumu in Kenya to overhaul and run up the engines; Shell oil-company staff had taken charge of the refuelling. Hugh Gordon went to the mission hospital and fetched young Blake, who was ill with malaria, so he'd be able to watch *Corsair* fly away. The weather first thing on the fourteenth was cool and damp; the river current 2½ knots. Plenty of time – and space – for all the one-armed paper-hanging if you had the whole of Southampton Water or Lake Victoria ahead of you, but with the speed of the river here, its extreme narrowness, and a pronounced bend a little further down, it was vital to have the flying boat trimmed – stable and straight on the water – before it started moving. So once *Corsair* had been manœuvred to where she would start her run, a line was attached to the hook on her tail and tied to a tree behind her on the bank. That way Alcock could balance the throttles on the engines without the torque causing her to drift, and get the ailerons and rudder right before the river carried her downstream.

At 0605 GMT everything was ready. Hugh Gordon took up his signalling position on the left bank. 'Where I was standing,' he told me, 'I could only see the top of the flying boat – just part of the wing. I could see her lifting – even with the line astern she starts lifting up – and released, and now I could see more of the flying boat.' When Alcock had opened up the engines *Corsair* had answered well, and within 50 yards she was already coming up on to the step.

'And then I realized,' said Hugh, 'something was wrong. He wasn't doing what I thought he was going to do. Instead of coming over here' (to pass the dreaded rock on the left), 'he started going straight on.' About 120 yards into his take-off run – still well short of the rock – Alcock found *Corsair* swinging fiercely to starboard. He tried to correct it with the port throttle, but the narrowness of the river left no room for manœuvre. The starboard float was already hitting the right bank, and Alcock had no option but to cut the engines. Gordon watched the flying boat settle in the water, the machine's nose swung into the bank, and *Corsair* hit the very same rock Alcock had at least managed to avoid three and a half months earlier.

'That was bad luck, wasn't it?' Hugh remarked to me in a light, rueful way. The flying boat's first officer had poked his head up through the top hatch to call out, 'It was the outer engine!' Imperial Airways' trilby-hatted chief engineer from Kisumu had come running up blustering, 'He can't bloody well blame this on me!' Now the captain had torn a hole in *Corsair*'s other side. Young Blake, who'd got out of his hospital bed to watch the take-off, had just cried.

'Three months' hard work,' Hugh Gordon wrote back to Shorts, 'destroyed within the short space of nine seconds.' *Corsair* now had a new hole in her hull 11 feet long. A blurry photograph of Peter Newnham's, taken just after the impact, shows a forlorn white craft nose down like a child's paper dart at the edge of the river. Another, side-on, view: the rock on which the craft has newly foundered is huge – almost as high as the hatch in its side, nearly snagging the port inner prop. Around the flying boat, just high matted grass, and the still mirror behind, and the empty bush beyond.

'As you can imagine,' Hugh told me wryly, 'Imperial Airways weren't too pleased . . .' Recriminations followed swiftly. Their Central Africa manager, having checked with the pilot on the height of the river, declared that a take-off had been attempted in defiance of every instruction. Captain Alcock decided, in his own words, to wash his hands of the whole affair. Hugh Gordon never saw him again.

The cause of the second accident – not that, in the immediate aftermath, it really mattered to anyone involved – was debatable. Peter Newnham thinks it was a loss of power on *Corsair*'s starboard engines. Then again, it might have been the current of 2½ knots running across the River Dungu just after its bend that pulled the flying boat off course – and though Alcock had originally undertaken not to attempt a take-off until the river had been dammed to raise the water-level, he'd subsequently realized that a dam might only speed up the current, and thought better of the idea. In any case, before a new colloquium on how Imperial Airways were ever going to get their valuable Empire boat off this minor Central African river, *Corsair* was going to have to be mended all over again. And now there was more trouble. The river, with predictably perverse timing, had at last started to rise.

At least after the first accident the flying boat had been left stuck fast in the mud, safe there until the repair effort was ready to dig her out. Now she was marooned on the opposite side of the river from the temporary slipway, her hull flooded through another big leak in her side, and the damaged area that needed mending sinking further and further under water. It was a thoroughly unpleasant situation for a weary and bitterly disappointed salvage team – who in the event had not acted on their immediate request to return home, and instead agreed to stay on, and start all over again. But this time, before they could set about a permanent repair, Gordon's men would have to patch the gash so that the hull could be pumped out and the flying boat refloated to bring it across the river. With the river 2 feet higher already in the space of three weeks, and still rising, their hand-operated diaphragm pumps were now utterly inadequate. The prospect of working in and even under the water prompted worries about dysentery and bilharzia. Put carbolic soap up your backside, advised Kleinschmidt at the mission hospital, for protection from the bilharzia parasite – and stop up the front of your penis with it, too, if you can. There were also crocodiles in the Dungu. The local policemen arrived in their blue uniforms and red tarbooshes to tell Hugh that their native charges wouldn't go inside the flying boat for fear of '*serpents*' – water snakes. Lacovitch of the SHUN company came to the rescue again and took Hugh to the gold-mine at Watsa to get some heavy-duty water-pumps, but after just one day of toiling in the water of the Dungu, unpersuaded by Kleinschmidt's assurances that it was too fast-flowing to harbour the bilharzia-carrying river snails, Gordon's men called enough.

So, his young team on their way home after four months in the Congo, Hugh Gordon found himself alone at Faradje, the salvage effort still his responsibility, with just the local workforce to draw on. 'And I was sitting on top of the flying boat, wondering what I could do – you know you can do nothing but you still sit there . . . And then – a mirage! Someone coming! It looks like Peter Newnham, his khaki shorts! He'd got as far as Juba. "I couldn't go home," he said. "I couldn't leave you . . ."' The Hugh Gordon I met that June afternoon in 1997 at his Somerset cottage was a witty, urbane man and, though casting back sixty years and fearing he was creating a 'very confused' picture, he'd told his story with great panache. But even at that historical remove, still for a moment he couldn't speak. 'Even when I think about it now,' he said quietly, 'I think that's quite touching . . .'

We are now into August 1939. 'I am afraid I am very much overdue in writing again,' Hugh wrote to Shorts back in Rochester, 'but with the work and worry of the past three weeks, writing has not been easy.' The Dungu was still rising – and in another month was expected to be 3 feet higher again. 'The situation is somewhat critical. Progress is painfully slow owing to the poor visibility under water: it is certainly not more than 3 inches, which means that one has to work mostly by feel.' But Hugh had one last card to play. 'If this should prove successful,' he reported, 'then I think there is every possibility of saving *Corsair*: on the other hand, if it should prove unsuccessful, I am afraid it means that the hull will have to be abandoned.' The previous four days, he revealed, they had been 'working on an apparatus which we hope will enable one to remain under water for at least half an hour . . .'

For Gordon had had a splendid idea – his words. He'd enlisted again the ever-resourceful Lacovitch, whose workshop had knocked up a tubular framework of steel bands covered with rubberized canvas, inserted a Perspex visor for Hugh to see through, and attached a pair of inner tubes into which he'd put his arms. Not a diving bell but a *diving chute* – a scratch-built device that would protect him from both drowning and disease, and enable him to work deep below the surface of the water for long enough at a stretch to patch the damaged hull, while his two best native workers were simultaneously sealing it from the inside. Very clever chap, Gordon congratulated himself, to make something out of nothing! There were two patent safety features, in case anything went wrong once he'd been lowered under the water inside it. The first was a rope looped round his foot by which Peter Newnham, stationed on top of the flying boat, could haul him out. And, in the event of a crocodile nosing towards the submerged Gordon – Hugh laughed at the absurd memory – a flare would be fired from *Corsair*'s Very pistol.

'That was the theory,' said Hugh. 'Bloody awful idea, really.' But the river was still rising, and by the time the diving chute was ready Hugh needed to descend still deeper underwater to reach the damaged section. Lacovitch got some big iron bars out of his store, to add more ballast to Hugh's canvas cocoon. They had to affix extension rods to the chute's frame to lower him out over the thick weed clogging the riverbank. The canvas was already leaking. Suddenly, under the weight of water the whole contraption collapsed in on him, and amidst an awful scramble Hugh Gordon was hauled out of the Dungu in the nick of time.

At points like this in the story I have to pinch myself: here is the actuality behind the idyllic, pastoral legend. All this, to save a large piece of metal. And yet it is also at such points that the tale starts to seem like myth. Something more profound than an aircraft, surely, must have been at stake – there has to be an allegory! But perhaps the truth is simply that in isolated circumstances no one is on hand to moderate courage.

'You have to bear in mind . . .' mused Hugh, 'when there's nothing else . . .' And then he broke off, vehement with wonder: 'It *amazes* me now – that the firm used to send me to all these places, and they left me to my own devices, and they didn't seem to bother very much! But people did in those days. It was wonderful, really – all work, after a fashion – but now I think, why did they do it in such a casual way?' When he finally got back from the Congo, his superintendent at Shorts' Rochester works told him how he'd joked to colleagues, 'Oh, if old Gordon falls in the river I bet he comes up smelling of roses!'

Now history took a timely hand. Word came that the two engineers were to return home. Hugh Gordon left the Belgian Congo with mixed feelings. They'd done the job they'd gone out to do, and yet it was the only job he hadn't finished. Now he had to leave *Corsair* still marooned on the Dungu, no nearer flying away than five months earlier, 'and I hadn't got it home.'

Back on the Medway at last, he walked into the works superintendent's office to a perfunctory greeting from Shorts' top management, who were poring over something on the table, and asked them what was up. 'Did you come in with your eyes shut?' came the impatient reply. The factory had just been camouflaged; everyone was far more interested in appraising its effect from these new aerial photographs than in the long-lost arrival from Central Africa. Peter Newnham found himself offloaded *en route* a couple of times from the Empire boats to make way for various VIPs, and finally got home to find himself posted down to Pembroke Dock to modify military Sunderlands. War was declared the following day.

Centaurus

15

Alaska

There, temporarily, we leave *Corsair*, nose down in the Dungu. For a short time, the outside world loses interest in her. There are more important things to think about. We will go back to the Congo, but the outbreak of war offers a timely hiatus in which to go on another, in more than one sense final, flying-boat journey.

In a 2,000-page book I'd come across three small letters, *GRG*: under the heading 'Flying Boats and Amphibians', on the Aircraft Codes page of the *World Airways Guide*, were just two entries, and this was the first. In two volumes, thick as phone books, the *Guide* lists every single scheduled air service on the planet. For every place visited regularly by plane it details the destinations served, hours of departure and arrival, days and times of year the service runs, the operating airline and, crucially, the *make and model of aeroplane*. It is an intriguing facility – British Rail never bothers to tell you what kind of locomotive will be pulling your train to Glasgow – for who but a plane-spotter cares if an MD-88 is parked at the gate instead of a 737? But in Bethnal Green Library in the East End of London, amidst the crackle of newspapers, the woman opposite me snuffling loudly with a heavy cold, there was – I hold my hands up – a cabbalistic thrill in coming upon a tiny code that bespoke a recondite and exotic other world. No one else there knew. But I did.

GRM, the other entry, meant Grumman Mallard: this was the Pan-Am Air Bridge seaplane that had flown me out to the Bahamas. But in checking the timetable of when the flying boat went to Bimini and Paradise Island I'd cross-checked against the aircraft codes, and here was *GRG*, too. So there was at least one more place where flying boats were still the only way from A to B! Grumman Goose – second child out of four in the Grumman family of amphibians. Where in the world could you still ride on a Goose?

Several hours' fruitless poring over wispy pages of tiny type convinced me that these elderly Grummans could be scrap metal in Arizona's desert boneyard or I blind as Milton before I stumbled upon them by this method. But subsequently, Nigel Harrod of the *Guide*'s publishers, OAG, offered to run a search of his entire database against these two codes – and soon he had a result. A small Alaskan airline called PenAir. That was all: just the one. History hadn't quite run out on me. Not an airshow flypast, not a preservationist's joyride – sixty years after *Corsair* had got lost flying her northbound Africa service over the Upper Nile, somewhere in the world they were merely carrying on where they'd never left off. Here was a second, and probably last, chance to explore flying-boat country – by flying boat.

Appropriately, it was an island. The Galapagos had their giant turtles, Indonesia the Komodo dragon and St Kilda its wren: fastnesses within their natural moats, islands were tiny protectorates of evolutionary dead-ends and anachronisms. Aepyornis Island and the island of Dr Moreau – H. G. Wells knew where to find his fabulous beasts. And now I was bound for Kodiak Island: 290 miles south-west of Anchorage, or 40 minutes by 737. It had a second speciality to boot: its brown bears, a separate genus, were the biggest carnivores in the world.

It was also a very long way away: two days' flying. Ironically, the ceaseless technological progress of modern aviation, that had formerly shrunk the globe to bring Alaska within eight hours' flying-time of western Europe, has now made it recede again. Until the eighties Anchorage was one of the busiest international airports in the world. Northwest, British Airways, Lufthansa – every long-haul Jumbo on its way to Japan and the Far East stopped over there to refuel, and the town's top hotels did good business putting up overnighting crews. But the second-generation Jumbos, the 747–400s, had the range – aided by a short cut across Russian airspace opened up with the collapse of Communism – to do even the Tokyo hauls non-stop, and now Anchorage is bypassed. Unless you're coming from Zurich, you can't fly direct. I had to go to Seattle – eight and three-quarter hours from London – and change to Alaska Airlines for Anchorage – another three and a quarter hours, and the furthest you could get in one day. Then it was back to the airport the day after to retrace my route south one more time, the cloud floating in wraiths over the Chugach mountains, their western faces sheets of copper in the afternoon sun, to Kodiak. Put your watch back twice along the way, for Alaska's Yukon Time is a further hour behind even Seattle's Pacific time, and a truly comprehensive case of jetlag converts distance into tremulous dislocation.

Alaska became magical and weird for me before I even got to Kodiak. My first sight of Anchorage, as the cab drove me into town through a filthy evening, was a bedraggled man on the highway embankment, throwing bread to a milling throng of Canada geese in the pouring rain. At the hotel I opened the copy of *Alaska* magazine I'd bought in Seattle airport at a colour picture of a moose on fire. Flames licked up the back of its neck in an orange mane as it browsed oblivious in the snow. The accompanying caption found the spectacle mildly diverting: it appeared that a stray Roman candle from someone's firework display had accidentally ignited the beast, which had eventually put itself out with a roll in the snow. 'I saw one the other day,' said Patrick Cochran, who drove me back to the airport in the morning, 'had a whole string of Christmas lights all wound round his antlers. Don't know where he picked them up.'

Though these huge hunchbacked moose were meant to stray through downtown Anchorage, feasting on young trees – a big bull had been in Mr Cochran's garden only that morning making short work of his lettuces – I never set eyes on one, which only made them seem more mythical, like pumas on Dartmoor. *It was – you wouldn't believe how big!*

Anchorage was Alaska's only real metropolis, half the state's population living within the city limits. But this still amounted to only 250,000, and the downtown had a relaxed and mellow small-town feel, bright with hanging baskets, the languor broken only occasionally by the tootle of the odd car or bus. Just one part was crowded and teeming and oversize on an American scale: the seaplane facility. In Lake Hood, across the road from the airport – actually two lakes that had been knocked together – Alaska had the biggest seaplane base in the world. The lakeshore was lined with them – Beavers, Otters, Cessna floatplanes – for miles. Floatplanes rested on chassis up on the banks. Amphibians were ranked hundreds deep across a vast parking apron. Advertising boards for dozens of charter companies touted for hunters, wildlife-watchers, fishermen, prospectors or just freight to haul off the lake and over the snow-capped peaks fringing the city. It took a quarter of an hour to drive the lakeshore road around its circumference: long, winding trails, clusters and districts of them – well over a thousand craft, a mini-city of seaplanes. Skyways were the roads in this state, and Alaskans, so the saying went, 'the flyingest people under the American flag'.

I knew the Goose before I saw it. Late afternoon, and just after I'd checked into the Buskin River Inn, Kodiak's airport hotel, there was a rich drone of something coming in to land behind the terminal, and then a throaty clatter as it taxied over towards me. Jets screamed, Cessnas whined, but they didn't sound like this. A stocky bulldog of a plane parked itself behind the hangar, Oxford-blue-liveried with a yellow and white stripe, the dark colour all over making it look more dumpy and antique. The twin moon-shaped panes of glass in its split windscreen gave it the heavy-lidded innocence of Disney's Pluto. Sat back on the tail wheel, bow – it wasn't streamlined enough to call a nose – cocked at the sky, and two drum-shaped radial engines high on the wing squared up like a boxer's gloves: a Second World War vintage Grumman Goose.

By devoting his programme in an eighties television series on classic buildings to the Boeing 747, the architect Sir Norman Foster (a keen flyer) demonstrated that you can appreciate the design of a machine without sounding like a car enthusiast leering at the voluptuous curves of his Jag. V. S. Naipaul once said that fiction never lies: it reveals its author totally – but substitute an aeroplane for a novel and a certain truth remains. The 747 had authors, people who conceived and built it for other people to use – as a response to, and to modify, their lives. It needn't be sad idolatry telling you only that the beholder needs someone to love: a plane is human aspirations subjected to physics. Despite a profile with undeniable hints of a miniaturized Boeing Clipper, yet there was a bluntness about a Goose, in shape and mood, accentuated by the neat, even dainty architecture of PenAir's modern Navajos and Caravans parked near by. It looked built to go through anything. It was prepared for the going to be rough, elementally rough. You took a Goose as you found it.

'Jim and Graham?' There were two of us for the 0845 Friday-morning departure for Port Bailey, Village Island, Zachar Bay and Amook. Jim, a quiet-spoken mustachioed man clad in blue denim, was up from Seattle to value some equipment the salmon cannery at Port Bailey was selling – he said he travelled all over America and Canada on such assignments. He'd just sold some fish-processing equipment to Russia. Fishing was the major industry in these teeming waters, Kodiak the biggest fishing port in the whole of the US, and late September was the back end of the salmon run, when millions of fish swam up the rivers to spawn and die. When I stopped my rental car south of the airport one afternoon to train the binoculars on some goldeneye duck, the river was churning and thrashing with sleek humpbacks. The ripe stink of dead and decomposing fish reached to the airport gate. No need out here to fill the lakes and bays with cages of farmed salmon. 'I don't know how people eat that stuff,' said Jim. PenAir's two Gooses (they had another pair at Dutch Harbor at the western extremity of the Aleutian Islands) flew scheduled services on three main routes, covering most of the island at least once a week, and today we were heading out west.

If you were wavering over whether to choose Chalk's as your carrier out to the Bahamas, the leatherette seats and stained curtains inside their Mallards would be unlikely to tip the balance, but PenAir's Goose number 832 set new standards for basic accommodation. The airline had acquired it the previous year from the Alaska Fish and Game Department (whose blue and white colours it still wore, even though PenAir's were white and red), and inside, it was as unadorned as a parcel van. The interior was bare metal, sides and floor painted grey, ceiling a rebarbative custard-yellow; three low tip-up seats with thin, sagging cushions were slotted in down one side of the fuselage – you could have fitted in a few more where the sacks of mail and boxes of freight were now piled under securing netting. 'Do you want to sit up in the cockpit?' asked Bryan, the pilot. There was no side panel beside my seat to hide the wiring. This was an amphibious version of a Land-Rover post-bus.

It was a beautiful morning, the sun newly up and splintering ahead as we took off towards the sea. Kodiak was christened 'the Emerald Isle' for the deep green afforestation cloaking it during the summer months, but we were already into the golds, russets and ochres of the fall. I'd come to Alaska with warnings that the island's frequent autumn fogs might rule out flying altogether – maybe prevent getting on to Kodiak at all – but such Indian-summer weather was to last, miraculously, throughout my four-day stay. The American novelist Don DeLillo writes of how the comfortable passage of modern jet airliners has reduced the entire sensation of powered flight to 'a rudimentary tremble'. He cannot ever have caught a Grumman Goose. Hung between the two radial engines – the starboard right beside me – we rode a capsule of drumming thunder. The Pan-Am Mallard's turbines had set up a crazy deafening racket, so comprehensively to obliterate the headsets' tinkling reggae: this was a low-revving, hoarse roar. You were a participant more than a passenger. We flew at a mere 3,000 feet, wheeling westwards over hillsides of golden silver birch, through mountain passes between snow-tipped peaks sparkling like icing. There were just a hundred miles of roads on Kodiak, all in the north-east radiating out from the town, and unpaved beyond where the town ran out. Where the mountains rose up and the valleys closed in, the roads ran out. But the roads didn't lead to many more people, and only half the island's 15,000 inhabitants lived in the town. This was how to reach the rest.

I can still hear in my mind's ear the rubble-rattle of the water under the hull when the Chalk's flying boat had touched down at Bimini and Watson's Island – a day when wind and rain had stirred up the sea to juddering resistance. But in the sheltered bay at Port Bailey, a clutch of corrugated sheds on stilts, the Goose slid on to the water so smoothly, a planing, cushioning swish until we sagged in and the water flopped across the screen, that I can't remember the sound it made. As we taxied over to the shingly shore Bryan was reaching down beside his seat and winding hard on a handle. Was that, I asked when we'd swung round to a stop up on the beach, the undercarriage he'd been manually cranking down? Bryan nodded. 'Old planes. Nothin' fancy. None of that computer crap in them.' Jim called goodbye and climbed out, Bryan exchanged a couple of mail sacks with a couple from the cannery, and it was time to be off to the next stop.

That first morning out with the Goose I'd have liked to stop and stay over a day at each place we visited – Village Island, for example, where we went next. What lives went on at these tiny, mountain-locked settlements? A small low wooden cabin at the top of another lonely inaccessible beach, two tiny figures looking up in anticipation as we circled in, who turned out to be a couple of young women who carried on throwing driftwood for their excited black Labradors once we'd arrived: 'Oh,' explained Bryan, 'just another little place out in the middle of ab-so-lute-ly nowhere.' I just had time to jump out to take a couple of pictures – in one of them the shining dark-blue water framing the Goose stretches away like steel – and the younger of the women, with a cap of short blonde hair, shot me some suspicious looks at this intrusion. Her dark-haired friend told me she sure wished she was flying with us on a beautiful day like this, and now it was time to leave them, too.

That was our only contact: it wasn't just the demands of the timetable – PenAir's flying-boat service was perhaps unique, I subsequently learnt, in that the airline would sell you a ticket to any of its destinations on Kodiak, but at many you weren't allowed to alight. The salmon canneries, these individual lodges and cabins, were private property: they could accept the mail but reject you. But retreats like Village Island, I soon realized, were different and special anyway. It was not for a journalist to step off a plane straight into these two women's lives and demand a half-hour resumé of their every secret. That was why they lived out here. There weren't many places in the world where you could insulate yourself so completely. The Goose taxis out into open water and surges away into the thrilling gather of the take-off run: mail delivered and collected, and a glimpse has aroused and also had to make do for all that curiosity, but at least there are plenty of other places for us still to go and people to see. But the chunky blue flying boat booming across the bay, rising on its white skirt and floating off over the mountains, is also their only sight of us – or anybody – for several days.

At Zachar Bay, the Goose was a goods van: the cannery here had a delivery from the J. C. Penney department store. What was it about islands and duvets? Out of the nose of the Mallard at Bimini had come a whole pile of comforters, and now a flying boat was bringing an Alaskan island a load more. 'How many beds you got?' grumbled Bryan, tossing another large carton out on to the pebbles. Did island people get through duvets as loft insulation or something? Then it was Steve, Gisela, and their young son Tyler, clambering in at the last stop, Amook, with a clutch of fishing rods and boxes of salmon after a week's holiday at Munsey's Bear Camp watching the island's huge brown bears – they'd seen forty, from inside a hide, on their first day – for the ride back to Kodiak and a flight home to Anchorage.

But before we'd been able to turn round tail-first to unload at Zachar Bay, heaving ourselves up the beach on arrival, the Goose had come to a halt, engines thrashing, just on the edge of the water. Bryan was thumbing through a small pamphlet. A moment's thought, then he gave it the gun. This time we lurched up the shingle. 'Almost got stuck there,' he said: an unexpectedly soft beach. 'Took a chance.' Those were tide tables he'd been flicking through. And how long before the tide would have arrived to float us off? This was not a factor in the John Lewis van's rounds. Bryan returned me a bright look. 'About three hours.'

'I flew these airplanes sitting on my dad's lap,' Fred Ball told me, 'nine or ten years old.' Fred was a vice-president of PenAir, but more importantly he was the airline's chief Goose pilot. He was too modest to say so, but others told me this was 'the King of the Goose':

no one in the world could top the 11,000 hours' flying Fred had clocked up. 'In the Grumman community probably half the people know who I am,' he conceded. His business card was a colour photo of a Widgeon taking off. He got asked down to Texas to check out airplanes for buyers; he'd taught a guy to fly a Grumman in San José, California, and it was off to Seattle next week to give some lessons on a Widgeon. But, though he inquired affably about my jetlag, he'd never been abroad himself – Britain, Europe, anywhere – and it appeared he didn't much mind. He was even surprisingly hazy on other kinds of flying boat. 'Did Britain build the Martins?' he asked me – 'like the Martin Mars?' Even I knew that Martins were as all-American as Grummans. He was an expert on what he had to deal with, and that was that. Composed and bespectacled, a neat, small-built man like so many of the other flying-boat craftsmen I'd met back in England, I never saw him without his slate-grey baseball cap embroidered with a Goose that was PenAir's concession to a souvenir ($10) of their elderly amphibians.

'My dad was an Alaska bush pilot,' said Fred. Back in the thirties, when the Depression down south had reduced millions to poverty, his father could earn $300 as a trapper for a couple of days' work. 'There was no Depression up here! For five winters he ran dog teams, and the only reason he took up flying was because he got fed up with running dogs over the mountains!' Fred remembered from his childhood them having to drain the oil out of the plane every evening during wintertime and keep it indoors by the fire so the engine would turn over in the morning.

By 1958 air forces were starting to divest themselves of their Gooses. When production ceased in 1945 Grummans had built 350, mostly for military use on coastline search and rescue duties – 'but they did put bombs on them,' said Fred. 'Even in my day I've found a Goose that still had the little placard on the dash saying BOMB RELEASE. I've got it at home.' The French, I found out later, had used them in Vietnam in the early years of the Indo-China war, a kind of ponderous precursor to the Huey gunship. Fred's father and uncle paid $30,000 for their first Goose, with just 360 hours on it and, adding a second three years later, started their own airline, Ball Brothers, in Bristol Bay on the north-west side of Alaska's Aleutian peninsula.

Now there were only thirty Gooses left in the world, and the price had increased more than tenfold: $380,000 a time. In Anchorage I found two that had been restored as lovingly as vintage cars. One, at the Aviation Museum on Lake Hood, had been acquired, like PenAir's plane, from Alaska's Fish and Game Department – but this one was now magnificent in brilliant deep orange with a black hull, and through the cabin windows I could see sumptuous velvet seats. On the other, put back into its silver military colours, a local attorney had spent some $800,000 installing non-standard extras like a mahogany floor sealed with twelve coats of lacquer. 'I took my shoes off to get in that thing!' said one of his friends. 'It's his Winnebago.' They looked fabulous, but when you'd made your Goose such a collector's item that you wouldn't land it on salt water – what was the point of owning a flying boat in Alaska if you couldn't fly it to places like Village Island and Amook?

'This is all fly-by-the-seat-of-your-pants flying,' said the chief Goose pilot. 'Visual rules flying, daylight only. It takes a lot more conscious thought, rather than just droning along. In the wheelplanes we go to six different places, and the airport doesn't usually change every time you go there. In the Goose we go to *1,500* different places, and the sea's different, the tides, every single time. Where I grew up in Bristol Bay, if you move the tide up two feet the water'll move inland a mile and a half.'

Very specifically only a Goose would do for most of the places PenAir flew to on Kodiak. 'No one in their right mind would run a schedule to those folks,' said Fred – government subsidy underwrote these routes as an 'Essential Air Service'. Here it was the old story: no one was making a pot of money out of running flying boats. There were no long jetties alongside which a modern floatplane could taxi, and only a plane old-fashioned enough to be sat back on a tailwheel was capable of ploughing up Kodiak's shingle beaches. There were no shock absorbers on the landing gear, and PenAir cranked it up as high as it'd go for driving over rocks out of the water: that meant a good landing every time a pilot put it down on a runway – or a very hard one. And no two Gooses flew the same: Grummans hadn't used jigs, they'd hand-built every one, and getting out of one of PenAir's Gooses into the other, Brian said, was like flying a completely different kind of aircraft. *Nothin' fancy*: a Goose was all mechanical – 'I'm tired at the end of the day,' he told me, gripping the control column, 'from pulling this thing in and out.' For one of PenAir's pilots the Goose had proved just too strenuous. 'He sweated,' said Bryan, 'but he couldn't fly it.'

Nothing, it seemed, you couldn't fit inside a Goose. Fred Ball had hauled 20-foot bendy plastic pipes – you had to feed them in through the bow and snake them all the way through to the baggage compartment at the back; 600 lb people so broad across the beam 'we've had to load 'em through the cargo doors'; and many times at remote inlets and cabins the flying boat had become a makeshift hearse, the coffin sometimes so large you'd have to slide it in on its side and hear the body within shift with a *clonk*, turn it over with another *clonk* for the flight, and then *clonk*, *clonk* again in reverse to get it out for the interment.

There was a charter to do that afternoon – Fred had to go to Eagle Harbor, south of Kodiak, and pick up a party who'd spent a week fishing from a cabin. Another radiant day, and he thought we might leave a little early . . . In the pilots' office Fred offered me what looked like some kind of sweet from a tall glass jar, but turned out to be a chunk of smoked salmon tough as jerky and pungent as a kipper, that inhabited my mouth for hours after. As we walked out to the Goose one of the baggage handlers called out, 'What do you need that tackle box for, Fred?'

'Survival kit,' replied Fred without breaking stride.

There is that scene in the film *Groundhog Day* when Bill Murray suddenly realizes that no one is going to stop him driving along railway tracks or eating every last cream cake in the diner: *You're right – we can do whatever we want . . . !* Off over the mountains to the south we went, and soon the pilot was pointing out an oval of water that looked no bigger than a hand mirror. Miam Lake, announced Fred, and down we went. He put the Goose on the water in what seemed no more than a few yards, with the soft powdery *whumph* of a ski turning in snow; parked it up in the shallows and out we jumped. Once the engines had died the only sounds were the tiny lap of water around the hull and an eagle pealing in the hills. Fred cast his spinner and said, 'I *hate* it when I have to go fishing.' In a quarter of an hour he was reeling in a 15 lb salmon. The imperturbable pilot looked at his watch: yes, we'd probably better go get those guys at Eagle Harbor now.

A certain celebrity is usually one of the perks of the long-distance traveller. Thousands of miles away in another land you become a strange bird, a special event. 'They have whole features about Vaughan Williams!' exclaimed an artist called Mike when I turned up in Hays, Kansas, once, bearing a copy of the *Sunday Telegraph*. What am I doing here? is the first despairing thought in a new place; the second is often, *I'm the ambassador.* But the smaller the place you visit, usually the less, not the more, your celebrity. Small towns have no interest in big distances. Kodiak's insularity seemed at first positively offhand. *I'd* be curious to talk to me! I thought as the district attorney cut me dead one evening during a Chamber of Commerce wine-tasting at the Buskin – 'The Man Who Travelled

9,000 Miles Across the World to Ride on a Fifty-Year-Old Sea-plane!' Apart from the representative from the Visitors Bureau, I think I only met two people in Kodiak who genuinely registered where I'd come from, and they were a helicopter pilot and his wife from the US coastguard base who were considering a posting to Cornwall. All the rest were interested only in each other's business. 'I put out a lot of disinformation,' the local Toyota dealer, John Gregory, joked to me – 'it's one way of staying ahead of your competitors.' The worldliness of Portland, Oregon, his previous abode, had given him the measure of Kodiak's introverted world. A town of some 10,000 souls, Kodiak was a community that got along quite nicely, thank you, by itself.

I couldn't figure out the stop-light. There was only one in town, right in the centre, and it flashed red all the time. At first I sat tight in my rental car until I could see it was never going to change – but did it mean stop, or proceed with caution, or what? 'Oh, it's broken,' said Bryan, the Goose pilot. 'They said it was going to cost twenty thousand dollars to fix it. So we decided we *really didn't need it that much.*' Giant blubbery sea lions lolled all day over one of the docks in the port: 'They seem to have taken it over as their own,' Evan, the helicopter pilot, informed me. So theirs it was – no question of Kodiak throwing them off. The biggest houses in town, I heard, belonged to its schoolteachers – they were able to use their long summer vacation to charter a fishing boat and haul in catches worth $300,000. The *Kodiak Daily Mirror*'s regular 'Public Safety' digest of crimes and breaches of the peace reported one day that 'a loose dog was chased from a supermarket parking lot to its home on Murphy Way.' Who needed news from elsewhere?

Kodiak, by its very parochiality, by what I didn't find there, taught me why the romance surrounding the flying boat was so exclusively British. Britain never had any local flying boats. Ours connected us only with far-away; their haunts had the delicious melancholy of vast distance and isolation. It is surrounding water that defines an island; every British flying boat, burring out over Southampton Water, gave us the aerial perspective to feel ourselves a sea-lapped island, and set its compass for the secret place on the other side of the oceans. *Cassiopeia* rocking on the water, *Canopus* circling overhead, portended a sad goodbye, a long parting, a treasured letter, an unknown future. Planes lay out cities and landscapes below you like a map – a static prospect: a tableau, not a drama – and they can do the same with your life. The big white flying boat gave you the long view; freeze-framed your whole life.

America, its small fleet of Pan-Am Clippers aside, had nothing else. Its Mallards and Catalinas and Gooses and Widgeons were all local, hopping out to islands, around archipelagos – feeder flights, commuter services, short-haul. For me, travelling more than half-way across the world to come upon these rumbling Grummans, and touch down with them at a tiny empty inlet like Village Island, was to feel something of the lonely bafflement that had stayed with Patrick Spencer from his arrival at Cape Maclear. But I was bringing 9,000 miles' separation to that short flight over Kodiak's mountains: for PenAir's pilots it was their backyard. Sometimes its office seemed more like a minicab office, with calls coming in requesting a last-minute pick-up here and a box delivered there – even a shopping list radioed in, the goods to be picked up at Safeways – and the Goose's schedules changing by the minute.

The Baranov Museum in Kodiak had a photograph of the first aeroplane to visit Kodiak: 1925, a Curtiss biplane flying boat that looked like a box-kite attached to a canoe. Seventy years' continuity – but my sense of history was not shared by the men who flew the Gooses. Bryan said he'd seen pictures of the fabulous Boeing Clippers. 'The cockpit, chart table and everything – it's like a room. It's bigger than my living room! It would have been real neat to go in that.' But it was fourteen years now since he'd flown himself and everything he owned up from Washington state in his little Supercub plane, and these days it seemed to me the flying boat was taking him to places and people he'd come to know only too well. A droll saturninity accompanied him to work. When one passenger joshed, 'Don't argue, don't complain,' Bryan mourned, 'That's the bit that usually gets me into trouble.' A delivery of wood for that afternoon prompted a gloomy prediction of how we were going to be caught unloading on a falling tide and had I got some lunch with me in case we were stuck there for six hours? 'I'm like a truck driver or cab driver in town,' said Bryan. 'It's just what I do.' I tried out on him the tale of how some of the Imperial Airways' Empire boat captains used to have their white-suited crew line up at the quay to click their heels and salute them aboard. 'Like going on a ship?' he said, and considered a moment. 'Round here we're a little more . . . casual,' and he fired the engines.

The flying boat took me to places, though, from which the town of Kodiak seemed a prodigious metropolis. Had anything but an amphibious Goose been able to get to them – road builders, runway graders – they'd have become communities. Instead we circled in each time, banking above the shiny olive water, peering down until suddenly you caught the tiny scurry of red that was someone's waterproof jacket. In my free time between flights I'd been trying to track down another exotic attraction – Kodiak's tufted puffins, remarkable for their weird blond pony-tails copied off Hulk Hogan. Eventually (Evan and his wife Barb generously gave up some of their Sunday afternoon to show me a deserted, secret beach in Middle Bay) I found a flock, bobbing stiffly like a line of Captain Pugwashes – but every trip in the flying boat came to seem like going human-watching. I saw flocks of bald eagles at Anton Larsen Bay, harlequin ducks sprinkling the water at Fort Abercrombie, mergansers on the rivers – birds you expected in this wilderness, rare species required a wider search – but to come upon people was always a surprise. Yes! down there! Definitely a very rare . . . person!

Also I found my perspective of the remote constantly on the move: beyond even the empty coves we alighted in, it turned out, there was always more extreme isolation. Bryan and I flew down to Alitak, on the very southern tip of the island, where the landscape became treeless, pudgy grassmoor, and at the cannery there he said, 'How's the big city treatin' you, John?', to a white-bearded man waiting to pick up the mail. He meant this clutter of silent corrugated sheds and fishing boats hauled up the beach, where over the winter John and his wife were the only residents – for the Goose had already hauled the 160-strong workforce back to civilization, and when they returned the couple would retreat even further south to live by themselves on a lonely island. 'I guess he just likes the wild life,' reflected Bryan.

But then we flew on to Stockholm Point, where the three occupants were closing up for the winter and moving back into town. 'This is all you got?' Bryan exclaimed to the man, a salmon fisherman called Sid, once everything was loaded aboard. 'My wife'd fill the whole plane.'

'I been workin' on this for weeks,' said Sid. The neat green-painted cabin we were leaving, decorated with hanging baskets and window-boxes; the pot plants, Cellophane wraps of dried flowers and flagons of homemade wine stowed along one side of the Goose's cabin; the elderly Labrador flopped mournfully in the aisle – we could have been an estate car just leaving the weekend cottage in the Cotswolds.

Another day, I flew with Fred in the other Goose – number 911, royal-blue 'Spirit of Unalaska' that had clattered in the day I arrived, its small dark cabin of beige panelling and woolly brown seats more like an antique airliner was supposed to look than the troop-carrier austerity of the other – to Hidden Basin to pick up a party of fishermen. We headed south, towards the spine of snowcapped peaks that threaded the island's north–south axis. To the east, beyond three rock pinnacles spiking out from a promontory, was where we'd collected the fishermen at Eagle Harbor. With casual pride Fred pointed out a mountain tarn below: he'd even landed on that. Then his finger was directed ahead, to where we were looping down. 'See those black spots on the water?' They were like scuff-marks, bruise-shadows in the indigo bay. 'That's where the wind is denting the water – coming down over this mountain and kind of bouncing off it.' Cat's paws was the aviator's nickname for them, because they also looked like a scatter of prints: the sight of them warned you that as you descended below that mountain the gusts could knock you about. Over east in the next bay, towards Eagle Harbor, the water was fish-scaled silver – from up here rather beautiful, like silver-thread cloth, but, said Fred, that fish-scaling was the wind whipping up the water. Try to land near that and both descent and touchdown would be a lot rougher. 'We learn to read the water.'

Our destination was indeed a hidden basin, enclosed in its amphitheatre of cliffs. We scudded across the water towards what loomed up as a substantial three-storeyed wooden chalet, the size of a small block of flats. The owner, an expansive and loquacious wildlife guide called Nick Brigman, had built it all himself. He hosted groups on weeks of fishing, bear-watching and sometimes hunting. While last week's guests stowed their cool boxes, holdalls and rods inside the Goose, he wanted to take me on a helter-skelter tour. A brown bear-skin was spreadeagled across the pine-panelled wall of the huge living room: Nick had shot it himself in '88. 'It almost ate me,' he exclaimed. 'Not a big one – eight, nine hundred pounds – but I used too small a gun, a thirty-odd-six . . . *That's* a big bear' – he'd turned to a framed photo of a bespectacled man grinning sheepishly beside a vast carcass. 'A fifteen-hundred-pounder! He'd be hell in the NBA. He'd be gettin' all the boards and the rebounds!' Clinging to another wall was a big white goatskin: 'That's not huntin', man,' –

said Nick. 'That's survival! You're out for days! Every year I'm out there I say, this is the last time, and every year I do it again.' We bounded upstairs to take in several bedrooms of bunk beds, back down to peek outside at Nick's recent installation of a *banya* – a traditional Russian steam bath – and then into 'my pride and joy', a spacious modern kitchen, to behold his latest acquisition.

Nick Brigman had a dishwasher out at Hidden Basin.

Had that come out by flying boat? 'Yup. Everything in here except the couch. That wouldn't fit.'

Back at Kodiak airport Fred Ball beckoned me to follow him into the PenAir hangar. Marooned on top of the office roof, still wrapped in its delivery polythene, was a loudly striped sofa.

'Hey, Graham!' Nick Brigman had just hung up at a pay phone in the lobby of the Buskin. This was the day after we'd flown out to Hidden Basin. Nick and his assistant, Roy, had tidied up later by drinking dry the crate of beer a previous party of Germans had left, and had just come in today on the flying boat. Now there was time before their next flight to catch some medicinal hair-of-the-dog in the Buskin and two vast trenchers of cheeseburger and chips – an unaccustomed treat, it seemed, after all that fresh crab, halibut and salmon. A Jack Daniel's went on the tab alongside their Bloody Marys, and I joined them up at the bar.

An ebullient man with a Zapata moustache and a wide laugh, Nick was the kind of guy who answered your questions for you without your even asking them. His personality and opinions were as open-air and heedless of shelter as that big tall pile of a Lodge out at Hidden Basin. He was not a hidden basin. But neither was he a hectoring boor: what he wanted to tell me about Alaska was his way of saying, 'Welcome.' He and Roy were on their way to Anchorage, to collect an Eskimo man who, at the age of ninety, wanted his first ever crack at seal-hunting. 'If you put a million dollars in front of him he'd say, "Start a fire with it," ' Nick declared. 'But if you put a silverback salmon there he'd talk for hours.' He meant, *It's different here, isn't it?* Did I know that Alaska had 3 million lakes over 20 acres in area? That this was the only state in the Union that paid its citizens just for living here? Over the years it had banked the vast duties levied on the oil that flowed through the Trans-Alaska pipeline – not squandered them as the British government had with North Sea oil – and now such was the income from the investment fund that, shared out among Alaska's half-million citizens, it amounted to an annual dividend of $1,300 per head. Nick was proclaiming self-sufficiency, not bragging about riches. Until 1950 Alaska hadn't even been a state of the Union: just a territory, like the US Virgin Islands, and to listen to people like Nick and Roy it was Alaska that had done the United States a favour by allowing them to join. There was Alaska, and there was 'the lower forty-eight', and when you left for the rest of the States you announced, like Captain Oates, 'I'm going *outside*.' 'First, I'm a human being,' said Nick – up here there were so few of them it didn't seem a pompous statement. 'Second, I'm an Alaskan. *Then* I'm an American.'

This was the fall of 1998, and the reverberations of Kenneth Starr's report into President Clinton's affair with his White House intern, Monica Lewinsky, were still subject to blanket coverage by the news media. I'd travelled to the US with something of a heavy heart at the prospect of continual ear-bashing on the case. But Alaskans seemed genuinely, solipsistically detached. Indeed, to my amazement Nick was not the first person to chuckle, 'In Britain you had your Profumo case, didn't you?' – as though it had all happened yesterday. My head reeled. This was thirty-four years ago! I was four at the time! No one even in Britain was prompted by the Clinton scandal to parallels with Profumo. But now I wonder: maybe Profumo seemed no more foreign an issue than Clinton: for Alaskans, spectator-sport both. Or maybe after all this time news had finally reached Kodiak Island.

So when Nick spoke of survival and subsistence it was not the paranoid gun-toting secession of Montana militias or the Unabomber. They couldn't escape the Union; Alaska was already beyond the pale, always had been. The North-West brand of home-steading was a retreat into a bunker: out here it was flinging your life open to the elements. Nick said they were now completely self-sufficient at Hidden Basin – only that morning he and Roy had netted a 90 lb halibut. He kept a few bison, laid crab nets, grew all his own produce. 'Who knows what's going to happen in the world, Graham?' he appealed genially. 'You can have a million dollars in the bank, but you still gotta stand in line at the grocery store. *My* convenience store's the front garden. We've got guns,' he went on, 'but we don't use 'em on each other. I was just saying to Lisa here' – the woman minding the bar was readying up a last round of Bloody Marys – 'I've been out at Hidden Basin eleven years and I've never had a drive-by!'

Most of Kodiak Island was a national Wildlife Refuge, so using guns on its wildlife was neither common nor encouraged. If you couldn't eat it, you couldn't shoot it, was the general rule – bears, the principal exception, were strictly limited to two a year for the few permits issued, and I found plenty of islanders who thought a single one was too many. Even deer-hunting attracted the oppro-brium of some of Nick's wildlife-watching guests, as one lady last week had made plain. 'She said to me, "How can you kill those deer?"'

Well, Nick replied, those they shot provided enough meat for a week, and besides, culling ensured the population didn't grow beyond the numbers the habitat could support.

'But that beautiful big buck over there,' the woman had persisted, 'how can you shoot him?'

'And I was thinking how to explain to her,' said Nick – 'she was quite an old lady – so I said, "Ma'am, have you *any idea* what he's gonna go and do to his granddaughters?" She said, "Shoot every last one of the sonsabitches."'

Kodiak town I'd found a slightly dour place; quiet and hesitant, as though waiting for but not expecting something to happen; its people inclined to a grim taciturnity. After a single afternoon driving round it I'd thought, right: seen that – and I was only living on the island for four days. But once I got out on the flying boat, and we could go out beyond the mountains, and then a ways more, I found wit and laughter and freedom – relaxed, easy people like Nick, and Fred Ball, and the young women at Village Island. Bryan's pessimism stayed behind on the runway at Kodiak when we took off. A fisherman we picked up at Moser Bay in the south pretended to fuss about suffering from motion sickness: Bryan pointed at his wellies and said, 'You got your boots . . .' I never met anyone out in these wilds who seemed to be running away, withdrawing, or retreating. Alan Moorehead's sense as he recalled the Empire boat touching down at Malakal that he was seeing the land as Livingstone saw it: out here on Kodiak Island it was as though you were being given an earlier look at things, back in a calmer, sanguine time.

'Did you see the sunrise?' asked Bryan. Just before nine on my last day out with PenAir's Gooses, and we were heading north over the dark mysterious spruce forests of Afognak Island. He pointed east: 'It was deep red all the way across. You sure lucked out on the weather.' Every morning had dawned with great slashes of coral and rose. Now the sun was spilling over the eastern horizon in a trench of liquid gold. 'Boy, it's a really clear day. Beyond those humps – they're islands – you can see the mainland. That's Anchorage ahead, King Salmon's over to the left.' A view of 300 miles to mountains dreamy powder-blue with distance.

That day we flew the whole length of the Kodiak archipelago, from the northernmost port of call on Afognak to Alitak in the far south. We changed Gooses at Kodiak in the middle; we were out from early morning until the afternoon. There came just one moment, as we corkscrewed down the air into the bay at Alitak, when suddenly – those hours of hammering noise, the sheer physical participation of flying in this old flying boat – all the energy went out of me, and for the first time I thought, imagine flying in something like this all the way to Africa . . . !

But at Kitoi Bay we touched down in a glassy olive-green inlet where seagulls thronged the beach and white-striped humpie salmon jack-knifed and squirmed around the hull. Bryan said, 'Last week the place was just hoppin' with 'em.' Joseph and Greg got out, Joseph to work in the salmon hatchery, Greg the Fish and Game inspector, who said he was unused to this scheduled flight and check-in business – 'I'm used to chartering a whole Goose to bring me and my camp out!' In the terminal the two of them had fallen to discussing a ghastly variant of carpal tunnel syndrome, a deformation of the wrist afflicting hatchery workers who slit open millions of salmon for a living to release the eggs – it was why Greg himself had got out of hatchery – and I'd been treated to a ghastly evocation of how the operation to drill out the calcified bone left you looking like a failed suicide.

The waters we landed on around Kodiak were so calm that, strangely, it is not touchdown's thrilling intermittent thud under the keel that I most remember from flying with the Goose, or the booming, swelling scramble of take-off: rather the sudden lilt and quiet of just-having-landed, the white suds chasing and scrambling across the glass: the weightless moment of becoming a boat. But no one was up at the next stop, except a small sandy dog trotting around the cabin's verandah to stare. 'I think they're still sleepin',' said Bryan. 'Well, I'll go around a couple times and then they'll have to wait till the next time.' The droplets of water shone like glycerine on the windscreen as we picked up speed. In the Caribbean the seaplanes I'd flown with had shared their element with turtles and pelicans; here I looked down on a seal breaking the surface, slick as a wetsuit. 'This is Seal Bay,' Bryan reminded me. We had some mail for a man living all alone among the gaunt rusting sheds of the abandoned Port Williams cannery, the sun temporarily effaced, most melancholy outpost of all, and now further north was only the sea.

That was the dark-blue Goose's last flight before a major overhaul; 832 was ready for us back at Kodiak for the run south, and when I climbed in I found its cabin so full of wood – 14-foot planks, boards grazing the roof – that we could barely squeeze through to the cockpit. Kiavak Bay was the first choppy water we'd landed on, white-crinkled and granular under the hull. Water leaked in around the edges of my side window on to my lap; Bryan said, 'Now you're definitely in a boat.' At the third attempt we managed to roar up the shelving, shifting beach, and an elderly man with rosy weather-beaten cheeks ambled down to meet us. Behind him was the skeleton of a small wooden cabin. This was Andy, who led goat-hunting expeditions in the hills (according to Nick Brigman it was the flying boat, of course, that had brought in the first of the mountain-goat population back in the fifties). The rest of the time he lived out here, all by himself, building this house. He'd been at it four years already, said Bryan: still no roof on the main part yet. Once in a while the flying boat turned up to tip a load more lumber out on the beach for him.

As we were unloading Andy kept up a genial mumble about how this year he really hoped he'd get the rafters on. His soppy Labrador, lolling all over the planks even as we were setting them down, was the only other sign of life. A circular saw and a box of metal brackets came out of the Goose's nose, and finally two large boxes of cheese. Andy regarded the lumber and mused, half to himself it seemed, 'Guess I've got something to do for the rest of the day.'

Back on board the flying boat I said to Bryan, 'In twenty years you can bring him a dishwasher.' He was eager to be gone – just grimly pleased we hadn't got stuck on the beach with a falling tide for the rest of the day. He watched me brushing the sawdust off my sweatshirt – I hadn't really come dressed for manual labour – as he ran the engines up to a roar and pointed the Goose out into the ink-blue bay. The lone figure and his gambolling dog were already small and receding behind us. 'Still seem romantic, does it?' asked Bryan.

Canopus

16

The Dam

'When war broke out over Europe, a party of British aircraft engineers must have been among the Englishmen most remote from conflict. They were living in huts of planks and thatch on the banks of a remote river in the heart of Central Africa, toiling at the hull of a flying boat that lay damaged on the swampy river bank.' With Macaulayan sonority HMSO's Dudley Barker sets the scene for the last act of the saga – even if all the stuff about huts of planks and thatch is picturesque invention. German armies marching into Poland from the west, the Russians from the east; battleships engaging on the River Plate; Britain's main railway stations thronged with bewildered children being evacuated to the countryside; blackouts, the issue of gas masks; the British Expeditionary Force leaving for France. And, 4,000 miles away, Empire flying boat *Corsair* still wallowing in the Dungu.

But what seems like the extreme isolation of this solitary aircraft – indeed, its utter irrelevance to the wider tides of world war – would in fact assume a felicitous irony. The world had suddenly changed around *Corsair*. In the short term, it would be the outbreak of war in Europe that would save her to fly on into the future. And in the long term it was to be the Second World War that would put paid for ever to the strange historical phenomenon of the flying boat.

The substantial *Times* obituary for Sir Roy Sisson makes no mention of Corsairville. He died in February 1993 at the age of seventy-eight, his career in the aviation industry having spanned some fifty-five years, from an apprenticeship at Hawker's in 1930 to the eventual chairmanship of the avionics and electronics combine Smith's Industries, and a knighthood in 1980 for services to British exports. The *Times* notice emphasizes three particular achievements. In 1941 he was a flight engineer on the Boeing flying boats that flew BOAC's wartime transatlantic run. After the war he was involved in its introduction of the Lockheed Constellation, and in the fifties, seconded by the airline to De Havilland's at Hatfield, he'd 'played a significant role in assisting BOAC to put the . . . Comet into service as the world's first jet airliner'.

But in September 1939 the then Roy Sisson was a ground engineer for Imperial Airways, stationed at Alexandria in Egypt – the 'Clapham Junction' of flying boats, as he put it, with Empire boats coming in from the UK, the Middle East and Africa. 'I was just getting used to this rather lovely place,' Sir Roy told me when I went to see him, eighteen months before he died – in retirement he lived not far from the former De Havilland works in Hertfordshire – 'and bathing down at Stanley Bay . . . and I had a beach hut – oh! Then the chaps said, "There's a bit of a problem down in the Congo . . ."'

The Times commemorates, in that stiffly respectful way of obituaries, 'one of the industry's best-known characters' – but in this case the tribute seemed simply apt. I found a jovial, imperturbable man with a boyish sense of humour, and a resonant baritone that rose to mirthful falsetto as he almost cried with laughter in recounting the story of Hugh Gordon's ducking in the diving chute. If the final instalment of the *Corsair* saga seems to have been penned by Evelyn Waugh rather than Bruce Chatwin, it is due to its new protagonists like Roy Sisson, whose younger ebullience, obvious throughout his reminiscence that sunny morning, set the pervading tone.

Once Shorts had recalled its engineers from Faradje at the start of the war, for *Corsair* that looked, finally, like the end. If Imperial

Airways wanted anything done about her, they would now have to do it themselves, and initially, it seems, the company threw the towel in. Sisson and five other engineers under foreman Jock Halliday were dispatched from Alexandria to the Belgian Congo, to take the engines off her, rescue any other parts that could be used for spares, blow up the hulk and abandon it there. That's how Sisson and Alf Cowling, one of the other engineers, remembered their original brief.

But now there was a war on. Britain had already declared against Germany in support of Poland. In May 1940, of course, the Germans invaded Belgium, and from then on Britain and Belgium were on the same side. But this was still eight months earlier, during the uneasy 'phoney war', and back in 1936 Belgium had returned to a position of strict neutrality. And now, with the French Maginot Line looking unlikely to hold for long against the westward German advance, a flying boat belonging to one of the combatants was languishing in the territory of its African colony. 'Well, we were going to salvage all the valuable bits, and transport 'em back to Alexandria or Cairo,' recalled Sir Roy. 'But they said, "You're not going to leave that here!"' *Corsair*, it appears, had become a diplomatic incident.

All I have is those Imperial Airways engineers' word for it. I could find absolutely no official proof of this tiniest, most recondite eruption in Anglo–Belgian affairs. Like so much in this story, in public-record terms *Corsair* seems to have flown off the edge of the world – not so much written out of history as never written in. The entire archive of embassy and consular correspondence between Britain and Belgium for the period from 1915 right through to 1940 was destroyed, presumably by a bomb, in 1940. Even Captain Alcock's original forced landing on the Dungu is oddly absent from the Foreign Office and Air Ministry records of air accidents – even though *Challenger* coming to grief in Mozambique harbour, the loss of *Cavalier* in the North Atlantic, and *Capella*'s collision at Batavia are all included for 1939. The only reference under '*Corsair*' in the encyclopaedic multivolume red-bound Foreign Office index for 1939 pertains to plans by the Admiralty to purchase a yacht of that name. Our flying boat, however, is out in no man's land; not on the map.

'But whilst we were going down to salvage all this,' insisted Sir Roy, 'the general messages coming back were that you've got to get it out of here!' He laughed. 'So we started again where Hughie Gordon had left off.'

The Imperial Airways team, like Gordon's before them, checked in to the SHUN resthouse at Aba, where Sir Roy remembered the Belgian officials who used to drink there in the evenings as 'pretty hostile', and not optimistic about Britain's chance in the war. But the new salvage crew seems to have been far from intimidated – indeed, their remote assignment appears to have been liberating, not oppressive, judging from the jocularity with which they set about their task. Already the obstacle on which the flying boat had foundered anew had been christened Alcock Rock. When wading into the river to feel around for the underwater hull damage raised worries about bilharzia, one member suggested that, for protection, they get Alexandria to send down three dozen condoms. Taken to the local convent hospital for a tetanus shot after cutting his hand, Roy Sisson inquired in cheery bewilderment of the pretty young woman who ministered to him, 'Whatever made *you* want to become a nun?' It is almost as though the flying boat that took Guy Crouch-back, Ritchie-Hook and the corpse of Apthorpe away from West Africa had later wheeled around and settled down on the Dungu.

The new team tried a different way of floating the boat off its rock. They removed all the engines and flaps to lighten it, then jacked it up under each wing, with the port wing supported on a raft of huge 1,000-gallon tanks taken from petrol-tanker lorries.

They managed to put a metal patch on the hole in the hull, and started pumping. At first it was slow going – and heavy rains didn't help. 'Boys bilging all night,' Alf Cowling recorded in his diary on 2 October. But inch by inch *Corsair* began to rise. 'And I always remember the day of victory,' said Sir Roy, 'because the thousand-gallon tank was bloody nearly *below* the water, and *suddenly*, as the boat began to have buoyancy, we could see it beginning to come up!' On 5 October 1939 Jock Halliday cabled the U K : '*Corsair* afloat stop.' Once floated across the river, with a lot of pushing and shoving *Corsair* was hauled up the slipway again. Now they were merely back to where Hugh Gordon's team had been five months earlier.

Once again, the rains were late. At the end of the month Imperial Airways' Central African manager was reporting them much below normal; by the middle of November the Dungu at Faradje was in places only 3 feet 4 inches deep – and the draught of the flying boat, even empty, was only 2 inches less. The elemental factor that had undone Alcock had not gone away. How was *Corsair* ever going to get out of the Congo?

Imperial Airways sent for Kelly-Rogers.

Jack Kelly-Rogers was another of Imperial Airways' most illustrious flying-boat pilots. A vigorous, thickset southern Irishman – 'the outstanding example of a strong personality' – he was later in the war to distinguish himself in two separate adventures. On 10 June 1940, when Italy entered the war, the Mediterranean suddenly became hostile territory for Imperial Airways craft. The Empire boat *Clyde* was moored in Kalafrana Bay in Malta that day, bound for Britain with a party of RAF officers. Despite a swell heavy enough to overturn her where *Clyde* would have to take off, and one engine only running on half power, her captain, Kelly-Rogers, boldly decided to flout every rule of take-off to try and get away. He taxied out into the swell, and then swung round for a take-off run directly into the smooth water of the bay. He got *Clyde* off just 200 yards from the shore – 'the last civil-registered aircraft,' he subsequently confirmed, 'to traverse Europe for a long time.'

Then, in January 1942, by then the Flight Captain of BOAC's Boeing fleet in charge of the transatlantic run, Kelly-Rogers was called upon to fly a secret party of VIPs in the flying boat *Berwick* from Norfolk, Virginia, to Bermuda. He and his crew had to clear customs in Baltimore (the BOAC Boeings' base) and fly out as if commencing a routine crossing, such was the need to decoy enemy attention – for the principal passenger was to be Winston Churchill. The British Prime Minister had crossed the Atlantic by battleship to meet with Roosevelt at the White House, and now was returning home with his chiefs of defence staff. The Boeing flight would allow their ship to start out from Bermuda and further decoy German attempts to torpedo it.

It sounds, from Churchill's long and enthusiastic account of the flight in his *History of the Second World War*, as though he found a kindred spirit in Kelly-Rogers, with whom he quickly struck up an acquaintance on *Berwick*'s flight-deck:

I took the controls for a bit, to feel this ponderous machine of thirty or more tons in the air. I got more attached to the flying boat. Presently I asked the Captain, 'What about flying from Bermuda to England? Can she carry enough petrol?' Under his solid exterior he became visibly excited. 'Of course we can do it . . . We could do it in twenty hours.' I asked how far it was, and he said, 'About three thousand five hundred miles.' At this I became thoughtful.

Each man had been thrown a challenge, and for each the response was instantaneous. Though it had previously been thought too dangerous to entrust a British prime minister to the air for a trans-atlantic crossing, Churchill's mind was made up. Five days would be saved! In Bermuda Kelly-Rogers was subjected, in John Pudney's words, to 'one of the most momentous cross-examinations of any

BOAC pilot in history', at which the captain acquitted himself so ably on the capabilities of his craft that Churchill remarked in conclusion, 'He seems to have all the answers, doesn't he?'

So at 11.36 the next morning Kelly-Rogers took off again from Bermuda to fly the British war leader and his entourage across the ocean in the giant flying boat *Berwick*. In *Merchant Airmen* there is a magnificent moment when, darkness having fallen, Churchill and Lord Beaverbrook, the Minister for Aircraft Production, ascend to the flight-deck after evening dinner:

they stood for some while gazing through the windows at the brilliantly starlit sky through which Berwick was riding, with stardust brushed across the carpet of cloud below. In such serenity, they told Captain Rogers that they envied him his job.

Then they hit dense mist, and Churchill himself writes of watching the 'great flaming exhausts pouring back over the wing surfaces', and the ice splintering off the de-icing tubes. The steward – it was to become a regular custom – warmed Churchill's slippers for him in the galley's oven.

The following morning dawned clear and blue, and Kelly-Rogers had to give a blithely evasive answer when the soundly-slept VIP inquired what they'd do if they sighted enemy aircraft. Afterwards he confessed that in that cloudless sky he'd felt a little too exposed for comfort. Complete radio silence imposed throughout the flight had made keeping to their course difficult, and had the captain not turned north promptly as soon as the Scilly Isles did not appear where they should have, *Berwick* would have been over the German batteries at Brest in minutes. Radio silence also caused the flying boat to be reported in Britain as an enemy bomber: fortunately the half-a-dozen Hurricanes scrambled on the news failed to find her. Ultimately Kelly-Rogers touched her down at Plymouth, bringing the Prime Minister home just 17 hours and 55 minutes after leaving

Bermuda, and earning himself lunch at Downing Street to receive the thanks of an admiring Clementine.

This was the redoubtable individual who received an order on 20 November 1939 to fly out to Juba and make his way to the Congo.

The great man arrived in Faradje first thing on 2 December, and straight away set about a preliminary survey of the profile of the river bed. This involved all the Imperial Airways engineers marching out into the Dungu and wading down the middle of the river in a human chain. 'So when a chap came up to his ankles, that was a rock; and when you suddenly saw his topee floating down the river,' laughed Sir Roy, 'that was deep water.' From this exercise, in which the local Africans understandably declined to participate, Kelly-Rogers established that there were rocks less than a foot below the surface, and far too little water for take-off anywhere. 'No appreciable rain expected before April stop,' he cabled back – but even if it did arrive, neither did Kelly-Rogers fancy handling a flying boat on a swift-flowing river in spate. Only one thing for it: 'Recommend building of barrage.'

Here the story takes on another dimension. From now on it is not only *An Outpost of Progress* that comes to mind, or the Sword of Honour trilogy: we have entered the world of *Fitzcarraldo*. Werner Herzog's megalomaniac hero set about the manhandling of a vast longboat across the mountains of the Amazon: now, to get *Corsair* out of the Congo, if her surroundings wouldn't permit a successful take-off, the surroundings had to be remade. Dam the river!

There was, however, a context. The Belgians had done well back in the last century when the recurring border dispute with Britain over the north-eastern border of the Congo had been settled. Both nations had been seeking gold in this part of Africa – mostly alluvial gold – and eventually the demarcation had been agreed, logically, as the shelf between two great rivers' drainage basins. Everything that drained into the Nile was the Sudan; everything that drained into the Congo was the Belgian Congo. From this arrangement the Belgians ended up with most of the gold. To extract it they'd cut a diversionary channel temporarily to re-route a river, dam up its original course to create a lake, pump out the water, and filter the gold flecks out of the mud. If the 130-foot-wide River Dungu now needed a barrage to get a stranded flying boat out, the Kilo Moto mines down at Watsa – whose pumps had already emptied her flooded hull – could get straight on the job.

Victor Pitcher told me a story of how, while a navigator on the wartime transatlantic Boeings, and recurrent bouts of tonsillitis at last forcing him to go sick, he found himself called into Kelly-Rogers' office at Baltimore airport. 'Have 'em out! boomed the big Irishman. 'I've booked you in the hospital. Out!' That was that. A doctor's informed diagnosis appeared to be redundant. Kelly-Rogers had decided, and that was that. Vic's tonsils were removed, and Kelly-Rogers came to see him in the hospital to declare, 'That's put an end to your nonsense!'

Kelly-Rogers didn't wait for a response to his recommendation. Within two days of his arrival at Faradje he'd paid a visit to Watsa, been quoted a price of just under 23,000 Belgian francs – about £165 at the time – and the Kilo Moto mines had received his order. The impatiently pencilled note covering his handwritten letter to Imperial Airways' wartime headquarters at the Grand Hotel in Bristol, accounting for his expeditious action, reads:

Because of the heat, discomfort, mosquitos, cockroaches and lack of ink I have no alternative but to send you the enclosed for typing. I've tried a French typewriter but had to give up.

To allow for the dam to be keyed into each bank of the Dungu for strength, calculated Kilo Moto, it would have to be 72 metres across – about *240 feet*. A framework of tree-trunks was to be driven into the river bed, and a basket weave of thin branches in between would contain the lining of boulders. A metre-square box of the same construction at regular intervals would further reinforce it. Twenty tons of wood and 170 tons of stone would have to be brought in by truck to each riverbank, and about 200 men would be needed on site. But not only was there hardly a tree in sight around this stretch of the Dungu: to create a lake of still water long enough for *Corsair* to take off without hitting the dam itself, it would have to be built a way downstream – and down there, on both sides, was just the same thick bush as all around.

So as for those extravagant evocations I'd read in more recent accounts of the *Corsair* episode, of engineers 'hacking their way through virgin jungle'? 'Oh, yes indeed,' replied Sir Roy. 'We had to do a lot of hacking through jungly bits. They had to make about three miles of roads through pretty rough country to get the trucks down there, and a lot of dumping had to be done to make the road suitable for bringing all the timber and rocks. And we had to go a bloody long way to find trees and cut 'em down – the right sort of trees.' Kilo Moto seconded four of its African foremen to the project, and the Belgian authorities released 200 of their convicts, from prisons all over, to form the main labour force. But where were they to stay? A native village was built for them beside the Dungu – 'a transit camp' in Sir Roy's phrase – twenty grass huts so that they could sleep on the job. The Imperial Airways team christened the new settlement they had placed on the map *Corsairville*. Historic riparian cities: Leopoldville; Stanleyville; and now Corsairville. The name was always meant to be a bit of a joke.

By the middle of December the team had repaired *Corsair*'s hull and overhauled her soggy engines. 'In spite of the length of time they have been here and the almost insurmountable difficulties under which they have been labouring, their air of happiness and co-operation,' wrote Kelly-Rogers to Alexandria, 'is an example to the rest of the company.' Perhaps this is the most surprising thing: the extent to which these new castaways took the whole strange business in their stride. Various Imperial Airways personnel came down to Faradje to check on their progress: 'they'd never stay very long,' observed Sir Roy. Then again, these were Africa veterans already – not displaced young cockneys from Rochester in Kent – and they were able to take up the priceless links with local Europeans like Lacovitch at SHUN and those with the American missionaries that Hugh Gordon had forged. Once a week one of the African Inland Mission's Chevy trucks, JESUS IS COMING blazoned on the side, would come down to the resthouse to collect them for dinner – a welcome change from the usual poor diet of yams, sweet potatoes and tinned stuffs. The team would look out of the window and see the cloud of dust coming down the hill just outside Aba and say to each other, 'Hooray, here comes Jesus!' Sir Roy remembered a very long grace, thanking the good Lord for providing food in a strange land. 'Well, you only had to open the back door and you fell arse over tip over a guinea-fowl!' But with a leader of men like Kelly-Rogers at the helm you weren't left to work out your own salvation.

Having been on the Dungu for nearly nine months already, *Corsair* had also become a fixture in the lives of the local community. 'I think everybody wanted to come and lend a hand,' said Sir Roy, handing me a photo of two young African women who helped to cook for them down at the flying boat. The local man who served as their *askari* had been kitted out in a suit made from *Corsair*'s seat upholstery. The radio officer, Wycherley, who had joined the team to keep daily contact with Alexandria, was known locally as 'Mokoto' – the King. Alf Cowling recalled for me how the local population would collect up old rivets from the flying boat to wear as ear-studs. Piston rings from the engines made good ear-rings for the native women, split pins were worn through the nose, and Duralumin bracelets on their arms. 'As Captain Kelly-Rogers says,' remarked the *Aeroplane* magazine fondly several months later, 'the *Corsair* may be gone now but bits of it will live on in the Belgian Congo.'

Christmas approaching, the barrage now looking to be completed by the end of December, it was time to launch *Corsair* on the Dungu. The engineers had built a mud bank along the water's edge to keep the water back from the slipway – but now the time came to knock it down to refloat the flying boat, the river had dropped! How to get it across the swamp into the water? If only the team had acted on the first and best idea . . .

One day Kelly-Rogers had given the salvage team a day out – a visit to La Ferme pour la Domestication des Eléphants near Lake Albert to the east of Faradje, where, as at Nagero on the north bank of the Dungu, African elephants had been trained for farm work and to carry officials and baggage. Remembering that docile parade of elephants lined up after the bath in the river that concluded their day's work, coiling their trunks to lift visitors on to their backs, the team wondered – send for a team of four, station them on the opposite bank of the Dungu harnessed to ropes and . . . heave! Elephants hauling the big white bird back into its element; timeless Africa coming to the rescue of the modern metal vagrant – regrettably this is one episode we can't write into the secret history. In the event, Belgian officialdom obliged by organizing a mass tug-of-war of over 200 people, from villagers to mine workers, to pull like mad. With the engineers opening up all four engines, *Corsair* slithered across the mud.

But other African wildlife did play a truly indispensable part in the saving of the flying boat. The wood-and-boulder dam now stretched across the Dungu, designed to raise the depth of the water to 8 feet. But how to seal it? There was no cement out here – no question of concreting the walls to make the dam watertight. In this part of the world, as the Kilo Moto gold-mines had discovered, there was only one alternative sealant. Anthill mud was non-porous. 'We had to go round about a hundred miles knocking down anthills,' said Sir Roy. 'Lot of angry-looking ants got poured into that dam!'

Christmas, 1939. Imperial Airways sent down half a dozen hampers packed with turkey, Christmas puddings and crackers, and the whole salvage team repaired to Yei, the small Sudanese town 30 miles from Aba, and the house of Jack Bartram, the British prison governor. Kelly-Rogers stood the drinks, and Bartram, popular locally for his custom of allowing native prisoners' wives in every evening to prepare their husbands' meals, laid on what was billed as a 'fantasia'. All wearing their paper party-hats, the Imperial Airways men attended what Sir Roy Sisson recalled as a 'native love dance' performed around the bonfire. Kelly-Rogers blasted off red and green flares from the flying boat's Very pistol as impromptu fireworks, and briefly set fire to the chief's hut. Loud murmurs among the local crowd were caused when *Corsair*'s first officer, Geordie Garner, a great conjurer, turned the 5-piastre piece clasped tight in one village girl's hand into a 1-piastre piece. The situation was redeemed when he produced the 5-piastre piece from under the left breast of the chief's wife – a prestidigitatory feat exciting the chief's great interest in the possibility of more wealth from the same source.

The dam was complete by the end of the year – an unfortunate by-product of all this water-engineering the flooding of several native villages upstream. Most of the salvage crew, including Sisson and Cowling, reluctantly departed for Juba to catch the next Empire boat north. A photo in Cowling's album frames a jaunty tableau of his four colleagues, in topees and shorts, mugging at the camera – while behind them, atop the flying boat moored out in the Dungu, stands a single quizzical African. Kelly-Rogers, meanwhile, worried about the bend in the river along his planned take-off run – acute enough that, from the flight-deck, the two grassy riverbanks appeared to meet – had a series of 20-foot poles erected along them to help him judge his course, each surmounted with a basket.

'I always regret I wasn't there,' mused Sir Roy. Early on the morning of 6 January 1940, the banks were lined. Hundreds of people had come from miles around – word had spread that the great white bird was going to try and fly away. At 7.15 a.m. Kelly-Rogers ran the engines up, and slowly slipped the tail hook. *Corsair* smoothly rounded the bend in the Dungu, and now the captain gave it the gun. The flying boat lifted off the water and thrummed away into the sky. The crowds lining the banks shouted 'Hooray!' Kelly-Rogers circled overhead and dipped his wings to say, as one of the African Inland Missionaries put it, 'Goodbye, folks.' Lacovitch, who'd been standing on the dam giving a last wave, dived in.

Later in the war, when Victor Pitcher was on a few days' layover in Baltimore in between transatlantic runs of BOAC's Boeings, he switched on the local radio station one day, and heard the voice of his flight captain. As an Irishman Jack Kelly-Rogers was well loved in America; as the Commodore of the Baltimore Yacht Club he enjoyed further local esteem. He drove around in the Jaguar SS8 he'd had imported specially from the UK. And now Victor found he'd chanced upon the middle of an epic radio drama – a documentary enactment of the *Corsair* saga in the Congo, and a certain flying-boat captain's amazing feat of bravery. He recalls the climactic moments as something like this:

Chorus of concerned bystanders: 'Captain Rogers! Captain Rogers! It's too dangerous! You can't take off! –'

[Firm Irish voice breaks in] *Kelly-Rogers*: *'I can do it!'*

Concerned bystanders [voices now piping with anxiety]: 'Captain Rogers! Captain Rogers! No! No! –'

[Adamant Irish voice] *Kelly-Rogers*: *'I can do it!* I'm not afraid . . .'

Thus was the story improbably mythicized for the citizens of Baltimore, Maryland, with the man in the leading role playing himself.

Sir Roy Sisson had found one small photograph to show me from the day of the celebrated take-off – taken, he explained, by Jack Bartram, over at Yei. Slightly blurred, the clean pale outline of *Corsair* sails overhead on her way to refuel at Juba, and thence to Alexandria for a full overhaul. A touch of dysentery that morning had not impeded Bartram's presence of mind to take his camera with him when he had to dash – and capture the historic moment through his open toilet door.

Sisson and Cowling both received silver cigarette-cases for their part in the rescue; so did Lacovitch (monogrammed); Harry Stam was sent a modest donation to the funds of his mission at Aba. The episode even made a page in the *Illustrated London News*. Within a couple of months the factory that supplied interior fittings for Imperial Airways' planes had received an order for *Corsair* to cover everything from a promenade carpet to nineteen lapstraps, two shaving shelves and two Elsan lavatories.

And that was that. Imagine Kelly-Rogers' eagle-eye view from that eastbound flying boat, performing a valedictory circle above the thronged banks as he gained height: a 200-foot stone, wood and anthill-mud dam; a new lake; a wooden slipway; 3 miles of roads; a grass-hut village called Corsairville. 'What's left there,' said Sir Roy, 'Heaven only knows' – and he poured me quite the largest pre-prandial gin and tonic I have ever seen.

Hugh Gordon had promised to show me his ciné films. He'd taken a clockwork ciné camera with him on all his pre-war salvage assignments for Shorts, and he had two reels of 16 mm film from the *Corsair* episode. (Kelly-Rogers, according to Sir Roy Sisson, had shot another during his time at Faradje – almost certainly the one Vic Hodgkinson had been shown at Calshott. But my luck in tracing

it was no better than his.) So in the summer of 1998 I drove down
to Somerset again.

He'd had a nasty moment that morning, Hugh admitted when I
arrived. It was so long since he'd last shown the films they hadn't
been where he'd gone to look for them, and he'd had an anxious
search. The projector screen was somewhere up in the loft – inaccessible since he'd hurt his arm a while back – so, ever the resourceful
engineer, he'd hunted around for a large piece of cardboard, painted a
white square on it, and propped that up at the end of the dining-room
table.

He wanted to take me to some other places first, he said, so we
found ourselves on a French hillside inspecting the splintered remains
of *Capricornus*, locals hauling mangled twists of metal away on
ox-carts, and a quick shot of a young Gordon dressed for some
reason in plus-fours. On a return visit to France, Hugh recalled,
he'd looked up the taxi-driver who'd run errands for the salvage
team. Ushered into the man's living room he was confronted with
the sight of a large pouffe, covered in the familiar green leather of
an Empire boat's seat upholstery. '*Souvenir Capricornus!*' announced
the proud taxi-driver.

Then we were in Alexandria, on the Nile, and beholding an
extraordinary contraption on the water – a kind of flying catamaran.
This was an Italian flying boat – 'No, they worked,' said Hugh, 'the
pilot sat in the wing between the two booms.' They were much
faster across the Mediterranean than Imperial Airways' old biplane
flying boats, in fact – Hugh remembered a cartoon at the time
showing a Calcutta lumbering along so slowly the sun managed to
set completely behind it. Now in colour – in remarkable condition
for such early stock – we visited the old railway hotel at Wadi Halfa
in the Sudan, a garden oasis of brilliant flowers, now submerged
under Lake Nasser; we watched pearl divers at Sharjah in the Persian
Gulf.

Hugh threaded another reel into the little projector. 'You're in the Congo.' It opened on a mess of mud and swamp and excavation half the size of a football field around the flying boat – trenches conditions. 'We had to dig our way out, really,' mused Hugh, as I watched his engineers and their African assistants at the hand-pumps in an effort to create dry land round *Corsair*. The pumps were amazingly small – tiny as car-jacks, expelling little squirts and slops of water. Here was a handsome dark-haired young Peter Newnham out in the open air using a blowlamp to normalize rivets. 'He didn't like doing that,' said Hugh.

Next we met Harry Stam with his family outside the mission at Aba – tall and lanky, a high forehead and receding hair-line, making a big play of smoothing down one of his sons' hair for the camera. He looked rather like Tom Hanks. Behind them the mission was a low, dark building, as was the squat SHUN hotel in another frame, the Shorts men's two chunky black shooting-brakes parked outside. Darkness was the predominant visual impression: the dark red soil, the low-browed buildings, the deep green vegetation.

'Now this is ironwood,' said Hugh. Several Africans were floating big logs across the tea-coloured Dungu, the wood low as a crocodile in the water. 'It only just floats, terribly heavy. Don't know what it would cost in a woodyard nowadays.' The team were digging deep shafts in which to set the logs as pilings to stabilize a slipway for getting *Corsair* up on dry land. It was only seeing these scenes of mud and water and swamp and wood and earth that I really appreciated what an elemental task the whole salvage had been. It had been a battle against natural forces with natural tools and means: that was almost all they'd had. 'I bet those shafts are still there,' said Hugh, 'and some day people will say – there'll be all sorts of theories, and they'll probably be wrong – they'll say, "Well, it's a ceremonial thing, a sacrificial . . ."'

The screen became busy with activity – oil drums being carted around, men striding to and fro: the day of the first take-off. 'And you recognize that?' asked Hugh: his *ad hoc* filming had engineered a pitiless jump-cut – to *Corsair* nose-down and newly sunk on the other bank of the Dungu. 'It was a very sad ending, really. Poor old John Alcock. That will *always* trouble me, always – less and less as you get old, but for a long time I wanted to go back.' The last frames were filled with blue sky and ivory fluffs of cloud beyond the underside of a silver wing, as Hugh had pointed his clockwork ciné camera through the window of the Empire boat taking him home.

Irene Gordon had joined us. Outside, the sun had come out, was peeping round the drawn dining-room curtains. 'It was quite an adventure, wasn't it?' she said. 'It becomes very much part of you, doesn't it, a thing like that?'

'Oh, it *does*, believe me,' said Hugh. 'I can't tell you how much really.'

Centurion

LIST OF ILLUSTRATIONS

Section One

1. Two Imperial Airways Empire flying boats over the Dead Sea
2. Croydon Aerodrome and an Imperial Airways Handley–Page HP-42
3. Lady Cobham with her canary
4. Captain Dudley Travers with the boxer Primo Carnera, 1932
5. *Caledonia* over New York, 1937
6. The Mayo-Composite, *Maia* and *Mercury*, 1938
7. Captain Arthur Wilcockson in the cockpit of *Caledonia*
8. *Cassiopeia* loading in Southampton Water, 1937
9. *Sylvanus*, *Scipio* and *Satyrus* at Alexandria
10. Brochure advertising the new Empire Air Mail service to South Africa
11. The observation deck inside an Empire flying boat
12. Rod-el-Farag at Cairo on the Nile
13. Ringing the bell at Wadi Halfa in the Sudan
14. Refuelling *Canopus* at Olvengo on the Congo
15. Laropi, Uganda
16. Three Imperial Airways flying-boat captains on the wing of an Empire boat
17. *Cleopatra* circles over Durban
18. Coming in to touch down in the harbour at Durban

Section Two

Acknowledgements

The author and the publisher are most grateful to the following for permission to reproduce photographs:

Imperial War Museum 1, 12, 13, 14, 15, 16, 17, 18, 19, 37, 41, 42, 44, 45, 46, 47; Flight International 2; Sir Alan Cobham Archive 3; Hall of Aviation, Southampton 5, 7, 10, 21, 48, 49, 52; Science Museum 4; TRH Pictures 6, 43 and endpapers; Hulton-Getty 8, 51; Adrian Meredith Picture Library 9, 11; Mike Taylor 50; Southern Newspapers 57; Eric Whitehead, Cumbria Picture Library 58; Pat Blair (taken by Alwyn Baker) 20, 24, 31, 32; Ian Henderson 22; Hugh Gordon 23, 28, 29; Alf Cowling (courtesy Mrs Bevis) 25, 33, 34, 35, 36, 38, 40; Peter Newnham 26, 27, 30; Illustrated London News 39; the author 53, 54, 55, 56.

Crossing-the-line certificate, given to Empire flying-boat passengers when they crossed the Equator, courtesy of Mrs Veronica Berry; boarding card for the BOAC Solent flying boat on the post-war Africa route to Johannesburg; postcard sent by Tessa Smith in 1942 after her flight to Johannesburg on Empire flying boat *Corsair*, courtesy of Mrs Tessa Smith; pages from Captain Alcock's pilot's logbook recording *Corsair*'s forced landing in the Belgian Congo, courtesy of the Southampton Hall of Aviation; badges of individual Empire flying boats reproduced from *The World's Airways*.

ACKNOWLEDGEMENTS

An enormous number of people helped to make my research for this book an unmitigated pleasure. I'd like first to thank Ron Wilson and Fred Huntley at the British Airways Archive, Laura Sole at the Shell Archive, Alison McAleer, Celia Cook and Mike Houston at the Friends of the Lake District, Dr Charles Swaisland at Rhodes House, Oxford, Norman Powell and Don Upward at the Hall of Aviation in Southampton, Andy Pickering at Royal Mail International, Andy Murphy and Nigel Harrod at OAG, Peter Kent at the Imperial War Museum Photographic Archive, Michael Oakey at *Aeroplane Monthly*, Allan King, Alan Tanner, John Mudge, Ian Redmond, Pat Blair, Bill Mortimer, Ray Wheeler, Norman Rutter, Revd Herb Cook Junior, Revd Herb Cook Senior, and especially Captain Vic Hodgkinson, Victor Pitcher, the late Alf Cowling, his daughter Freda Bevis, the late Sir Roy Sisson, Peter Newnham, and above all Hugh and Irene Gordon.

The assistance of the following was invaluable in placing appeals for reminiscence and memories: Terry Barringer of the Royal Commonwealth Society Archive at the Cambridge University Library, Mr David LeBreton of the Overseas Pensioners Association, Mr Philip Pawson of the Sudan Government British Pensioners Association, Mr Peter Sterwin of the Shell Pensioners Association, Lieutenant Colonel Richard Corkran and Captain Peter Stocken of the King's African Rifles and East African Forces Association.

Over the years a number of editors allowed me to write about flying boats, and thereby made much of my research and travel possible: I'd like to thank Jocelyn Targett, then at the Weekend *Guardian*, Angus MacKinnon, then at *GQ*, Sarah Spankie at *Condé Nast Traveller*, and Michael Kerr at the *Daily Telegraph* Travel section – and these newspapers and magazines, in which parts of my book appeared in an earlier form.

For helping with my travel to remote flying-boat haunts, or for talking to me about seaplanes once I arrived there, I'm very grateful to: Anne Foussé at *Condé Nast Traveller*, Adrienne Calver at Statesman Travel, Sean Smith of Pan-Am Air Bridge in Miami, Florida, Peter Green and John Wagner at Seaplanes of Key West, Kermit Weeks at the Fantasy of Flight in Tampa, Florida, Jaqi Todd and Sharon Gaiptman of the Alaska Division of Tourism, Pam Foreman at the Kodiak Convention and Visitors Bureau, Ken Morris at the Anchorage Convention and Visitors Bureau, Alaska Airlines, Fred Ball, Bryan DeBoer and the staff of PenAir in Kodiak, Alaska, Nick Brigman at the Lodge at Hidden Basin, Mike McChulskey at the Buskin River Inn, Mervyn and Fay Carnelley at Fisherman's Camp, Lake Naivasha in Kenya, Kes and Fraser Smith, Steve Wolcott and Mrs Joan Travers in Nairobi, and Mike Honmon at Victoria Falls.

I received crucial assistance from my friends Andrew Treip, who lent his Toshiba computer, Michael Cross, who scanned the text, Amanda Kelly, who keyed it, and Imogen Sharp, Sarah Thornton, Melanie Sharp, Alan Hay, Louise Restrick and Nick Fox, who all gave encouragement just when it was needed.

Clare Alexander, then at Penguin, originally gave me the chance to write a book about Corsairville. Mike Petty, Bloomsbury, had first encouraged me. From our first meeting, when Eleo Gordon revealed herself to have grown up in Uganda, watching the flying boats at Port Bell 'skidding down on to the water outside the yacht club', I knew she would be the perfect editor for it, and so she has been. Without the unfailing friendship of my agent, Antony Harwood, who read it as I wrote it, truly I couldn't have finished it.

And, finally, a big thank-you to everyone who wrote, rang with their memories, sent photographs and memorabilia, and talked to me about flying boats: Captain Ken Emmott, Captain 'Taffy' Barrow, Norman Parker, Les Hills, Edward Hulton, Dick Stratton, Madge Wilson, Tommy Boyce, Sir Ross Stainton, Jake Seamer, Frank Baker, Mr Jack Beagle, George Blake, Richard Kennedy, James Ambrose, Joan Hewitt, Marjorie Parrington, Stan Fearon, Rosemary Potter, Mrs I. G. Barnes, Mrs R. Webster, Jennifer Robson, Eileen Murray, Mrs B. Harrison, Helen Bray, Bill Bott, Gillian Ollerenshaw, Mrs Lyle, Molly Woods, Dr Mary Wilson, Mr Carter, Mrs Eileen Kilburn, Mr P. Lunt, Miss Walton, Mrs Tessa Smith, Bill Rhodes, Mike Taylor, Kenneth Gregson, Mrs Winnington-Ingram, Robert Lovell, Mrs Bettine Richardson, Lady Marion Sheridan, Dorothy Tow, Kenneth Gregson, S. A. Yates, Mr Evans, Mrs Piry Leche, John Godfrey, Mr Carter, Dorothy and the late Stan Prince, R. Adam, Alice Clarke, David Ashley Hall, Peter Chenery, Mrs Veronica Tagg, Mrs Pickering, Mrs W. Fisher, Mr and Mrs Hall, Richard Sherren, A. T. Ternent, F. John Franklin, Air Commodore E. S. Williams, the late Ralph Lawes, Dick Smerdon, Hilary Hall, Roger Blankley, Mrs Skelton, Mac Davidson, George Van, Anita Husband, Valerie Latham, Mrs Hilda Middleton, Sheila Rand, Sally Slaughter, Edith Taylor, Gavin Waddell, Reginald Collins, Hilary Watson, Bernard and Dorothy Babb, J. W. Smith, Rosemary Quantrill, Mrs Margery Piggott, Norman Ramsay, Professor Jake Jacobs, Veronica Berry, Willoughby Thompson, the late Professor Kenneth Kirkwood, Derek Gratze, 'Tim' Moore, Robert Lilley, Philip Clarke, Mrs M. Steel, George Hill, Dorothy Sunman, C. A. G. Coleridge, Christopher Collier-Wright, R. D. Crow, Winifred Hutton, A. E. Lorriman, Dr Joyce Lowe, Mrs Judy

Skerman, Mrs Lesley Harris, Mrs R. M. Hart, H. G. Hillier, Mr Jones, J. Roy Clackson, A. W. Waddell, Patrick Gillibrand, Dr Arthur Williams, D. P. Taylor, Barbara Creighton, Gwendolen Hughes, Peter Colmore, Dr Francis Smith, Mr Bunnens, John Wright, Mrs H. B. Arber, Inez Bowden, Roy Marriott, Marjorie Wild, 'Hodge' Barrett, M. S. Powell, Peter Tew, Mrs Joy Talbot-Smith, Ian Henderson, Molly Bunker, Elaine Forster, N. W. D. Dewdney, Roelf Attwell, Mrs B. J. Laurie, Mrs Buchanan, Dr W. L. Barton, Mrs H. W. T. Willoughby, Mrs D. H. Marquand, Victor Harvey, R. G. L. Wallace, Peter Burbrook de Vere, Mrs Olive Burkitt, Peter Hicks, Alexander McKinlay, Michael Crouch, G. H. R. Dunwoodie, John Harris, Joan Carmichael, Jean Entwhistle, W. E. Kendrick, Warwick Forester, Mrs P. M. Bennett, Mr Wagner, Mr I. M. Tring, J. B. Watson, L. W. Raven, Pete Charlton, Mr Collins, Ron Gray, Tony Skinner, Mrs Una Sangster, Dennis Ansted, Mrs J. J. H. Swallow, P. M. Johnson, the late Dr Geoffrey Elcoat, Mrs Phyllis Baker, Alison Weller, Brigadier Michael Biggs, Mrs Diana Owen-Thomas, Alfred Laxton, Ian Marshall, James Scrivener, Roland Mosher.

NOTE The Official CAA report on the circumstances of the accident to the Catalina in Southampton Water in 1998, referred to in Chapter 12, subsequently found the cause to be corrosion in an undercarriage door, and in no way pilot or crew error. The flying boat has since been acquired by a new team of preservationists who hope to restore it to flying condition.

BIBLIOGRAPHY

Alan Moorehead, *No Room in the Ark*, Hamish Hamilton, London 1959; Penguin, Harmondsworth 1962

John Pudney, *The Seven Skies: a Study of BOAC and Its Forerunners since 1919*, Putnam, London 1959

C. H. Barnes, *Shorts Aircraft since 1900*, second edition revised by Derek James, Putnam Aeronautical, London 1989

Dudley Barker, *Merchant Airmen: the Air Ministry Account of British Civil Aviation 1939–1944*, HMSO, London 1946

Brian Cassidy, *Flying Empires – Short C-Class Empire Flying Boats*, Queens Parade Press, Bath 1996

A. S. Jackson, *Imperial Airways and the First British Airlines 1919–40*, Terence Dalton, Lavenham 1995

Sir Alan Cobham, *My Flight to the Cape and Back*, A & C Black, London 1926; and *Twenty Thousand Miles in a Flying Boat*, Harrap, London 1930

Peter London, *Saunders and Saro Aircraft since 1917*, Putnam Aeronautical, London 1988

David Jones, *The Time Shrinkers – Africa: the Development of Civil Aviation between Britain and Africa*, Beaumont Aviation Literature, London 1977

Harald Penrose, *Wings Across the World*, Cassell, London 1980

Maurice Allward, *An Illustrated History of Seaplanes and Flying Boats*, Moorland Publishing, Ashbourne 1981

Adrian B. Rance (ed.), *Seaplanes and Flying Boats of the Solent*, Southampton Public Libraries, Southampton 1981

Ian McIntyre, *The Expense of Glory – A Life of John Reith*, Harper-Collins, London 1993

Tim Jeal, *Livingstone*, revised edition, Pimlico, London 1993

Marischal Murray, *Union Castle Chronicle 1853–1953*, Longmans Green & Co., London 1953

Tim Binding, *In the Kingdom of Air*, Jonathan Cape, London 1993; Vintage, London 1994

J. L. Carr, *A Season in Sinji*, Alan Ross, London 1967; Penguin, London 1985

T. Alexander Barns, *Across the Great Craterland to the Congo*, Ernest Benn Ltd, London 1923

'Lake Malawi's First Flying Boat Visit', 'Alan Cobham's Flying Boat Visit, 1928' and 'The "Solent" Flying Boat Service to Nyasaland, 1949–1950', all by Colin Baker, *Society of Malawi Journal*, vol. 41 no. 2, vol. 44 no. 1, vol. 48 no. 2

'Africa in the Colonial Period: Transport and Communications': papers given by Patrick Gillibrand and others at symposium held in Rhodes House, Oxford, edited by Dr Charles Swaisland

Alan Wood, *The Groundnut Affair*, Bodley Head, London 1950

SOURCES

Archival sources

British Airways Archive
Shell Archive
Public Record Office
Hall of Aviation, Southampton
Rhodes House, Oxford
British Commonwealth Society Collection, Cambridge University
    Library
Alan Tanner Video

Interviews

Norman Parker, Les Hills, Joan Hewitt and Marjorie Parrington, Stan Fearon, Madge Wilson, Tommy Boyce, Captain Vic Hodgkinson, Captain Ken Emmott, Captain 'Taffy' Barrow, Norman Powell, Alf Cowling, Sir Roy Sisson, Hugh Gordon, Peter Newnham, George Blake, Jack Beagle, Rosemary Potter, Patrick Spencer, Mrs Veronica Tagg, Mrs Pickering, Dorothy and Stan Prince, Mrs K. Hall, Mrs R. Webster, Hilary Watson, Veronica Berry, Derek Gratze, Ralph Lawes, Eileen Murray, R. D. Crow, Mr B. and Mrs D. Babb, Mike Taylor, Kenneth Gregson, 'Hodge' Barrett, Robert Lilley, Ian Henderson, Patrick Gillibrand, Professor Jake Jacobs, Joy Talbot-Smith, Victor Pitcher, 'Tim' Moore, Sir Ross Stainton,

Jake Seamer, Peter Colmore, Dr Charles Swaisland, Edward Hulton, Mrs Joan Travers, Mervyn Carnelley, Dick Stratton, Tessa Smith.

Unpublished memoirs

Veronica Berry, 'Superfluous Trifles'
Roy Marriott, 'Some Impressions of a Flight by Flying Boat, Victoria
    Falls to UK and Return, 1950'
A. E. Lorriman, 'To East Africa by Flying Boat – 13/14 July 1949'
Mervyn Carnelley, 'A Flight to the Equator'